For Mary Jane Keith Schildberg,
an early and sinister influence

∞∞

The
Gothic Novel
1790 – 1830

Plot Summaries and
Index to Motifs

ANN B. TRACY

THE UNIVERSITY PRESS OF KENTUCKY

Publication of this book has been assisted by
a grant from the Andrew W. Mellon Foundation.

∞∞

Library of Congress Cataloging in Publication Data
Tracy, Ann Blaisdell.
   The Gothic novel, 1790-1830.

   Includes bibliographical references and indexes.
   1. English fiction – 19th century – Stories,
plots, etc. 2. Gothic revival (Literature)
3. English fiction – 18th century – Stories, plots,
etc. 4. Horror tales, English – Stories, plots, etc.
I. Title.
PR868.T3T7   823'.0872'09   79-4013
ISBN 0-8131-1397-0   AACR2

             Scholarly publisher for the Commonwealth
        serving Berea College, Centre College of Kentucky,
         Eastern Kentucky University, The Filson Club,
        Georgetown College, Kentucky Historical Society,
      Kentucky State University, Morehead State University,
     Murray State University, Northern Kentucky University,
         Transylvania University, University of Kentucky,
   University of Louisville, and Western Kentucky University.

Editorial and Sales Offices: Lexington, Kentucky 40506-0024

Contents

Acknowledgments *vii*

Introduction *1*

Summaries *13*

Index to Motifs *195*

Index of Characters *206*

Index of Titles *214*

Acknowledgments

My principal indebtedness is to my mother, Brenna Tracy, whose voluntary functions have ranged from secretary to research assistant and have been undertaken out of sheer maternal affection; my work would have been very much more difficult without her. I am largely indebted as well to four good friends: Drs. Eileen Curran and Herman Doh, who have painstakingly proofread and edited many more Gothic plots than they ever wanted to know about; Barbara Doh, who has loyally maintained that she *likes* the mechanics of indexing; and Pat Hoffmann, who has provided moral support, occasional sanctuary, and a keen eye for bombast. Further, I am grateful for the help, support, and advice provided at various points by Lynn Valenti, and by Drs. Carol Ames, Gerald Bentley, Frank Carner, Jay Macpherson, and Philippe Perebinossoff.

A number of friends and relatives aided my labors by offering hospitality near university libraries — Olive Blaisdell, John Dottridge, Harriette and Steven Land, Gary and Peg Miles, Beverly and David MacNeill, Dorothy and Brian Parker, Ed Wortman, and especially and recurrently my kind cousins Frank and Grace Blaisdell of Charlottesville, Virginia.

Not least am I grateful to several people whose professional assistance was especially valuable and courteous, notably the staff of the rare book room at the University of Virginia's Alderman Library and John Langley of the University Press of Kansas. Finally I am indebted to Ruth Fecteau and Gina Patterson, whose clerical labors on my behalf were salaried, but whose interest and encouragement defied compensation.

Introduction

∞∞

After a deceptively modest beginning in the 1760s, Gothic
fiction had by the nineties acquired such vigor and momentum
as to carry it three decades into the nineteenth century.
What we now rather loosely describe as Gothic motifs and
plots invaded the brief literary sketch and the five-volume
novel, the chapbook and Dr. Nathan Drake's *Literary Hours,*
drama and verse. Gothicism crept into the libraries of men
of letters (Wordsworth anathematized the novels and Coleridge reviewed them), into the heads of the coming generation (Macaulay and Thackery seem never quite to have lost
the taste), and, judging by a fine shadow-toy of the Bleeding Nun which I have had the privilege of admiring, into the
toy-cupboards. Gothics and quasi-Gothics were written by
men and women who were also writing opera, history, biogra-
phy, scientific papers, Shakespearean forgeries, treatises
on beekeeping, sermons, newspaper reports, literary criti-
cism, poetry, recollections of Byron, political observations, and topographical works. Greats, near-greats, and
friends of greats tried their hands at various forms of the
Gothic; writers of ordinary if not exceptional merit flooded
the market with it. It was written tongue in cheek and it
was written tear in eye. It came studded with travelogues,
interspersed with poetry, quivering with sensibility, dark
with Romantic gloom, clad in fancy dress, dripping gore, embellished with piety or sensuality, and framed with assertions that it had been found on crumbling manuscripts. Most
of all, it came in enormous quantities and we may presume
that it was sold and read in analogous quantities, though
the popularity of traveling libraries would suggest more
readers than sales.

Nowadays there seem to be three critical questions most
often asked about the Gothic novel. Where did it come from?
What caused its emergence? How does it behave? The first
question seems to me not very interesting, though curiosity
on that score is understandable, given the rather flashy nature of the Gothic phenomenon. Literary historians have

been prone in general to see Gothic precursors in Smollett's *Ferdinand Count Fathom* and Leland's *Longsword*. They have observed in the Graveyard school tastes and preoccupations compatible to the development of the Gothic and have noted the influence of French romances and of German *Ritter-, Räuber-, und Schauerromane*. And yet the German novels that appear in translation among the English — *Horrid Mysteries* and *Necromancer of the Black Forest,* for instance — seem oddly fragmentary, quite a different breed of fiction from the complicated but smoothly resolved novels of such writers as W. C. Green, Curties, Ireland, Stanhope, and Pickersgill. As for precursors, where do we stop? Certainly some of the novels, besides appearing to owe their attractive villains to Milton and their comic servants to Shakespeare, are, in devices of plot, more like Revenge Tragedy than anything else. And how, in any case, are we to trace the ancestry of such a pastiche of historical, sentimental, and horrific as "Gothic novel" suggests? I am well content for these questions to refer the reader to such stalwarts as Birkhead, Railo, Summers, and Varma.

The second question — What caused its emergence? — interests me very much indeed, for the answer to that might tell us as well why the last fifteen to twenty years have witnessed a similar phenomenon. But I do not pretend to know the answer, and nothing so far has led me to believe that anyone else knows it either. Perhaps some day a psychologist-cum-historian with a grasp of philosophy and an unusual knowledge of the early Gothic novel will tell us why people at a particular point in history need to frighten themselves in a particular way, and precisely what circumstances trigger a need for the Gothic's peculiar titillations. Until then, we had better go on to the third question — How does it behave? — for this one is both interesting and possible to answer in some detail.

Gothic fiction has suffered a little, I think, from a tendency on the part of scholars to treat it as a curiosity. Curious it may be. but one misses a great deal of a novel by standing too far away from it. For this reason Robert Kiely's *The Romantic Novel in England* (Cambridge, Mass., 1972), which talks about such novels as *The Monk* and *Melmoth the Wanderer* from the inside, as though they were perfectly ordinary books, has always seemed to me to contain unusually valuable observations. These introductory remarks, therefore, will deal with the view from inside the novels. I have not discriminated for my generalizations here between "terror" and "horror" Gothic, or between those and the historical or sentimental Gothic, or any combinations thereof; rather, I have tried to discover what viewpoint, if any, all novels called "Gothic" might share.

The world represented in Gothic fiction is characterized by a chronic sense of apprehension and the premonition of impending but unidentified disaster. In this world, appearances frequently, though not consistently, deceive, the mind and the senses falter and fail, and the passions overwhelm. Tempters, natural and supernatural, assault in impenetrable disguises, precipitating ruin and damnation. Nobody is entirely safe; nothing is secure. The Gothic world is quintessentially the fallen world, the vision of fallen man, living in fear and alienation, haunted by images of his mythic expulsion, by its repercussions, and by an awareness of his unavoidable wretchedness. Further, it is a fallen world peculiarly without hope. Robert Kiely has noted this hopelessness, as it appears in Maturin's *Melmoth the Wanderer,* as a peculiarity of the author's theology,[1] but the hopelessness seems to be far more pervasive. The mistakes and lapses from rectitude resulting from various weaknesses and temptations become enormously important in a context like Gothic fiction which generally neglects to discuss atonement. Nor is this omission surprising, insofar as romance-writing, like poetry, may tap the unconscious mind of the writer; man's fallen state is a circumstance in which everyone participates whether he wishes to or not, and whether or not he identifies his difficulties in those terms. Redemption, in the theological sense, becomes part of the human condition only for the individual who chooses to participate in it. Therefore we may say that of the two circumstances, the fallen condition is the more universal and the more deeply imbedded in the mind; it provides the Gothic nightmare, from which some sort of redemption may or may not provide an awakening.

A particular qualification in my use of "fallen world" is advisable. Protagonists in the throes of concentrated Gothicism would be only too glad to enter a workaday world that would promise some kind of stability, however fallen and corrupt. In the world as we know it, theological problems may be comfortably deferred for deathbed consideration; the supernatural, both beneficent and malevolent, is expected to stay in its place, i.e., in the background. The discomforts of the fallen state are, on a day-to-day basis, not very dramatic. In the Gothic world, on the other hand, the supernatural is likely to thrust itself into the foreground and demand immediate attention. Such occasions do not permit deferment of questions about good and evil, the human condition, death and damnation. Rather, an immediate and correct understanding of these problems becomes crucial. Even in the more conservative fiction, the Gothic world is characterized by the concentration and magnification of fears and problems inherent in the "normal" world.

One of the most conspicuous traits that identify the Gothic world as fallen is the physical environment. Settings typical of the Gothic novel may be sufficiently familiar from Eino Railo's study *The Haunted Castle*. The desolation of the Gothic scene is striking. Castles that presumably once offered warmth, revelry, or at least security, stand empty and ruined, providing instead baffling passageways, unspeakable mysteries, and menacing or pathetic apparitions. Typically, the Castle of Udolpho (though relatively habitable, as fictitious castles go) has "towers, crowned by over-hanging turrets, embattled, where, instead of banners, now waved long grasses and plants, that had taken root among the mouldering stones."[2] Like other Gothic castles, it is surrounded not by gardens but by dark and possibly hostile forests. The ruined world of Gothic fiction must imply that something better once existed. Indeed, a number of novels (e.g., Sleath's *Orphan of the Rhine,* Stanhope's *The Corsair's Bride,* Godwin's *St. Leon,* Moore's *Grasville Abbey,* Ball's *The Black Robber,* and Montague's *The Demon of Sicily*) contain scenes that emphasize the process of desolation by bringing their characters home to unexpected revelations of loss and neglect.

A related circumstance that suggests the post-lapsarian is the curious sunlessness of the novels. The obvious use of the twilight and nocturnal scenes and of the shadowy or pitch-black halls and tunnels and forests is to establish an atmosphere in which any surprise may plausibly occur and anxieties about the unknown may be aroused. But conceivably the darkness of the novels, especially in conjunction with the signs of ruin, also suggests a world from which the light, with all its possible implications and symbolic values, has been withdrawn or in which it has been extinguished.

As for the natural world in general, though the prospects are often magnificent and melancholy in the Romantic tradition, passages from Gothic fiction frequently suggest a nature infected with insinuations of hostility. To cite two conspicuous examples, Lewis in *The Monk* describes the mountaintop from which Satan will later hurl Ambrosio to his death as a place altogether inhospitable to man, and for Ann Radcliffe's Emily, in the *Mysteries of Udolpho,* the beauties of the Pyrenees are impaired by such reminders of mortality as memorial crosses and a gibbet, while natural features are seen in terms of their potential as ambush.

The very notion of mortality (as above, and implicit in the ruined castles) also testifies to the nature of the Gothic world. Certainly the novels deal with death — sudden death, violent death, tragic death, death as punishment for villainy. This in itself would scarcely be worth noting, as one might take it for granted in novels so highly colored.

But the accompanying obsession with putrefaction, though
not exclusive to the Gothic novel, does suggest an interest
in death as something more than a lurid plot device. That
scene in *The Monk* in which Agnes puts her hand on a squashy
object and discovers it to be the head of a dead nun is more
representative than one might like to think. For comments
on the burial and decomposition of parents, children, lovers,
and employees, the reader may examine typical passages in
Roche's *Contrast,* Lewis's *The Monk,* Bonhote's *Bungay Castle,*
and Stanhope's *The Siege of Kenilworth,* respectively. Mary
Ann Radcliffe's one-handed villain has the unusual and moving experience of seeing his own lost member "rotting in
the blast."[3] The more famous and conservative Ann Radcliffe
supplies as one of Udolpho's mysteries a waxen image of
putrefaction complete with vermin. The point of all this
wormy circumstance is that death is a peculiar, even dis-
tinguishing, characteristic of the fallen world. Death is
perhaps the most striking difference between the Edenic and
the blighted worlds, and Gothic fiction has always at hand
some *memento mori* to remind us which world we are in.

The isolation of the protagonist is another principal
testimony to the fallen nature of the Gothic world and is
probably, next to the setting, the best-known characteristic of Gothic fiction. Gothic heroes and heroines are on
their own, stumbling alone, sometimes in foreign countries,
through appalling complexities of decision and action,
obliged to find their own solutions or go under; estrangement from all family ties is their normal condition. Indeed, it would be nearly impossible for protagonists in the
bosoms of their families to get into the scrapes common to
Gothic fiction.

Occasionally isolation is voluntary, as when a hero goes
off on some kind of mission, or perhaps simply takes a trip.
More often, it is involuntary, as when the heroine (e.g.,
Isabel in Green's *Abbot of Montserrat,* Rosaline in Mary Radcliffe's *Manfroné,* Ellena in Ann Radcliffe's *The Italian*)
or sometimes the hero (e.g., St. Leon in Godwin's *St. Leon,*
Leonard in Palmer's *The Mystery of the Black Tower*) is kidnapped. Protagonists are frequently orphans, or they are
foundlings or adopted, their family origins mysterious
(e.g., Theodore in Walpole's *The Castle of Otranto,* Theodore
in Stanhope's *Confessional of Valombre,* Edmund in Reeve's
The Old English Baron). Sometimes they are incarcerated in
monasteries or nunneries (e.g., Agnes in Lewis's *The Monk,*
Bernardo in Montague's *The Demon of Sicily*), voluntarily or
involuntarily, where they may be further isolated by the
hostility of the religious community (e.g., Monçada in Maturin's *Melmoth the Wanderer*). On other occasions they may
be locked in solitary cells by the Inquisition (e.g., St.

Leon in Godwin's *St. Leon,* Ambrosio in Lewis's *The Monk*), or
left to waste away in dungeons (e.g., Ethelwina in Curties's
Ethelwina, Verezzi in Percy Shelley's *Zastrozzi*), where they
sometimes suppose themselves to be forgotten by their cap-
tors and all the world besides. In short, the one place the
protagonist almost never finds himself is at home. (Like
mankind, according to some religious views, he is just a
stranger; his home is always somewhere else.) And one might
add the reflection that his lifelong isolation in his own
skin is capped by the even greater isolation of the grave.

The Wanderer, though he is deprived of death rather than
threatened with it, is the epitome of the solitary protagonist, and his state is often explicitly (as in the case of
Maturin's Melmoth in *Melmoth the Wanderer,* Croly's Salathiel
in *Salathiel,* and other Wandering Jews) and at the least im-
plicitly (as for St. Leon, or Alhamet in Green's *Alibeg the
Tempter*) a species of Divine punishment. He may be seen as
a perpetual exile, both homeless and alone in a world that
contains no other creature of his kind. Neither quite natural nor quite supernatural, he is analogous to fallen man,
who is alienated both from the beasts, which have learned to
fear him, and from pure spirits, because he is mortal, with
all the limitations that mortality implies. One might note,
too, that the archetypal Wanderer, Cain, is the first man
born into a fallen world.

The Gothic protagonists' dominant reactions — guilt and
fear — so permeate the novels that one is half tempted to
discuss them as aspects of the setting. Certainly they are
crucial to tone and pertinent to the nature of the Gothic
world. Guilt is personified in restless and conscience-
stricken ghosts (e.g., Viscensio in Montague's *The Demon of
Sicily,* Ditmar in "The Family Portraits" from *Tales of the
Dead*) and in ghosts which, like Ethelwina's murdered father
in Curties's *Ethelwina,* or Edmund's parents in *The Old English Baron,* or Arion in Green's *Alibeg the Tempter,* walk
in connection with someone else's guilt. There is also much
preoccupation, one way and another, with damnation and ruin
as the fruit of guilty deeds. Villains expire in mental
agony (e.g., Leopold in *Ethelwina,* De Weldon in Drake's "Sir
Egbert"), raving about their victims and about the devils
who will carry them off to hell. And, again, there is the
guilt-ridden figure of the Wanderer, who can never stop paying for his particular misdeed.

As for fear, it seems to be the novels' principal end.
Besides fearing — to name only a few things — murder, kidnapping, robbery, seduction, passion, damnation, bankruptcy,
bereavement, and falling into pits, the inhabitants of the
Gothic world are clearly plagued by the fear that has no
name, perhaps what Mary Shelley means by "the mysterious

fears of our nature."[4] Characters allude on numerous occasions to their fear of the unknown and demonstrate repeated-
ly a feeling that something is likely to jump them at any
moment, and has probably been stalking them all along. The
novelists sometimes emphasize that such fears are vague and
undirected, but more often provide them a focus in a number
of more explicit menaces, such as ghosts, the Inquisition,
apparently omniscient spies; these menaces share the charac-
teristics of stealth, apparent or actual invisibility, and
the ability to apprehend the victim at any moment and to in-
vade him in what he thought his safest strongholds.

Not only do the novels present an image of the fallen
world, but their plots are much concerned with the process
of falling. The tribulations of the protagonists have frequently to do with temptation, flattery, deceit, and a subsequent lapse from virtue. The agents of temptation are
various, but may generally be classified as demons, villains,
and illicit desires. Genuinely demonic tempters are not un-
common in the more spectacular fiction. They assume a variety of forms: for instance, Green's demon in *The Abbot of
Montserrat,* "half brute, half serpent,"[5] always begins its
appearances as a patch of yellow light, impervious to rain,
and increases its wattage as its victim participates in
evil; Dacre's Zofloya (in *Zofloya*) begins as a Moorish servant and becomes more beautiful with his victim's wicked
deeds, until he reveals his true ugliness at the moment of
her destruction; Lewis's demon, in *The Monk,* comes disguised
as a beautiful woman and perpetrates a most astounding and
subtle complexity of deceptions; Montague's demon in *The
Demon of Sicily* is described as a mixture of angelic and
infernal (reflected perhaps in an accompanying woodcut that
shows him with wings and a mustache) but works through a
rather crude if occasionally supernatural machinery of
erotic dreams, door keys, and such.

More often than demons, Gothic fiction provides villains, described in uncompromisingly demonic terms. *Fiend*
is a predictably frequent term of disapprobation, but both
serpent and *subtle* have a high level of incidence as well.
Male villains, in particular, tend to look a little satanic.
Several, like Holford's Wolfsteïn (in *Warbeck of Wolfsteïn*)
and Maturin's Schemoli (in *Fatal Revenge*), take pains to
persuade their intended victims that they are indeed supernatural. Many of them are beset by Satan's own flaw, un-
governable pride. Nearly all of them relish their wicked
work.

Temptations, like their agents, come in many forms —
murder (parricide is popular), renunciation of God, capitu-
lation to lust and passion, gaming and fiscal irresponsibil-
ity, and a host of lesser sins like suspicion, rudeness to

parents, and weakness of character. Authors make clear that all of these lead to disaster. Characters understandably remark that Satan seems to have been let loose to prey among them.

The task of the powers of darkness is assisted by some human weaknesses that are contingent on the fallen state. Man is the victim, first, of corrupted appetites and, second, of imperfect faculties. The novelists' views evidently coincide in this respect with those of Coleridge, who writes to his brother George in 1798, "I believe most steadfastly in original Sin; that from our mothers' wombs our understandings are darkened; and even when our understandings are in the Light, that our organization is depraved, and our volitions imperfect."[6] This seems a succinct statement of what the novels demonstrate — that the condition of being fallen renders one peculiarly vulnerable to snares and deceptions which should at all costs be resisted.

The principal passion that undoes Gothic heroes and heroines is predictably lust, though there are instances of anger, avarice, occult curiosities, and even gluttony, as well as more general sensuality. Especially for novelists who wish to avoid the more lurid effects achieved by demons and villains, passions play the role of demonic agents, treacherously internal. When Roche's Clermont asks a monk whether evil spirits really are let loose to tempt men to destruction, the holy man replies, "'tis not the ministers of darkness, but their own impetuous passions which hurry them to destruction."[7] Consequently we often discover that tempters have set elaborate traps, bowers of insidious bliss, baited with pleasures which arouse as many sensations as possible. In Lathom's *Astonishment,* for example, a virtuous young man is tempted by an older woman whose garden is heavily perfumed with the scent of orange trees, roses, heliotrope, etc., whose table is set with cakes, ices, and wines, and who hopefully inquires whether he likes music.[8]

The success of the tempters often depends to some degree on their ability to delude the victims. Sometimes the delusion is intellectual, as in the inculcation of what the novels call False Philosophy (usually some poisonous brand of libertinism). More interestingly, the delusion may be physical — the innocent and smiling face of a villain, the illusions of sorcery, the false appearance of a demon; the novels display a marked preoccupation with the unreliability of the human senses. In Maturin's *Fatal Revenge,* for instance, the sinister confessor Schemoli, pretending to be a specter, plays on the somewhat occult expectations of the two Montorio brothers, the more susceptible of whom is at one point falsely persuaded that he has seen the confessor turn into a skeleton. Schemoli's deceptions ultimately pre-

vail, and the boys, supposing their persecutor to be omnip-
otent, give themselves up to his direction. Or consider
Lewis's *The Monk,* which demonstrates deception by the senses
at its most dangerous. Although Ambrosio's mind is warped
by pride and passion, his visual equipment is normal; yet
it perceives only the disguise and not the demon hidden underneath. He is taken in, to his eternal damnation, by Matilda's disguise as a young man, by a demon's disguise as
Matilda, by Matilda's resemblance to the Virgin Mary's picture, by Satan's appearance as a handsome boy, and by the
conclusions based on these false perceptions.

A few additional details are particularly reminiscent
of the Edenic myth. Gardens (and related man-made scenes of
luxury, as above), on the occasions when they do appear, are
likely to be the scenes of temptation. In Maturin's *Melmoth
the Wanderer,* Immalee's island paradise, into which Melmoth
insinuates his horrid knowledgeability, is an obvious representation of Eden, with Immalee as the innocent Eve. Other
conspicuous garden-temptations can be found in *The Monk*
(Matilda reveals her identity, and her bosom, in the abbey
garden, and Ambrosio is bitten by the snake) and in Dacre's
The Libertine (where Angelo the libertine enters the bucolic
paradise designed to keep Gabrielle innocent, and seduces
her). The preternatural and Edenic innocence of the average
Gothic heroine has been burlesqued too often to require
elaboration.

Disaster in the novels, as in Eden, strikes swiftly and
relentlessly and is irreversible. Much is made of this; the
plots are predictably full of murder, sudden death, kidnapping, and so on. They are full, as well, of philosophizing
on the sudden and evil turns of fate and are particularly
given to imagery involving falling into pits and off the
edges of precipices. Related to the notion of pits opening
beneath one's feet, and even more pertinent to temptation,
is the vortex image that accompanies the assertion that one
false step can lead straight to endless ruin. Lust is of
course an especially dangerous sin in this respect. In
Hamilton's *Montalva* alone, three quite separate girls fall
victim to this evil passion, succumbing in weak moments to
what the novelists call "guilty transports." "One unguarded
moment," explains one of the sinners, "plunged us both into
guilt, and robbed me of peace for ever."[9] Dacre warns her
readers, "The temptation to evil once admitted, it is no
longer easy to repel its insidious advances; a dreaded step
once taken, another quickly follows; and the wretched victim of error seldom awakens, till repentance is in vain."[10]
Dacre's casual assumption that repentance is in vain is a
good illustration of the oddly hopeless tone one perceives
in the Gothic world; man has a soul to lose, but no expecta-

tion of mercy or possible atonement. Innocence occasionally
resists the snares laid against it and wins through to a
happy ending. But the evadable snares are usually rather
crude and superficial ones. The heroine may triumph over
attempted kidnappings and rapes thanks to the firmness of
her principles and the fortuitous arrival of help. When
confronted with a tempter, natural or supernatural, of any
psychological ingenuity, however, the frail defense of the
darkened understanding is exceedingly likely to give way.

In addition to the evidence of deprivations, ruins,
failures, and hazards, one pleasant circumstance helps to
identify the Gothic world as fallen. The recognition and
reunion scenes that provide resolutions to a number of the
novels, especially the milder ones, are not peculiar to the
genre, but the search for one's origins, identity, and family connections is certainly one of the commonest quests in
Gothic fiction and may be seen as an attempt to impose order
upon a chaotic environment. The moment of discovery constitutes, with the reunion of lovers, the greatest and indeed
the only notable source of joy to be found in the Gothic
world, perhaps because it promises an escape from the world
as the poor wanderer has known it. The Gothic world, like
the fallen world, is blighted, a place of danger, sorrow,
and exile, in which the protagonist's only salvation is a
rediscovery of and reunion with the father or the beloved.
In certain of the novels, however, the discovery of one's
ties means the discovery of sin (e.g., incest, matricide)
and leads not to joy but to despair.

The ambience of despair and degeneration that charac-
terizes Gothic fiction, though it finds its widest and most
concentrated expression in that form, also runs suggestively
in one way and another through much of the literature of the
period. Surely we must stop dismissing Gothic fiction as
a frivolous manifestation of the Romantic fascination with
the supernatural, the mysterious, the medieval, and see the
genre as a principal part of Romanticism's darker side. Although the novels assert only intermittently a qualitative
claim to the company of Coleridge or Keats, by sheer bulk
and wealth of detail Gothic fiction provides much the most
comprehensive literary expression of the present, dark, and
fallen world against which Romanticism must measure the
brightness of its Edens and New Jerusalems.

Notes

1. Robert Kiely, *The Romantic Novel in England* (Cambridge, Mass.,
1972), p. 197.
2. Ann Radcliffe, *The Mysteries of Udolpho* (Oxford, 1970), p.
227. First edition, 1794.

3. Mary Ann Radcliffe, *Manfroné, or, The One-Handed Monk* (London, 1839), p. 94. First edition, 1809.

4. Mary Shelley, *Frankenstein, or, The Modern Prometheus* (Toronto, 1965), p. ix. Reprint of the third edition, 1831.

5. William Child Green, *The Abbot of Montserrat, or, The Pool of Blood* (London, 1826), 1:107.

6. Samuel Taylor Coleridge, *Letters of Samuel Taylor Coleridge*, ed. Earl Leslie Griggs (Oxford, 1956), 1:396.

7. Regina Maria Roche, *Clermont. A Tale in Four Volumes* (London, 1968), p. 294. First edition, 1798.

8. Francis Lathom, *Astonishment: A Romance of a Century Ago* (London, 1821), 1:170, 171. First edition, 1802.

9. Ann Mary Hamilton, *Montalva, or, Annals of Guilt. A Tale* (London, 1806), 2:121.

10. Charlotte Dacre, *The Libertine* (London, 1807), 1:72.

Summaries

Students of the Gothic will at once recognize that the synopses which follow represent a very small portion of the
Gothic novels published between 1790 and 1830, or there-
abouts, and will inevitably lament the exclusion of some
title or wonder at the inclusion of a novel that seems not
to be Gothic at all. My guiding principle was to produce
the reference work that I sorely needed, and did not have,
when I began my Gothic research some years ago. Wishing at
that time to read a great many of the more lurid Gothics,
preferably ones with demons and other supernatural person-
nel, I set off to rare book collections with a copy of Montague Summers's *A Gothic Bibliography* and never a clue as
to what might lie behind the titles. Some quite promising
titles led to disappointingly bland novels, while some rather neutral titles (e.g., *Mary Jane* by Richard Sickelmore)
proved satisfyingly horrid. This discrepancy accounts for
the not-very-Gothic summaries included in this collection;
having learned what is behind the titles, it seems best to
tell, thereby saving someone else the experiment. Since de-
ciding to publish my notes I have tried to fill in obvious
gaps and to supply useful titles — the Northanger novels,
for instance, and the novels republished by Arno Press,
those being perhaps more readily accessible to readers than
other Gothics. When feasible I have made notes on novels
especially cited by the handful of authorities on the Gothic; *The Castle of Niolo* and *Gondez the Monk* are examples.
I have tried, too, to fill in missing novels by particularly
reliable and prolific authors like Stanhope, W. C. Green,
and Curties. One particular omission and one inclusion require explanation. I have not done summaries for any of the
novels of Sir Walter Scott, though some, like *The Bride of
Lammermoor,* have as good a claim to be Gothic as other novels here. But there is no difficulty about finding out the
content of a Scott novel, and they seem to me not so Gothic
as to demand inclusion. I have included a few chapbooks,
especially a selection from Isaac Crookenden and Sarah Wilkinson. It is unlikely, though not impossible, that a reader will come in search of a particular chapbook title, but
these outrageous little stories are part of the Gothic phenomenon and may be useful to someone wishing to acquire an
overall view.

The synopses vary in length and specificity; less Gothic
novels will sometimes have less elaborate notes, as will
novels that are already relatively well known. The reader
may feel confident about the information which is included
(barring the possibility that I have somewhere been lured
into a trap set by the author and have not gotten out again)
but must bear in mind that much has necessarily been left

out, for the novels are full of subplots and reminiscences, and sometimes run to five volumes.

I must offer my apologies for any untoward lightness of tone that I have been unable to excise from the summaries. The novels themselves are almost always perfectly serious about their principal goings-on; as George DeMaurier says in "A Lost Illusion," "Passion hallows each page — guilt ennobles each line." Alas, I have found that suitable gravity is hard to maintain through some of the more remarkable details of plot. To avoid confusion between the novelists' amusement and my own, I have omitted from the summaries such burlesques and tongue-in-cheek productions as Barrett's *The Heroine,* Dubois's *Old Nick,* Sarah Green's *Romance Readers and Romance Writers,* and several of the novels of Jane West.

Readers wishing to pursue the originals of the novels summarized may appreciate a few words about North American availability. The University of Virginia's Sadleir-Black collection of Gothic novels is much the most extensive on this side of the Atlantic, and the staff is especially courteous and reasonable. Harvard and Yale both have Gothic holdings well worth a visit. Most good graduate libraries — I used the University of Toronto's — should be able to produce a surprising number of useful titles, both in nineteenth-century editions and in the modern reprints or editions, especially the Folio Press Northanger Novels, the three-part Gothic series from Arno Press, and the Oxford English Novels.

The novels that follow are summarized alphabetically by author; in the event that the author is not known, the novel is listed alphabetically by title.

1: Ball, Edward   THE BLACK ROBBER. A ROMANCE   3 vols. London: A. K. Newman, 1819

Ulric St. Julien, a younger son, resents having been put into a monastery by his parents while his elder brother is still at large. He falls in love and elopes with a novice named Julia on the proceeds of her diamond rosary. When Julia, some years later, is carried off by vengeful monks whose execution of her is prevented only by her spontaneous death, Ulric joins a band of robbers. He and his comrades kill the guilty abbot and burn the monastery, after which he goes on to become a local legend — the robber dressed in mourning who appears and disappears at will and may be in league with the supernatural.

When Ulric joins the robbers he leaves his child Valentine to the grudging care of its uncle Reginald, whose wife, Matilda Fitz Ormond, is also secretly married to Evlin de

Granville, a previous commitment. She and Evlin have a daughter, Issena, with whom Valentine will be in love later on. Evlin is a foundling, but before the end of the first volume he has been identified as the child of an aristocratic hermit. (The hermit, after having been sold into slavery in Constantinople, married a woman named Zelinda just in time to save her from a harem. Evlin as an infant fell through a hole into an old mine and was given up for dead.)

The story has three villains. The first, Ulric's brother Reginald, is perhaps the least vicious of the three. He is unkind to Valentine, permitting him to suppose himself a "victim of icy charity" rather than a nephew, and he dies in his cups, after which Ulric becomes Earl. The second and principal villain is Oswald, who is responsible for and profits from Evlin's murder in the forest. Desiring Issena, who loves Valentine, he has her kidnapped and proposes to her; when she refuses he tries to stab her but is prevented by the specter of murdered Evlin, her father. He does stab her mother Matilda, whose body he throws into a glen, and has Valentine imprisoned for the murder. When, after a melee between the bandits and Oswald's men, Ulric is captured and put in an adjacent dungeon, father and son are reunited and escape by the aid of a faithful servant. Issena escapes too, separately. The escape of Ulric and Valentine introduces the third villain, or villainess, for the useful servant recommends them to the care of the noblewoman Rodolpha, whose life he once saved. After Valentine goes to hunt for Issena, Rodolpha's growing passion for Ulric leads her impulsively (she is sorry immediately afterward) to murder her husband. Ulric is horrified and leaves as soon as he can. He finds Valentine, who has already found Issena, but soon Rodolpha comes and finds all three of them. Through her influence with the king, Valentine and Ulric are brought to trial for various crimes and condemned to death. Matilda's timely arrival clears Valentine of charges that he has murdered her, and Ulric is pardoned for his banditry. But clemency comes too late for the latter; the sight of his son on the verge of execution causes him to die of shock. Rodolpha goes mad, and the severed heads of Oswald and a criminal associate are stuck on the battlements.

2: Barbauld, Anna Laetitia   "SIR BERTRAND. A FRAGMENT" from *MISCELLANEOUS PIECES IN PROSE*   London: J. Johnson, 1792

Sir Bertrand, traveling across a heath, loses his way in the dark. He blunders into a ruined house equipped with gliding lights and tolling bells. There he encounters a series of horrid stimuli — blue flame, detachable hand, mysterious shriek, armed figure — which culminate in his kissing a lady who rises from a coffin. When he kisses her, the building falls down and he finds himself in a luxurious benqueting room with a beautiful woman and attendant nymphs. The woman thanks him for releasing her from enchantment.

3: Beckford, William   VATHEK. 1 vol. First published as AN ARABIAN TALE, FROM AN UNPUBLISHED MANUSCRIPT, WITH NOTES CRITICAL AND EXPLANATORY   London: J. Johnson, 1786

The Caliph Vathek, whose evil eye can kill with an angry glance and often does, has five special palaces, one for the gratification of each sense, but despite his passionate and self-indulgent nature his subjects seem to love him. One day a demonic stranger, a Giaour, arrives in the kingdom with a collection of magical knives, sabers, and slippers for sale. Vathek acquires, among other things, some sabers with inscriptions which change daily. That the inscriptions are undecipherable except by one old man does nothing to improve Vathek's disposition; he falls ill with frustration and is obliged to drink enormous quantities of cold water.
　　The Giaour, who has reappeared to cure Vathek on the one hand and to torment him on the other, promises at last to take the Caliph to the Palace of Subterranean Fire on condition that he adore the terrestrial influences and abjure Mahomet. Pleased with the bargain, Vathek throws the hungry Giaour the fifty most beautiful little boys in the kingdom, and when some of his subjects later forgive and attempt to rescue him from a fire (a magical one, of his mother's devising), he offers them up as well.
　　Vathek sets off for the Palace of Subterranean Fire with an uncommonly splendid retinue but is soon exposed to bad weather, wild animals, and forest fire. Parched, in the midst of a wasteland, his entourage fairly annihilated, he decides to ignore the Giaour's edict not to enter any habitation. Soon Vathek and Nouronihar, his host's beautiful daughter, are mutually attracted despite Nouronihar's engagement to and love for her soft and babyish cousin Gulchenrouz. She too is eager to see the treasures of the subterranean Palace and despite her father's efforts to stop her — he drugs her, carries her away, and persuades her that she has died — she leaves home to revel with Vathek in the delights of sensuality. At last, after some goading by his mother and some attempt by benevolent supernaturals to make him change his mind, the Caliph comes with Nouronihar to his destination. There they meet Eblis, see the treasures of the Pre-adamite Sultans, and encounter Soliman Ben Daoud himself, but they are unnerved to find all the inhabitants of the Palace pressing their right hands over their unquenchably burning hearts. In the few days remaining before

their own hearts catch fire they wander apathetically hand-
in-hand through the treasures that once tempted them to make
their journey, but even their companionship at last gives
way to the agony of their flaming hearts and they begin to
hate each other.

Vathek's witch mother Carathis, whom he summons in order
to berate her for his upbringing, is obliged to stay in the
halls of Eblis and burn with the others. As for Nouronihar's cousin Gulchenrouz, he was earlier rescued (from Carathis, who wished to sacrifice him) by the benevolent Genius and is leading a happy life in a magically protected land
of never-ending childhood, as are the fifty little boys whom
we supposed the Gaiour to have eaten.

4: THE BLOODY HAND, OR, THE FATAL CUP. A TALE OF HORROR!
   24 pp. London: Kemmish and Son, n.d.

The Bloody Hand is a first-person narrative ostensibly by
the son of an Irish family that earlier emigrated to France.
Reginald O'Mara (a pseudonym, he says) was born in 1766 to
a French mother, Antoinette Beaufois, daughter of a Marquis.
O'Mara has been promised to the Catholic church in expiation
for indiscretions committed by his maternal grandfather.
(The grandfather was in his youth professedly a Catholic but
really a deist who belonged to a sect called the Illuminati.
He and his friends carried off from a convent a girl whom he
wished to marry and who had been cloistered against her
will. In the course of the rescue he cut off a priest's
hand; the girl, who was taking communion when her chance
for escape occurred, inadvertently ran off with the chalice.
They were both punished severely and after his release from
prison were permitted to marry on condition that the church
be given half their property and their eldest son. The narrator's mother was their only child, so O'Mara is the first
available sacrifice.) O'Mara manages to avoid his ecclesiastical obligations but is more than once put into the Bastille for political and quasi-political reasons, having become conspicuous for his essays on the rights of the people.
The priest whose hand was cut off by O'Mara's grandfather
is still intent upon vengeance but at last dies a bizarre
death: a prisoner whom he is poisoning spits the poison back
into his eye and kills him. Finally O'Mara manages to leave
France and go to England, which he says is much nicer.

5: Bolen, C. A.   THE MYSTERIOUS MONK, OR, THE WIZARD'S
   TOWER   3 vols. London: A. K. Newman, 1826

Bolen's novel takes place in the reign of King John and involves much of the royal family. An explanation of family

relationships had better be made at the start, though they are not revealed until the end of the story. Ella di Mortimer, the heroine, and her brother Eric have been raised by Lady Gertrude, who turns out to be their aunt, sister to their father, Lord Pembroke. Lady Gertrude dies at the beginning of the novel and commends them to the keeping of Adolphe, who is the mysterious monk of the title and, as they discover later, their maternal uncle. As Lady Gertrude is dying, two armed men come with a warrant from King John to take Ella to a place of "better security," but on the way she is rescued by Philip Fauconbridge. Since he finally marries Ella (though King John's daughter Matilda would like to have him) his pedigree should be clarified at once. His mother, Lady Fauconbridge, has been twice married, the first time to Philip's father, Philip de Clairville, who subsequently appears to have been murdered. But we discover that he is not dead and that he is really Richard Coeur de Lion, so Philip becomes Earl of Monmouth.

A great deal of frenetic activity goes on between Lady Gertrude's death and Ella's marriage to Monmouth, and there are quantities of minor but royal characters, including the dowager queen Elinor and Prince Authur. Unsettling experiences mark Ella's long struggle to discover her identity and maintain her chastity. Thrice imprisoned, she is pursued by a number of men with dishonorable intentions, including King John — at that time she believes him to be her father — and the Pope. Her arm is accidentally broken by the dowager queen. Her brother is imprisoned and her lover wounded. She also survives the lesser shocks of seeing her first black woman (she has nightmares afterward), discovering that her page is a woman in disguise, and being several times convinced and then unconvinced that she has identified her father. There are some macabre touches as well, for during one imprisonment she sees a villain going past her cell with a dead body, and there is a sibyl who tells her about unearthly and prophetic blue flames. In the end Eric as well as Ella makes a suitable marriage as does Virginia, formerly the page. The rights of the innocent are restored and the bad come to justice.

6: Bonhote, Elizabeth   BUNGAY CASTLE. A NOVEL   2 vols.
   London: William Lane, 1796

Sir Philip de Morney has two children, Edwin and Roseline. Roseline is being educated in a convent but comes home to Bungay Castle for a holiday, bringing her friend Madeline. Although Madeline and Edwin fall in love, Madeline considers herself betrothed to God. Nevertheless the three young people enjoy themselves and go exploring the castle in hopes

of finding a prisoner to succor. They find a handsome one
named Walter, who begins writing poems to Roseline about his
loss of interest in escaping ("No More for Liberty I Pine").
Roseline's father wishes her to marry a particular baron, a
widower much older than she. Though unmoved by her father's
threats of a nunnery, when he intimates that he will liter-
ally die of disappointment, Roseline promises herself to the
Baron. The Baron is eager to marry her and leave Bungay
Castle, where he has been having some rather horrid experiences. (Once, for instance, he heard a voice inside a coffin. When he broke open the lid he found only bones, but
the voice went on speaking.) Roseline's wedding is disrupted by Walter, whom the Baron briefly supposes to be the
ghost of his wife. In fact, Walter is his son, said by his
scheming stepmother to have died in childhood; his identity
is established by a birthmark. The Baron gives Walter and
Roseline his blessing. Edwin and Madeline elope with the
aid of Albert, a servant who understands ventriloquism and
has been responsible for the castle's Gothic sound effects.
They go to see Walter, who is to travel for a while before
his marriage and has unwittingly become involved with the
daughter of the proprietress of a local brothel. Albert
arrives just in time to prevent their marriage; Walter has
been inveigled into the brothel and confronted with a clergyman. So there is a happy ending for Walter after all, and
for Roseline, and for Madeline, whose father forgives her
for eloping.

An inserted tale about two lovers called Narford and
Lucy, however, ends dismally, with Lucy's untimely death and
Narford's consequent lunacy.

7: Bonhote, Elizabeth   ELLEN WOODLEY. A NOVEL   2 vols.
   London: William Lane, 1790

Ellen Woodley and her brother Valentine are the intelligent
and upright children of a poor rural clergyman. A wealthy
farmer from the neighborhood sends Valentine to Cambridge to
study for the ministry. Their richest neighbors, Sir Henry
and Lady Alford, who made their fortune in India by some extremely unscrupulous means not specified, invite the Wood-
leys to dinner to see whether the clergyman will undertake
the education of their son Edwin. The boy is vain, feeble,
foppish, and inclined to be sadistic with animals, but Sir
Henry endorses Woodley's stern approach to his training and
Edwin so improves that Ellen falls in love with him. His
family disapproves of the match for reasons of class, but
Edwin stays faithful through the temptations of London,
Bath, and Brighton, while Ellen pines at home. After Woodley dies, Ellen goes as a paid companion to Lady Lexington

in London, but her background and temperament render her new environment uncongenial.

Edwin and Ellen are at last permitted to marry. They have five children and little money. Edwin worries about losing his ancestral home; Valentine tutors their children without pay. Then one day four-year-old William pulls a string that he sees in an India cabinet, and a secret drawer opens to reveal gold and diamonds and a letter signed Omiah. The letter is from an Indian whose family have been raped and killed by Europeans; it counsels mercy and warns against pride and luxury. Edwin and Ellen are enabled by this windfall to continue their happy and virtuous lives in the family home.

8: Bonhote, Elizabeth   THE FASHIONABLE FRIEND. A NOVEL
   2 vols. London: T. Becket and P. A. Dehondt, 1773

Henrietta Melville and Colonel Beaufort are secretly married; only her friend Caroline Tylney and his friend Henry Courtney know about it. In fact, the neighbors think that Henrietta is being kept, and Caroline's parents will not permit her to visit. (The novel is epistolary.) Henry is supposed to take care of Henrietta while her husband is away on military duty, but he falls in love with her and burns Beaufort's letters as they arrive. When she realizes what is going on she runs away and leaves her child with Henry, who repents. Her marriage is fragile, for she and Beaufort were underage and he can abandon her if he chooses. When he comes back he mistakenly believes her to be a loose woman, but his father has faith in her, and Henrietta's name is finally cleared.

Her friend Caroline has trouble with suitors. She is pursued by Mr. Danby but loves Mr. Cornwall. Her father has offered to Mr. Cornwall Caroline's elder sister Lucy; the anger and confusion generated by that misunderstanding require no description. Caroline is sent into the country to be guarded by a vengeful and hostile Lucy, but Lucy's conspiracy and sexual intimacy with Danby are opportunely brought to light. Danby and Lucy are compelled to marry, and Caroline is permitted to marry Cornwall.

9: Brewer, James Norris   A WINTER'S TALE   4 vols. London:
   William Lane, 1799

Edward the Black Prince is attracted to a girl whom he meets at a tournament, but as her social rank is lower than his he tries to overcome this inclination. The girl, Selina, is an orphan living with a distant relative, the Earl of Ilford. (Ilford has been given the title and residence that formerly belonged to Selina's father, who was banished for insurrection.) Invited to Ilford's house, the Prince is frustrated by Selina's absence from festivities and stirred by secret doors and gliding figures in the picture gallery, which contains a portrait of Selina's mother. At last the Prince finds Selina in her room, in which the Earl has requested her to remain. After a number of nocturnal visits, which Selina and the Prince fondly regard as merely friendly, they are undone by their reciprocal passion. The Prince is distressed that his position does not permit him to claim her, and Selina is distraught by her own turpitude. His attempt to marry her secretly is interrupted by the ghost of Selina's mother. They have been warned, too, by the articulate and levitating armor of Selina's father, which threatens them with death if they meet again, and by a dream of the Prince's in which Selina's mother comes out of her coffin and leads him to Selina lying on a bed with a dead child turning green on her bosom. Selina is, in fact, pregnant and later writes to the Prince to tell him so.

Selina has additional troubles in the Ilford household. Lady Ilford, after receiving a somewhat obscure warning from a wild woman in the forest, is murdered by her husband, who hopes to possess Selina himself. His son Lord Desmond nourishes similar desires and has once drunkenly tried to rape her. Her baby is delivered in secrecy while the Black Prince paces in an anteroom; he has continued to provide moral support even though the relationship has been chaste since the night of the child's conception. The Earl, after unwittingly stabbing his own son, whom he perceived merely as someone trying to rape Selina (Desmond's second such attempt), is more than ever determined to have her. He locks her up to consider his marriage proposal. A good priest helps her escape with her baby to France, where they cross battlefields to get to the Prince's army. She is captured en route by Sir Emeric, Ilford's old friend. The Earl of Ilford arrives later and they lock her in a dungeon, hoping that she will do anything to move the baby into a healthier place. Sir Emeric has decided to betray his town to the French army, and in the resulting fracas (the English win) Selina is rescued by her father, who was in the dungeon just above hers. Ilford is killed and Emeric captured. Selina's father is upset about his daughter's illegitimate child but forgives her.

10: Brewer, George THE WITCH OF RAVENSWORTH. A ROMANCE
     2 vols. London: J. F. Hughes, 1808

Ann Ramsey, "better known by the title of the Hag," has one tooth, a gray cat that drinks blood, a large raven, and a

reputation for eating babies. Snakes and toads slither
through the poisonous plants that grow around her cabin.
Her neighbor, Baron La Braunch, though more attractive, is
comparably wicked; he is dissolute and deceitful, and rumor
says that he has been cruel to a woman called Gertrude. As
the story begins he marries Bertha, a virtuous widow with a
small son. At the wedding feast a previously empty chair is
suddenly occupied by the Hag, who raises the toast "Misery
to the bride." She appears again at the christening of La
Braunch's new son Hugo and is about to baptize the child
herself when they take it away from her. After the birth
of Hugo, the Baron begins to wonder whether his little step-
son Edward, whom he has begun to dislike, will live to grow
up; should he die, Hugo could inherit his estates. Hoping
that the Hag will predict an untimely death for Edward, La
Braunch asks for a look at the future. The Hag requests a
child as payment for her help and the Baron obligingly supplies Edward, which makes his principal question more or
less unnecessary; she takes the boy away and returns with
a bloody knife to announce that he has been sacrificed to
Askar. La Braunch is shown the demon Ugall and a specter
woman who terrifies him much more than the demon does.
Though invited to a meeting with Askar, he does not return
to the Hag until eleven years later. By that time his son
Hugo has died and he wishes to be rid of Bertha in order to
marry his seductive neighbor Alwena.

The Hag tells La Braunch that this time he must certainly come to the meeting with Askar. There his initiation requires him to stab a loathsome corpse resembling the specter
which so terrified him eleven years earlier. Now the Hag
promises to kill Bertha, and Bertha suddenly disappears.
The marriage to Alwena is not happy, for the two are equally
vicious; after an unexpected lecture from the Hag about the
sources of felicity, La Braunch feels miserable and somewhat
penitent. He and Alwena murder each other — she poisons
him, he stabs her — and the castle by La Braunch's will goes
to a local woodcutter whose wife has expressed a wish to be
rich. A stipulation in the will sends the woodcutter to a
tower where he finds the bodies of a woman and a child, and
a written confession of La Braunch's crimes, beginning with
the seduction and poisoning of Gertrude. Further, the woodcutter discovers that a foundling left by the Hag on his
doorstep is the missing Edward. Bertha, too, is alive.
Nor is the Baron dead, for the Hag did not provide Alwena
with real poison; he has gone into a monastery. The Hag
herself is Gertrude, heavily disguised. Edward inherits the
castle, which assures the fortunes of both his real and foster parents, and Gertrude, formerly the Hag, enters a convent.

11: Brown, Elizabeth Cullen   THE SISTERS OF ST. GOTHARD. A
     TALE   2 vols. London: A. K. Newman, 1819

Blanchard, esteemed for his virtue and benevolence, is leading an obscure life in Switzerland with his two adolescent
daughters, Adelaide and Rosette. Rosette is amiable, warm,
pliable, and a bit giddy; her father worries about her and
tries to teach her that vice can look like felicity.   There
is a representative and, one suspects, highly symbolic incident in which Rosette leaves her flock to follow the music
of a passing regiment, causing a pet lamb to fall over a
precipice and her father to injure himself in a futile attempt to recover it. Rosette subsequently meets and finds
herself attracted to Montalvo, a passing nobleman with no
honorable intentions. Despite the precautions of her father, Montalvo one day lures her into a carriage with the
promise of a secret wedding; she is not heard of again for
some time. Adelaide, meanwhile, has met another and very
different sort of nobleman. Clementine and his mother, the
widowed Countess Rimini, have a vehicular mishap on their
way home from Bern and are assisted by the Blanchards. When
the Countess asks to borrow Adelaide for a visit, her father
(or foster father, as he suddenly reveals) consents, if reluctantly, for Adelaide is a much steadier character than
Rosette.
     Clementine and Adelaide fall in love, but Clementine was
engaged in infancy to his proud and insensitive cousin Valetta. He is trying to respect the wishes of his dead father, compounded by the injunctions of his rapidly declining
mother. Further, he will be disinherited if he does not
marry Valetta, so Adelaide refuses him for his own good.
He loses his head and offers her a separate establishment as
his mistress, causing her to run away, accompanied for protection by a reliable priest. Fortunately Valetta herself
breaks the contract and the couple marry with clear con-
sciences. One day, through sheer chance, Adelaide finds Rosette, gravely ill, with her baby; Montalvo gave her a wedding with a counterfeit clergyman. Clementine demands that
Montalvo marry Rosette properly; a duel ensues. Nobody is
killed, but Montalvo acquires a permanent limp which embar-
rasses him greatly. Rosette goes home and dies on her father's grave, embracing the turf. Adelaide and Clementine
bring up Rosette's little girl, who grows up to marry their
son and unite the families of the foster sisters.

12: Brydges, Sir Samuel Egerton   LE FORESTER. A NOVEL
     3 vols. London: J. White, 1802

Hugh Le Forester, an ancient profligate, long ago succeeded
to the titles and estate of his elder brother by having his
nephew Eustace raised in a cottage, kidnapped, and sent to
be sold into slavery. Saved by a shipwreck, Eustace came
back to England and spent the rest of his life trying to regain his father's estate. Eustace's son Godfrey is the hero
of the novel. A bookish and sensitive boy, he is taunted at
Cambridge by Hugh's spies and finally attacked and knocked
out by ruffians despite the preventative efforts of Emily
Mason, to whose looks (sixteen and melancholy) he is attracted. As a result of the attack he suffers a long illness and some resultant imbecility but recovers at last.
Emily coincidentally visits the house where he is recovering.
     At one point Godfrey is obliged to kill an assassin (for
which he will later be prosecuted) and is afterward subject
to tearful depression. The narrative is interrupted in the
second volume, most of which deals with the tribulations of
Godfrey's father Eustace, a record of which is preserved in
manuscript. With the resumption of the principal plot, Godfrey suffers further persecution, including kidnapping, imprisonment, and trial for murder. After his acquittal he
and Emily elope, since there seems no hope of winning her
father's consent. But her father and Hugh, she discovers,
are the same man; as he is dying, apparently of a stroke
brought on by attempting to shoot Godfrey, he gives his consent to their marriage. Godfrey's claim to the estate is
validated.

13: Brydges, Sir Samuel Egerton   MARY DE CLIFFORD. A STORY
     INTERSPERSED WITH MANY POEMS   1 vol. London: Whitting-
     ham, 1792

George and Mary are the last son and daughter of the De
Clifford family and are very fond of each other. Mary's social life takes a lively turn when George's set notices that
she is no longer a child. Only two of the young men are important to the plot. Woodvile, brilliant and eccentric, is
George's favorite and ultimately Mary's. There are disturbing rumors that he will marry Emily, his sister Elinor's
friend, but these are dispelled when Mary and Woodvile admit
their love for each other. Peter Lumm, a nouveau riche
neighbor whom George barely tolerates, proposes to Emily
with her mother's encouragement but is turned down. Lumm
is a pretentious dunce who claims to admire Milton and asks
whether he has written anything lately. (Brydges tells us

that Mary's library includes Petrarch, Spenser, Milton, Cowley, Thompson, *The Castle of Otranto,* and the novels of Mrs. Smith.)

A dispute over an old debt, settled by Woodvile's father without receipts and revived by Lumm's steward, leads to a duel between Lumm and Woodvile. Woodvile is killed. Lumm flees to the continent. Woodvile's mother dies of grief, as does Mary after several months of shock, fits, and lunacy. At the end of the novel Woodvile's sister Elinor is low in health and spirits, and Mary's brother George is not expected to recover from his melancholy.

14: Brydges, Sir Samuel Egerton   SIR RALPH WILLOUGHBY. AN HISTORICAL TALE OF THE SIXTEENTH CENTURY   1 vol. Florence: I. Magheri, 1820

Sir Ralph Willoughby, whose father Lord Uffington is in political exile from England, goes to the court of Elizabeth I and falls in, first, with Lord Burleigh. Burleigh is contemptuous of Willoughby's poetic tendencies and at last dismisses him, though not altogether for that reason; various people have conspired toward his downfall. Essex next takes him up (Willoughby has a precognitive dream of him with an open and bloody neck), and after further machinations he falls into Raleigh's hands. Raleigh hopes to extract the secrets of both Burleigh and Essex. Willoughby is beginning to be disillusioned with court life and with ambition in general. Before he can thoroughly embrace the simpler life he contemplates he is shipwrecked and becomes temporarily lunatic with fever; while he wanders and raves and hallucinates, people imagine that he is Essex in disguise. Later, when James comes to the throne and knights him, Willoughby finds himself involved in court intrigue again, for Salisbury thinks he aspires to Lady Arabella Stuart — he does find her very attractive — and takes the opportunity, when Raleigh accidentally implicates Willoughby in a trial, to destroy him. His manuscript scheme for an epic poem counts heavily against him. He is executed for treason.

15: Burney, Sarah Harriet   CLARENTINE. A NOVEL   3 vols. London: G. G. and J. Robinson, 1796

Clarentine Delmington, an orphan, is about thirteen as the novel begins. She lives with her uncle's family. Her foster brothers Edgar and Frederick are so fond of her that they resent the caretaking she voluntarily lavishes upon their youngest sister Emma; they wish that Clarentine would have more fun. Young Somerset, another cousin, appears as the story begins and inquires about her welfare, as he too wishes to take care of her. Later the household is enlarged by the temporary acquisition of Julia, whose mother has gone abroad with an ailing son. Although limp and spiritless at first, Julia improves under Clarentine's influence and develops an interest in Edgar. Edgar, however, wants Clarentine and proposes to her, which gets her into serious trouble: he does it at night, alone, in the parlor, and they are seen. At last he promises himself to Julia, and Clarentine is forgiven. She receives a proposal also from a Mr. Eltham, who continues impetuously to pursue her after her refusal. After a variety of troubles, Somerset and Clarentine decide to marry each other, and Clarentine's foster sister Sophia accepts Eltham.

16: Carver, Mrs.   THE HORRORS OF OAKENDALE ABBEY   1 vol.
    London: William Lane, 1797

Laura is sent to haunted Oakendale Abbey by Lord Oakendale, who wishes to seduce her. She is alone in the world except for one female servant, for not only her parents but her subsequent guardians are dead or missing. (Her earliest recollections are of being put on a ship by people in exotic clothing; the ship was captured and she was taken to a French prison where her identity papers were taken from her. The surgeon De Frene, who liberated and adopted her, has lately been decapitated for political reasons. Madame de Frene and Laura, who left Paris together after De Frene's head was delivered on a pike, were somehow put on two different ships. Eugene Rayneer, whom she loves, has sent no word since he was called back to England by his guardian. Oakendale has acquired Laura by pretending to send her to his sister in London in order that she may better search for her adopted mother.) Laura is brave, but it is a frightening abbey; it is later revealed to be the headquarters for a body-snatching business, which accounts for some of her nastier discoveries.

Lord Oakendale arrives at the Abbey to find that Laura has escaped. Not an altogether wicked man, he worries a little about her safety, but in fact she is being cared for by a philanthropic female neighbor. Sudden revelations of identity show Eugene Rayneer to be the bastard son of Lord Oakendale's wife, and Laura to be the daughter of Oakendale's brother William. Grateful at having avoided incest, Oakendale repents and becomes respectably avuncular. He does make trouble by opposing the marriage of Laura and Eugene and indeed nearly tries to force a renunciation from Laura when he is dying, but he relents. The marriage takes place and Eugene is permitted to inherit from his natural father, Lord Vincent.

17: THE CAVERN OF HORRORS, OR, MISERIES OF MIRANDA. A NEAPOLITAN TALE   72 pp. London: T. Hurst, 1802

This chapbook concentrates on the establishment-of-identity plot, producing along the way a fine assortment of coffins, bones, blood, daggers, and creaking doors. The heroine Miranda is ostensibly the youngest daughter of a Neapolitan vendor of fruit and ice snow. She ordinarily lives in a convent but has been extricated to help with the family business. She attracts the attention of several men, most important of whom is the young Cavalier Napolo di Logano, who later sends notes to her convent. After adventures that include being kidnapped by a father and son who wish to sell her to the Moors, she discovers the identity of her real parents, establishes her legitimacy, and marries Napolo.

18: COUNT RODERIC'S CASTLE, OR, GOTHIC TIMES. A TALE   2 vols. London: N. Lane, 1794

Roderic the Hardy retires from public life because Astolpho, the new king, seems to be hostile toward him. With Roderic goes his son Rhinaldo, though Rhinaldo is in love with Isabel, the previous king's daughter, who is still at court. Rhinaldo finds adventure even in retirement, for while sheltering in a ruined mansion he encounters assassins, one of whom he kills and consequently is obliged to impersonate. There are exciting times at court too, some of them due to a villain named Rhodolpho, who among other outrages tries to rape Isabel. Quite a lot of the conflict is political, and in the end the usurper Astolpho is delivered into the hands of the rightful king Emmanuel, who is not, as people had supposed, dead. Roderic is not dead either, though he too was supposed to be so; on one occasion Roderic intended to assassinate Astolpho in his bed but found that his accustomed fealty had made him unequal to the task, and Astolpho, seeing him hover by the bedside, supposed himself to be receiving a ghostly visitation. With the political world in order, Rhinaldo and Isabel are free to marry.

19: Croly, George   SALATHIEL. A STORY OF THE PAST, THE PRESENT, AND THE FUTURE   3 vols. London: Henry Colburn, 1828

Salathiel covers only the beginning of Salathiel's career as Wandering Jew, from the Crucifixion to the Destruction of

Jerusalem. Salathiel explains that the latter event marks
the end of his life as a family man and the beginning of his
real wandering. Many of the events that take place in the
early years are political, since Salathiel is a Jewish Na-
tionalist and a leader of rebellion. Other incidents are
more recognizably Gothic. More than once Salathiel or members of his family fall into pits, holes, or dungeons. He
has fantasies of nautical isolation like the Ancient Mari-
ner's and suffers real shipwreck as well. Various members
of his family are kidnapped and recovered. Once he supposes
himself to be buried alive eternally. Some of his family
become Christian and he defends a previously despised son-
in-law from Nero's lions. Until the fall of Jerusalem, Salathiel manages in some degree to overlook the reality of his
Wanderer curse, though he is pursued by rumors that he has
had some kind of accursed dealings with the supernatural.
However, when the Temple falls on him and he thinks that
death will extricate him from Christ's curse, he once again
hears the words "Tarry thou till I come" and is miraculously
extricated from the ruins; then he knows that his wandering
is inescapable. He speaks of his later years only briefly,
as when he mentions paying homage to Luther, watching Raphael paint, and so on.

20: Crookenden, Isaac   FATAL SECRETS, OR, ETHERLINDA DE
      SALMONI. A SICILIAN STORY   36 pp. London: J. Lee, 1806

Count Ormando Beraldi takes in his dissipated cousin Ricardo, whose own father has cast him off, and rashly leaves him
alone with his wife Theodora. Theodora even more rashly
squeezes Ricardo's hand in gratitude for some kindness,
which lights "a flame of libidinous desire" in his heart.
Ricardo's libidinous impulse comes to nothing at the time,
but during a later absence of the Count's he replaces all
the servants with his own followers, locks up and threatens
Theodora, and subsequently kidnaps and imprisons the Count
himself. Theodora dies. Ricardo, now lord of the castle,
brings home and raises Etherlinda, his illegitimate child by
Alicia, the daughter of his neighbor Salmoni. The Count's
child Ormando Jr. is raised as an orphaned dependent while
Etherlinda is to inherit the estate. Alicia, after she was
earlier abandoned by Ricardo, went to the Count for charity
and so attracted him that he entered into an affair with her
and set her up in another castle; when Ricardo learns of
this he adds her to his prisoners.
      Young Ormando and Etherlinda fall in love. Ricardo of-
fers his consent to their marriage on condition that Ormando
murder Alicia, but Ormando refuses. At the end, Ricardo,
who never in the course of their relationship learned Ali-

cia's last name, discovers that she is his own sister, whereupon he kills himself. This genealogical information is kept from Etherlinda, who is permitted to marry Ormando. Alicia enters a convent.

21: Crookenden, Isaac   HORRIBLE REVENGE, OR, THE MONSTER OF ITALY!!   36 pp. London: R. Harrild, 1808

Neglected Amanda is good, her spoiled brother Julien bad. When Julien marries, he locks his wife in a dungeon and brings her food in a skull; she dies. Julien makes advances to his sister, but she flees and finds a pious recluse who turns out to be her father. Julien kills him and then kills himself.
   With HORRIBLE REVENGE is bound HOPELESS LOVE. AN INTER-ESTING TALE
Horatio is smitten with a married woman whom he sees in church and starts writing her notes. Unaware that her husband has died of the flux, Horatio takes poison and goes to die at her feet. Someone pumps out his stomach and he has a happy life with the widow.

22: Crookenden, Isaac   THE ITALIAN BANDITTI, OR, THE SECRET HISTORY OF HENRY AND MATILDA. A ROMANCE   36 pp. London: R. Harrild, c.1811

Henry the foundling is informed that his foster sister Matilda, whom he fancies, is his real sister; their father has been murdered for his estate by their stepfather (who is also their uncle). Wishing to escape this awkward situation Henry goes to join the army but is captured en route by Italian banditti. During his escape from them he finds his father alive and discovers that Matilda is really the banditti captain's daughter, substituted for a stillborn child of his mother's.

23: Crookenden, Isaac   THE MYSTERIOUS MURDER, OR, THE USURPER OF NAPLES. AN ORIGINAL ROMANCE. TO WHICH IS PREFIXED THE NOCTURNAL ASSASSIN, OR, SPANISH JEALOUSY   36 pp. London: J. Lee, 1806

Both stories dwell upon incest, imprisonment, and badly decomposed corpses. In *The Mysterious Murder,* a girl is locked up in an attempt to force her into marriage, but the intended groom is discovered, just in time, to be her father. In *The Nocturnal Assassin,* a young man is imprisoned by his wicked uncle; the latter desires the hero's sweetheart and is discovered to have raped and murdered the hero's mother and murdered his father.

24: Crookenden, Isaac   ROMANTIC TALES   46 pp. London:
    S. Fisher, n.d.

1) *The Revengeful Turk: or Mystic Cavern*. Augustus, after
his father dies, is troubled by his aunt, Madame Venome; she
is "malignant," "turbulent," "crabbed," etc., and tries to
make him court a girl who is likely to get him into trouble.
He joins the navy to escape and is captured and imprisoned
by the Spanish. The Spanish governor's daughter Circesia
sees Augustus, pities him, loves him, and arranges his escape. Since she has been guilty of helping a prisoner and
a Protestant, she must go along, and she tells Augustus that
he may bring one additional friend. He chooses badly. His
friend makes him swim ashore at gunpoint and rows away with
the protesting Circesia. Augustus comes ashore near Bassa
the Hermit's lavishly furnished cave, formerly the quarters
of pirates whom Bassa joined after he killed a sultan for
kissing his wife. (Illness kept him home from an expedition and the other pirates never came back.) Exploring the
caves, Augustus and Bassa find the villain attempting to
rape Circesia. She is Bassa's daughter. Bassa kills the
would-be rapist and suddenly a blue vapor appears, accompanied by music, with his wife's angelic spirit in the midst
of it. She says that the kiss was the Sultan's fault, not
hers, and that she was murdered by the same rapist; then
she evaporates. Circesia and Augustus marry, and Circesia
converts — to Christianity, says Crookenden, though she
appeared to be Roman Catholic when we first found her in
Spain.
    2) *The Distressed Nun, or, Sufferings of Herselia di
Brindoli of Florence*. Herselia's troubles are caused by
her brother Vincentio, who believes her to be his father's
favorite. He arranges a secret meeting, even a clandestine
wedding, for her with Henri, son of a poor nobleman, and
then betrays them. Both fathers are furious, and Herselia
is clapped into a convent. When his father dies, Vincentio
as head of the family demands that she take the veil. But
she is rescued by Henri and marries him at last, while Vincentio takes an Italian courtesan who ultimately poisons
him.
    3) *The Vindictive Monk, or, The Fatal Ring*. Calini is
a foundling; he was left on the seashore to drown, accompanied by a ring inscribed "Ollorini." After he grows up he
is kidnapped and chained to a wall by Sceloni, an employee
of the villain Holbruzi, who wants Calini's beloved Alexa.
Alexa continues to refuse Holbruzi, despite Calini's strange
absence, and is consequently kidnapped herself. Sceloni is
about to kill Calini when he notices the ring and stops; he
is Calini's father. The ring belonged to his wife, an avun-

cular gift misunderstood by Calini to mean that she had a
lover. Hence he killed her, left their child to drown, and
became a monk. Calini rescues Alexa and they marry.

25: Crookenden, Isaac   THE SKELETON, OR, MYSTERIOUS DIS-
    COVERY. A GOTHIC ROMANCE   38 pp. London: A. Neill, 1805

Rotaldo and his sister Eleanora live in a castle with their
aged father and are attracted to extraordinarily refined
peasants, Almira and Adolphus. Rotaldo's clever and hypo-
critical friend Maurice tries to kill him and is himself fatally wounded, whereupon he confesses to several misdeeds:
he arranged Adolphus's kidnapping and hoped to have him convicted of Rotaldo's murder; he tried to rape Eleanora (Adolphus stopped him) but wept and persuaded her to forgive him.
Adolphus discovers that the castle in which he is imprisoned
really belongs to him and that he and Almira are cousins.
The real Baron has been murdered; his skeleton is the one
that figures in the chapbook's title. The usurping Baron
dies amid visions of specters clanking their "infernal
chains." The couples marry and virtue triumphs.

26: Crookenden, Isaac   SPECTRE OF THE TURRET, OR, GUOLTO
    CASTLE. A ROMANCE   32 pp. London: R. Harrild, n.d.

Aspasia's betrothed Florilmo is imprisoned by a wicked uncle
and forced to write a note breaking the engagement. He is
comforted by the bleeding ghost of his mother. The wicked
uncle manages to become engaged to Aspasia, but the wedding
is canceled by a spectral figure which stands between the
bride and groom and says "Forbear." Florilmo escapes from
prison and accuses the uncle, who kills himself and has dying visions of the hell that awaits him. Aspasia and Florilmo have a double wedding with Aspasia's cousin and his
bride. The two ladies give birth on the same day to children of opposite sexes, who are promptly betrothed to each
other.

27: Crookenden, Isaac   STORY OF MORELLA DE ALTO, OR, THE
    CRIMES OF SCORPINO DEVELOPED   24 pp. London: S. Fisher,
    1804

Scorpino is the villain, Morella the innocent victim. She
is kidnapped for purposes of rape. Scorpino is burned by
the Inquisition. The good people make appropriate marriages
at the end of the story.

28: Cullen, Stephen   THE HAUNTED PRIORY, OR, THE FORTUNES
OF THE HOUSE OF RAYO. A ROMANCE FOUNDED PARTLY ON HIS-
TORICAL FACT   1 vol. London: J. Bell, 1794

On a December day sometime in the fourteenth century a large
stranger with a harp and a white beard appears in a little
village in Castile. Assured that he will be welcomed by the
local philanthropist, Don Isidor de Haro, he goes to the
castle; his host recognizes him as his old guardian, the
Baron de Rayo. Rayo's daughter Maria and his nephew Henry
(sometimes in the novel called Henrico) Gonsalvo married and
had a child, Alphonso. The baby was put to nurse so that
Maria might follow her husband into war. Peter the Cruel
(the enemy) won the war and put Gonsalvo in prison for treason, permitting the family estates to be confiscated by
Punalada, a deceitful friend of Gonsalvo's. Now Rayo is
hunting for his no-longer-infant grandson, having heard that
Gonsalvo has been executed. He hopes that Don Isidor's son,
who resembles Gonsalvo, is the missing boy, but the resemblance is apparently coincidental; however, he is invited
to stay and help educate the boy, who is also called Alphonso.

When Don Isidor's Alphonso grows up and is presented at
court, he wins the confidence of the king but makes enemies
in consequence. Sent on a trip to Lisbon while the king
tries to catch the troublemakers in their deceit, he saves
two women from kidnappers. One is beautiful and causes him
to fall in love, despite the brevity of the acquaintance.
Later he finds himself at the haunted priory, where he hears
mysterious organ music and the sound of immense wings, sees
an unnatural light, and is confronted with a bloody and
sighing figure. A goatherd tells him that the place belongs
to Punalada and explains some elaborately nasty family history involving the accidental impalement of a young man intent upon raping his sister. Alphonso goes home and tells
Rayo the story, which for various reasons seems of possible
relevance to the death of Gonsalvo.

When Alphonso and his household return to the priory
they clear away rubbish from a flight of stairs to the ac-
companiment of spectral sighs and music. At the bottom of
the stairs Gonsalvo's ghost leads them to his grave and to
various pieces of evidence which they confiscate. Later
they discover in the dungeons of the priory, chained in his
mother's cell, a local charity boy who looks like Don Isidor. The woman, who is indeed Maria, makes a lunge at young
Alphonso, crying "My husband!" The others have to restrain
her. She recovers from her shock and is able to nurse Alphonso when he is near death from a wound and deranged from
the shock of being informed that the woman with whom he fell

in love is his sister; she had been raised in a separate
household. The nursing is fortuitous, for Donna Maria discovers on his body a birthmark like a bunch of grapes and
knows him for her own son; thus he is not after all the
brother of Don Isidor's daughter. An old nurse confesses
to some well-meant babyswapping. Punalada has cut his
throat after writing his confessions and an evil confederate
of his is sent to the Inquisition.

29: Curties, T. J. Horsley   ANCIENT RECORDS, OR, THE ABBEY
    OF SAINT OSWYTHE. A ROMANCE   4 vols. London: William
    Lane, 1801

Sir Alfred St. Oswythe arrives at his decaying abbey with
his small daughter Rosaline. He has been reduced by the
villainy of his own brother Rudolph to this gloomy residence
where his life and his daughter's will be complicated, as it
turns out, by the proximity of two women (one good, one bad)
who have loved him unrequitedly. He is pleased to discover
that the good one, Lady Ruithvina Urbandine, is his near
neighbor. She has been sent to that place by the Baron, her
husband, to live with her son Constantine and with Gondemar,
her husband's son by a previous marriage. Constantine grows
up to be good, Gondemar bad, Rosaline beautiful. Gondemar
nurses for Constantine a growing hatred founded in jealousy:
Constantine will inherit from his mother; as a child Gondemar was rescued from a fire by a servant while Constantine
was saved by the mother; Lady Paulina, whom Gondemar wishes
to marry, fruitlessly prefers Constantine. Paulina is important to the story, for (we discover at last) "the House
of Edmondville," which mysterious warnings tell Rosaline to
beware, refers to her. At the beginning of the novel, however, Paulina is using another title available to her and
is living in the Baron's household on the understanding that
one of the boys will marry her and thereby enable her to
keep her fortune.
    Ultimately both of the boys and also their father the
Baron want Rosaline for their own, but Constantine is the
one she loves. On the side of the lovers is only Lady
Ruithvina (Rosaline's father has been called away), and her
attempt to marry them secretly is interrupted by the wicked
Baron. Gondemar chases and attempts to rape Rosaline and
tries, apparently successfully, to murder his brother; subsequent assaults on Rosaline are prevented by Constantine's
"ghost." In the midst of these difficulties Rosaline's father dies, leaving her to the care of the Baroness. The
caretaking is ineffectual, however, as the Baroness has been
locked up by her husband, who also divorces her in order to
propose to Rosaline. Paulina surprisingly offers to rescue

Rosaline from the Baron's forceful advances but has her carried off to the custody of a fearsome woman named Agnes, who
was the other woman unrequitedly in love with Sir Alfred.
Since Rosaline is in fact imprisoned in the remoter reaches
of her father's own abbey, she finds some family papers
which she peruses in the intervals between Paulina's fum-
bling attempts to poison her. She discovers that Paulina
is her half-sister, incestuous product of her wicked uncle
Rudolph and her own victimized mother. Paulina has been
brought up to hate her. Behind this circumstance lies a
complicated tale of religious orders and apostasy: Matilda,
Rosaline's mother, was sent by her family into a convent;
Sir Alfred St. Oswythe, who wished to marry her, was talked
into a monastery by an ecclesiastical agent of his brother
Rudolph, who had economic motives; Agnes took the veil to
demonstrate her love for Sir Alfred. All three thought better of it and escaped, the former two to marry and Agnes to
join Rudolph in villainy which included the subsequent in-
carceration of his brother, sister-in-law, and niece. Sir
Alfred paid Rudolph and Agnes to release him and his child
after Matilda had been raped and murdered. Some of this
information comes from Agnes herself, who is dying as the
result of a fall and repents enough to show Rosaline a way
to escape. After a few more adventures Rosaline is restored
to her rights and titles and is reunited with Constantine,
whose wound was not fatal after all. Paulina is obliged to
enter a convent.

30: Curties, T. J. Horsley   ETHELWINA, OR, THE HOUSE OF
    FITZ-AUBURNE. A ROMANCE OF FORMER TIMES   3 vols.
    London: William Lane, 1799

Two orphans, Augustine and Emma, are taken in by the Fitz-
Auburnes. Augustine and his foster sister Ethelwina fall
in love. Godfred, the father, is lost in a military expedition, and little Arthur Fitz-Auburne is kidnapped. The
obvious villain is Cousin Leopold Lord St. Ivor. Emma is
devoted to Arthur's memory, but Leopold desires her. The
ghost of Ethelwina's murdered father pursues Leopold and
makes Ethelwina swear vengeance. She keeps the murder weapon, a switchblade dagger, with which she confronts Leopold.
He falls into fever and madness but first shuts her up in a
dungeon where she is comforted by the ghost of her mother.
She finds Arthur in an adjacent dungeon; he says that his
father used to be there as well. Ethelwina feels that she
is the cause of all the trouble because Leopold lusts after
her, but the ghost tells her not to worry. After throwing
herself between Arthur and an executioner's ax, Ethelwina
finally has to save him by promising herself to Leopold.

(She plans to back out and apologizes to God for her perjury.) She and Arthur escape, fleeing Leopold and the voice
of a putrid corpse which demands burial. On the way home
they find and rescue imprisoned Augustine, but then Leopold
captures Emma, so the others go back to rescue her and kill
him. The young people bury the insistent corpse, marry each
other, and are happy.

31: Curties, T. J. Horsley   THE MONK OF UDOLPHO. A ROMANCE
    4 vols. London: J. F. Hughes, 1807

Hersilia is awakened by her father, who has just taken poison and wishes to confess that he is the slave of vice, especially gaming. The sinister family confessor, who wears
on his forehead a linen band with a death's head motif, sym-
bol of an order of monks that he has founded, pretends to
give him an antidote but in fact makes certain that he dies.
Hersilia has always mistrusted the monk and is appalled by
his announcement that he and the Prince of Parma, her father's bitterest enemy, are to be her guardians. They for-
bid her to marry Lorenzo Val-Ambrosio, though his father
encourages the match. She is two years under age, has supposedly been disinherited by a deathbed will, and is trying
hard to do the proper thing, so the monk has a high degree
of control over her. When Lorenzo's father discovers the
circumstances (suicide) of her father's death, he renounces
Hersilia and prevents an attempted wedding. Having sworn
herself to silence for the sake of her father's honor, she
is unable even to discuss the topic with him.
    When Parma comes to take her property she refuses to
fight, though her subjects do not at all wish to transfer
their loyalty. Parma is accompanied by a female ward, Hortensia, who was formerly ruined by his nephew Sanguedoni and
is now enlisted to aid in the undoing of Hersilia. Parma
wants Hersilia to marry Sanguedoni, who is far too importunate for her taste. She refuses. Parma then demands her
for himself. The monk offers to take her away and leaves
her in a ruined castle. He returns later to reveal his
dual identity — he is also Sanguedoni — and to say that Parma has been killed and his body burned in his room on the
night she left, a circumstance meant to look incriminating
for her. The castle is Sanguedoni's, headquarters for his
monks, whom he claims to be the local arm of the Inquisition. He has bandits too. He was instrumental in her father's ruinous gaming. And Sanguedoni has captured Lorenzo,
planning to kill him despite Hortensia's eagerness that he
be given to her. Sanguedoni and Hortensia threaten each
other and bargain for the objects of their lust. Hersilia
is awakened from a drugged sleep, in which she is about to

be raped, by a voice and a providential dagger. The rape
is also deterred by the intervention of the ghost of Eloisa,
previous occupant of the room. Later Hersilia discovers Lorenzo's father starving in a dungeon. Lorenzo has been wed-
ded to Hortensia disguised as Hersilia; rejected even under
this legal sanction, Hortensia attempts to poison Hersilia
and is stabbed by Sanguedoni. Just as Hersilia gives in
to Sanguedoni, in order to save Lorenzo from the rack, the
monks all unmask and are revealed as soldiers belonging to
Lorenzo's family. Hersilia's page Astolpho adds to the confusion by revealing himself as Eloisa, not dead after all,
and the illegitimate half-sister of Hersilia. Sanguedoni,
who had taken Eloisa out of a convent under false pretexts,
stabs both himself and her. The moral is that "Heaven may
afflict, but man must not complain."

32: Curties, T. J. Horsley   ST. BOTOLPH'S PRIORY, OR, THE
    SABLE MASK. AN HISTORICAL ROMANCE   5 vols. London:
    J. F. Hughes, 1806

In Cromwell's time St. Aubuspine goes with his wife and
their daughter Roselma to live in a moldering priory with
a bad reputation. The household is nervous, given to ghost-
seeing and general jumpiness: St. Aubuspine is hiding and
expects harm and ruin of some sort; Roselma is a reader of
bloody manuscript romances. Some shipwrecked people admitted to the priory from charitable motives include De Rochemonde, a stranger whom Roselma's father suddenly urges her
to marry, despite the distress of her mother. Roselma is
willing to marry De Rochemond, though she does not love
him, but is frightened by his passion and haste. The ceremony takes place in the ruined chapel and is disrupted by
the servant Pierre, who makes a stifled effort to say something about the bridegroom; by a party of Independents who
arrest the father of the bride; and finally by a huge figure in black whose voice turns the bridegroom pale. Upon
reading a packet handed him by the mysterious figure, De
Rochemonde says that he and Roselma must part forever.
Then, apparently changing his mind, he says that they will
not part, that they are married; but in any case he is
obliged to leave before the marriage is consummated.
Roselma's mother dies, raving about a secret. When, two
volumes later, the secret is revealed, we discover the De
Rochemonde is "iniquitous Adolpho," a former royalist turned
agent for the Independents, and Roselma's uncle. St. Aubuspine supposedly killed Roselma's real father in order to
acquire her mother, but the father did not die after all and
was the figure in black who warned against the incestuous
wedding. Roselma marries the Marquis of Valmont, a heroic

young man who has behaved well at various points in the
story.

33: Curties, T. J. Horsley   THE WATCH TOWER, OR, THE SONS
    OF ULTHONA. AN HISTORICAL ROMANCE   5 vols. Brentford:
    P. Norbury, 1804

Morcar, the evil Chief of Stroma, comes to Ulthona in the
middle of the night to kill its Earl, who has married the
woman he loves. The Earl's widow, told that she can save
her children's lives by marrying Morcar, immediately stabs
herself. She dies asserting that her spirit, and God, will
protect her boys. (Here the narrative breaks off while an
editorial voice explains that the story is written on a
moldy manuscript and describes events c.1300, a very wicked
period.) Morcar sets fire to the castle, which subsequently
falls to ruin and acquires the reputation of being haunted,
perhaps because it contained a number of bodies that could
not be retrieved for burial. The Earl's two little boys,
carried off by Morcar's hired ruffian Uglio, are saved and
raised by Uglio's wife Unna, daughter of Ulthona's faithful
servant Uberto.
     The boys, Sigismorn and Adelbert, spend their lives hid-
den in Ulthona's watchtower until Sigismorn's adolescent
restlessness drives him to see the world and to hunt for his
relatives. Adelbert goes with him. Escaping from a storm
they chance to shelter in the ruins of Ulthona itself, where
they discover, but naturally do not recognize, their mother's brother Certaldo and his daughter Imogen. Sigismorn
and Imogen soon fall in love, but they are at first secretive about it and in any case they have little time to enjoy
the condition, for a number of alarming things are going on
in the ruins. Certaldo, for one thing, is at best on the
brink of lunacy and has been like this ever since his second
and much beloved wife Ermangarde disappeared. Sigismorn is
wounded by Certaldo, who mistakes him for a villain, and
while recovering from his wound is awakened by a specter of
his murdered father. It appears the second night in a more
alarming shape — blue with fiery eyes and a dagger in its
bosom — to lead him around the ruins and make him swear vengeance. On his way back to bed he finds old Uberto, who
shows him his parents' grave, the family treasure, parental
portraits, and later his father's armor. One night Sigismorn dreams of specters who say that Adelbert is lost, and
indeed when Sigismorn awakens, his brother is gone from
their bed and cannot be found. Sigismorn, sorry that he
ever took Adelbert away from the watchtower, goes with Uberto to see Unna again. The tower, however, is empty, and the
staircase smeared with blood; it looks as though Unna has

been murdered and thrown over the nearby precipice.

Imogen, whose troubles occupy a large part of the plot, is matrilineally a niece of King Robert Bruce. She is pursued ruthlessly and clumsily by Etheldart, Lord Dunbeth, who keeps inventing excuses to save her by carrying her away. Once she was nearly married to him by force, for Edward I had conquered the Scots and given her to Etheldart as a reward for his help. She was rescued just in time by her father, who hid with her in Ulthona; he has since then taken her to a convent. When she declines to take the veil, her only certain way to evade Edward I's orders that she be given up, the abbess refuses to shield her; she escapes in the night but en route to a great-uncle's is overtaken by Etheldart, who apologizes for past behavior and offers to return one of her family's castles and protect her there. (She and her father are accused of treason.) Etheldart's character has not after all changed, and she is obliged to be uncooperative during a marriage ceremony, saying "No" to the vows and tearing up the king's order. Just in time the English troops ride up and she turns herself over to them, thinking that imprisonment would be better than further harassment by Etheldart. Hearing that the king is dead, the leader of the troop is persuaded to take Imogen to the home of her great-uncle. At the castle she is told that her uncle is gravely ill and sees no one, and that a nephew (he has none) has taken over the castle. Though warned by a mysterious nocturnal visitant against curiosity, she creeps to her uncle's room just in time to see him murdered by his "nephew," who turns out to be Morcar. He carries off Imogen and also Sigismorn, who has turned up at the castle and been wounded by Morcar's men. At his own castle Morcar has a sixteen-year-old daughter, Etheline, who has led a sheltered life and believes her father to be lovable and who is at once attracted to Sigismorn. Her efforts to get him out of his dungeon give her a new view of her father. Morcar, like Etheldart, wishes to marry Imogen; when Etheldart appears in the guise of a sentry and once again offers to take Imogen someplace safe, Morcar kills him. Imogen discovers that Morcar's wife is still alive and is the missing Ermengarde, her stepmother; Ermengarde, who according to Curties has more good intentions than brains, was tricked into believing Certaldo dead in battle and is distraught to learn that she is a bigamist. Yet another man, the villain Uglio, whom Imogen has known under a different name, offers to carry her away and even to take along Sigismorn instead of killing him, as he will do if Imogen does not cooperate.

Meanwhile Sigismorn has been taken to Morcar's judgment room. Etheline hides in the shadows and watches. When Sigismorn refuses to abjure his parentage and to acknowledge

Edward as king, Morcar shows him the torture alcove, where he sees a pile of mangled corpses with Adelbert, apparently dead, on top. Etheline forestalls Sigismorn's death by rushing out to accuse her father. Later she tries to rescue him by putting on armor and calling herself Donaldine, but they speechify too long and Sigismorn collapses from poison or drugs. Morcar tells Imogen that only by signing herself over to him can she save the life of her now altogether lunatic father. Overcome by filial piety, she gives in at last, and just in time, for Morcar knows that Certaldo is nearly dead from more or less natural causes. He torments his future bride by sending her a bleeding human heart labeled "Sigismorn"; she secretes it in her bosom and faints. Later she follows two guards to her father's cell, lest they kill him, and discovers Ermangarde, for whom a grave is already prepared. (Imogen nearly falls into it.) Before they both die, Certaldo forgives Ermangarde her mistake and asks Imogen to bury them in one grave.

Because King Robert is winning again, Morcar needs to marry Imogen and hastens the wedding. Imogen comes to it with a dagger in case suicide should seem the only escape. Sigismorn arrives as the point is at her bosom and takes Morcar to the king for trial. Etheline begs for her father's life but is told that he is not her father, that she is the sister of Sigismorn and Adelbert, kidnapped in infancy by Morcar and secretly substituted by his wife for an infant of their own which had died while Morcar was out. Unna, not dead after all, supplies much of this information and brings with her Adelbert, who was only drugged. After staying in a convent for some time to rest, Imogen comes back and marries Sigismorn. The halls of Ulthona are restored and refurbished.

34: Cuthbertson, Catherine   SIR ETHELBERT, OR, THE DISSO-
    LUTION OF MONASTERIES. A ROMANCE   3 vols. London: Long-
    man, Rees, Orme, Brown, and Green, 1830

The story begins in 1516. It is St. John the Baptist's Eve and people are celebrating with bonfires near Dunraven Priory in Wales. Suddenly they hear a tolling bell and see a ship burning with blue flames and a small boat escaping the conflagration apparently unmanned. The priest Kenrick Blundel, who is devoted to truth, sees through the supernatural appearance of these events to discover their natural causes, and, what is more important to the plot, he rescues Lord St. Oswald, who is heir to the local castle. Lord St. Oswald's daughter, Lady Adela de Mandeville, marries De Rhone, and *their* daughter, Lady Mary, is the heroine of the novel. She is a delightful little girl, sturdy and genial and not at all ladylike, but her father seems not to love her. When Adela apparently drowns (in fact she is forcefully detained by some Ursuline nuns who like her fancy work), De Rhone brings home his mistress Rosamond, who takes over supervision of the nursery, and their illegitimate daughter Rhona, a crafty and beautiful little girl whom Lady Mary learns to hate. The foundling Algernon Fitzrivers is the other most important character. Because of the obscurity of his origins, Rhona withholds from him any affection, but Mary and Algernon help each other out of various dangers and fall in love. Their romance is imperiled by the news that Algernon is the true heir to Adela's honors and estates, for Mary feels that she cannot conscientiously marry Algernon and assume the position wrested from her mother. When the final mysteries are unraveled they are discovered to have included baby swapping as well as assassination and other villainy, and Algernon is able to marry Lady Mary after all. Rhona marries too and emigrates to the continent.

35: Dacre, Charlotte   CONFESSIONS OF THE NUN OF ST. OMER.
    A TALE   3 vols. London: J. F. Hughes, 1805

The nun's narrative is addressed to her son, Dorvil Lindorf; he is not to read it until after her death.
    As a child, Cazire, daughter of the Marquis Arieni, is attached to a man named St. Elmer. Though she is only eleven when she and her father move away, both she and St. Elmer are affected by the separation. He is perhaps the last good influence she is to know. Her father, who has earlier run away from debtors, leaving her mother behind, has taken up with the loose-principled Countess Rosendorf. The Countess has two children of her own and in time turns Cazire's father against her by making her the topic of conjugal disagreements. Cazire is sent to board in a convent, where she reads dangerously romantic novels. When she is sixteen St. Elmer comes back and is worried about their effect upon her imagination and principles.
    Cazire leaves the convent to live with her real mother, who is depressed and uninteresting. Discussions of philosophy with Fribourg, the exciting freethinker next door, lead to mutal passion. Her religious principles withstand his suggestions that they run away together, but she cannot quite leave him alone. There are renunciations and reconciliations and a lot of emotion. And all the time she is getting warning and moral notes signed "Ariel." In an effort to discourage Fribourg (and reassure his wife) she plays up to his visiting friend Count Lindorf and gradually becomes attached to him. When he goes home, presumably to a forced marriage, she suffers "a sort of partial lunacy"

and nearly cuts her throat. On the same day that her con-
ciliatory gestures to her father and the Rosendorf woman are
turned down, Lindorf comes back and she goes away with him.

Lindorf takes her to the house of a woman he calls his
sister Olivia, and Cazire pretends to be his wife. One
morning she wakes up to find both her and Olivia's "hus-
bands" gone. Olivia is willing to take care of Cazire, who
is pregnant, but they quarrel when Olivia offers her a new
lover. Cazire leaves and nearly starves until she falls
in with a neighboring widow, Janetta. Olivia, angry and
insulted, submits a bill for room and board, and Cazire is
sent to debtor's prison, where the baby is born. St. Elmer,
who has been the "Ariel" of the warning notes, frees her and
takes her and Janetta to a beautiful house with servants.
She hesitates to marry him because she looks up to him and
feels entirely unworthy, but because he is pale and tearful
she finally gives in. One day Fribourg comes to the house
wounded and St. Elmer invites him to stay after he is cured;
he wishes to show his confidence in Cazire, but she is terrified. She and Fribourg are left alone too much, and after
some buildup of emotion and handholding she loses her head
and succumbs to him. Frantic with guilt, she is about to
shoot herself when St. Elmer finds and stops her. She confesses and he runs out to duel with Fribourg. St. Elmer is
killed and dies forgiving Cazire. After screaming at Fribourg, who subsequently shoots himself, she falls into convulsions and is insane for two years. After her recovery
she goes into a convent.

36: Dacre, Charlotte   THE LIBERTINE   4 vols. London:
    T. Cadell, 1807

Gabrielle Montmorency, though raised in a Swiss cottage
"free from contagion of society" by her misanthropic ex-
gamester father, is secuced and impregnated by the Count
Angelo D'Albani, who stopped for shelter and prolonged his
stay. When her father learns of her disgrace he dies (lit-
erally, judging by the symptoms) of a broken heart; his
death induces Gabrielle's labor and the child Agnes is born.
Gabrielle finds Angelo and, in male attire, takes a job as
his page; she plans to acquire child support. Both Angelo
and his mistress Oriano rather fancy the page. Oriano tries
to kill Angelo, first with poison, then by hired assassins,
but Gabrielle foils both attempts. When, on the second
occasion, she is wounded, her identity is revealed and Angelo takes her to live with him again. Still unmarried,
they produce a son, Felix. Angelo later runs off with Oriano's half-sister Paulina.

Millborough, an unscrupulous female domestic who knows

the family secret, lures already spoiled Felix from his mother and corrupts him, and has a blatant affair with his father, whom she finally deserts after he is ruined by gaming. Gabrielle takes Angelo in again, out of pity. They starve until a friend leaves Angelo the money he won from him; at last they marry. Soon after, Gabrielle herself dies of heartbreak. Having promised to hunt for their children, Angelo goes to Paris, where he finds his daughter (recognition via miniature) as he is about to seduce her. Learning that she has already been deflowered, he puts her in a convent to repent and, in the midst of an argument about which of them has been more cruel to her, stabs her lover before her eyes. Escaped to England, he ignorantly helps to apprehend and sentence to death a highwayman who turns out to be Felix. Angelo finds that he cannot pray and commits suicide. Dacre points out that fathers' sins are visited upon children.

37: Dacre, Charlotte   THE PASSIONS   4 vols. London: T. Cadell and W. Davies, 1811

There are six principal characters in this novel: Baron Rozendorf, who speaks for reason; Count Wiemar and his beautiful wife Julia; Count Darlowitz and his virtuous wife Amelia; Countess Apollonia Zulmer, the villainess. Apollonia, who is a sort of Viennese bluestocking, misconstrued the attentions of Count Wiemar in his bachelor days and determines to get revenge for her embarrassment by destroying the thing he loves most, i.e., Julia. To effect this she befriends Julia, introduces her to feminism, anthropology, and relativism, and tries to make her read *La Nouvelle Heloise;* though Julia is so innocent as to be almost unteachable, these ideas enable Apollonia to make her secretive with her husband and somewhat unwary about her growing preoccupation with Count Darlowitz. Rozendorf sees it all coming but is unable to stop it. When Darlowitz, who reciprocates and feels terribly guilty, decides to solve the problem by fading away, Julia confesses her love and persuades him to live, secretly planning to pine away herself. Revived by an exchange of high platonic notes, neither dies after all. Amelia, however, does; although encouraged by her mother to live and be reconciled to her basically decent husband, she has visions of angels and expires. Darlowitz commits suicide. Wiemar, though he has not in fact been cuckolded, thinks Julia is polluted and refuses to live with her anymore. When Julia writes to Apollonia for help, she receives from that lady a cold note of dismissal and revelation and goes mad. Rozendorf is unable to persuade Wiemar to do more than send Julia money, though he seems to love

her still. She escapes from her keeper and dies, barefoot,
in a storm, on the doorstep of her old home.

38: Dacre, Charlotte   ZOFLOYA, OR, THE MOOR. A ROMANCE OF
    THE FIFTEENTH CENTURY   3 vols. London: Longman, Hurst,
    Rees, and Orme, 1806

Ardolf, an evil count whose hobby is breaking up good marriages, seduces Laurina, the wife of his host the Marchese
de Loredani. Dacre suggests that this influences the future
bad behavior of the Loredani daughter, Victoria, but Victoria seems never to have been very nice. Despite strong supervision, she runs away to Venice to join her friend Berenza. Because of her mother's scandal he cannot marry her,
but he scrupulously gives her a separate room until he is
certain that she loves him. She thinks this odd of him but
pretends to languish. One night she saves him from assassination by a man who turns out to be her brother Leonardo.
(Leonardo ran away after his mother's abduction and has been
taken up by a sinister mistress named Megalena Strozzi. The
affair is genuinely passionate, marred chiefly by Megalena's
insistence that Leonardo prove his love by stabbing or promising to stab various people whom she dislikes.)
    Finally Victoria marries Berenza, but principally as a
kind of vengeance. She soon covets his brother Henriquez,
who is engaged to an innocent little blonde, and has bizarre
dreams about Henriquez's servant Zofloya, in which he effects the deaths and displacements she desires, on the promise that she will be his. This is a dream from which there
is no awakening, for Zofloya does fulfill her wishes by providing poisons and potions, and he grows more frightening
and seems more supernatural all the time. She poisons Berenza, drives Henriquez to suicide by her ruthless pursuit of
him, kills his fiancée Lilla, and, discovering her own dying
mother, refuses to comfort or forgive her. She loves no one
but herself and fears nothing but the Inquisition. The end
of the novel provides a kind of reunion for all the living
characters. Leonardo and Megalena, who have become bandits,
both commit suicide to avoid capture. Zofloya offers to
save Victoria from worldly misery and, after she has given
one more pledge to be his, saves her by throwing her off a
precipice.

39: Dallas, Robert Charles   SIR FRANCIS DARRELL, OR, THE
    VORTEX. A NOVEL   4 vols. London: Longman, Hurst, Rees,
    Orme, and Brown, 1810

Sir Francis Darrell and his friend Vernon in their correspondence say a lot about the Vortex, by which they mean the

social whirl, the maelstrom of fashionable dissipation; Darrell warns Vernon that the Vortex is dangerous and not at all a game. Darrell himself is not received in "scrupulous society," but he attracts the notice of Augusta Saville, an upright young lady who thinks she should try to steady him. Dartford, who is already steady, wants Augusta, but he does not seem to interest her very much. Influenced by Augusta, Darrell begins exploring his Bible. He has trouble with the problem of evil, for he wants a God of Love but can see little evidence of dominant goodness in the world. Correspondence with Vernon is now full of reports about his progress with biblical studies (excess of black bile, says Vernon), and he begins to correspond with Augusta as well. Augusta's father would like her to marry Darrell, but she feels that she cannot marry someone from whom she differs on so important an issue as religion. At last Darrell feels that he is obliged to believe in the devil if he is not to lose the God he has so painstakingly found. He sends Augusta a manuscript account of his past sins and waits in suspense to see whether she will have him. Just then someone stabs him and he seems likely to die. Augusta goes to pieces, says she was overzealous to think everyone should be Roman Catholic, promises to be whatever religion Darrell likes (though she has him confess and receive the sacrament), and marries him on what she thinks is his deathbed. His unexpected recovery provides a happy ending. The author explains that he intended to let Darrell die at the end but was dissuaded by a friend.

40: Davenport, Selina   AN ANGEL'S FORM AND A DEVIL'S HEART
     4 vols. London: A. K. Newman, 1818

The angelic form referred to in the title belongs to the Marchioness of A, formerly a Miss Fitz-Arthur. The novel is full of complicated love affairs, old jiltings, mysterious godparents, and people who look like other people. Edward, the hero, is much taken with the friendly overture of the Marchioness, who not only is old enough to be his mother but turns out really to bear that relationship to him. He has been raised by her ex-servant Alice, by Alice's admirable husband, MacKenzie, and by Alice's mother. He also possesses a mysterious godfather, Maurice Colville, who turns out to be his paternal grandfather. Because of his considerable artistic talent, Edward is sent to a London art school where he makes additional complicated social connections. At last a housekeeper tells secrets, Edward's true father claims him, the Marchioness commits suicide with laudanum, and Edward discovers that Janet, the girl he loves, is not his sister. A particularly interesting secondary character is

an unpleasantly headstrong girl named Clara, who pursues
Edward, ruins her family with extravagance, and finally
misses her mother's deathbed blessing by eloping at the
wrong time with a man who later takes mistresses while she
turns to gaming.

41: Davenport, Selina   ITALIAN VENGEANCE AND ENGLISH FORE-
     BEARANCE. A ROMANCE   3 vols. London: A. K. Newman, 1828

Relationships in this novel all go on simultaneously but had
best be explained one at a time. First, Belgrave brings his
bride Evelina home to Belgrave Abbey. She is young and unhappy and not in love with her husband, but her friend Marian Gorden is some comfort to her. Belgrave is a libertine
(though Evelina does not know it at first) with a rather
scandalous background. He has earlier carried off an Italian woman named Hippolita (not, by the way, his first abduction), wooing her with promises of marriage. He does in
fact love her, but was obliged to marry Evelina to avert financial ruin. Hippolita has been in a rage, returning his
letters and trampling on his miniature. Later on Hippolita,
using the name of Rosalie de M____, contrives to meet Marian and, playing on the other woman's sense of honor, swears
her to secrecy about her plans for vengeance. Hippolita has
Belgrave's child, which she sends home to Italy. She becomes enormously grateful for Marian's kindness and nursing;
later, as a cloaked stranger, she rescues Marian from an attempted kidnapping. Hippolita's final scheme for vengeance
is to kidnap the Belgraves' newborn son and to tell them
that she has it. Marian is at last permitted to raise the
baby on condition that she not reveal its identity until
Belgrave is dead. At the end Hippolita effects his demise
by shooting him.
    Marian becomes involved as well with an apparently deaf-
mute Sunday artist, a stranger who calls himself Mr. Howard.
He is really Henry Arlingford, who has been disinherited
through Belgrave's manipulations. He offers Marian various
bits of good advice and protection, and she sends him anonymous gifts of money. In the end he is restored to his
rights and they marry.
    Another romance involves Rose Delaval, whom Evelina
hires as a companion. She was much loved during her childhood by an aristocrat named Edward, Lord Fortescue. He
appears in the neighborhood one day, clearly still in love
with Rose and still hunting for her. Because she is now so
much older and is calling herself Rose Aylmer he fails to
recognize her, though he is much drawn to her and finds that
she reminds him of his other Rose. At last he recognizes
her and they marry.

42: DeQuincey, Thomas   KLOSTERHEIM, OR, THE MASQUE   1 vol.
London: T. Cadell, 1832

Klosterheim is a German city run by an unscrupulous Landgrave and a pack of villainous soldiers. The caravan in
which Paulina, the heroine, is traveling, is one of many
attacked outside the city walls. Paulina loves Maximilian,
who is off on a mysterious mission. While she is in Klosterheim some terrifying things happen. An unknown man who
calls himself "The Masque" takes such thorough control of
the city that he can cause up to a dozen people at a time
to disappear without a trace. He leaves warnings and notes,
and nobody feels safe even at home. The Landgrave traps him
once but emerges so shaken from a conference with him that
he faints. Meanwhile, Paulina is being pursued by people
who want a trunk of mysterious and important papers with
which she has been entrusted. She is duped away from a
convent haven and imprisoned, but the Landgrave's daughter
helps her escape. The Masque has threatened to hold a trial
of the Landgrave on a certain date and on that night reveals
that he is Maximilian and the true heir of the late Prince,
whom the Landgrave murdered. Wishing to make a counterreve-
lation, the wicked Landgrave unveils the corpse of a young
woman which so far as he knows is Paulina; it is instead the
body of his own much beloved daughter, whom the guards shot
by mistake. The Landgrave repents and dies, and Maximilian
and Paulina marry.

43: Drake, Nathan   LITERARY HOURS, OR SKETCHES CRITICAL,
NARRATIVE, AND POETICAL   Third Edition. 3 vols. London:
T. Cadell and W. Davies, 1804

Drake's collection includes poetry, essays, and prose narratives. The narratives of principal interest to students of
the Gothic are
    1) "Henry Fitzowen": At a staghunt the hero is led
astray by a phantom light. Meanwhile, evil Walleran, who
has some kind of supernatural connections, kidnaps Henry's
beloved Adelaine. When Henry gets home he finds his door
draped with black, dead servants in a dark castle, his mother and sister locked up, and Adelaine gone. In pursuit of
her he is led to a castle by a witch-woman and undergoes a
series of horrors and illusions. He falls into a vault and
encounters corpses, skeletons, and specters. At last he
finds and kills Walleran, whereupon all the apparitions disappear. He finds Adelaine in a cavern and revives her with
a kiss. At the kiss the castle collapses and the pair are
led by music to some good woodland fairies who identify
themselves as helpers of the virtuous.

2) "Montmorenci": Drake intends to show here the mechanics of nonsupernatural horror. Montmorenci and his friends are suspended over a chasm by some bandits. One friend, in armor, is thrown in and the others can hear him bounce all the way down. In order to prolong Henry's agony, the bandits half cut the tree from which he is suspended. In the end, however, he escapes.

3) "The Abbey of Clunendale": Edward de Courtenay comes back from the wars and goes to visit his father's grave. There he sees an old man saved from suicide by a beautiful girl. As it turns out, the man is a brother officer prematurely aged by grief and remorse, for he has killed his brother-in-law in response to gossip that the man was his wife's lover. The gossip was false. The wife died. The beautiful girl, who is the potential suicide's sister, persuades him to believe in the forgiveness of God. Then she marries Edward.

4) "Maria Howard": This tale is written as a letter and has no ending. Maria Howard is essentially virtuous but loses her virginity to the Squire's son. His father, disliking the connection, has sent him off, so he is not at hand to marry her. She has been living at the Squire's and is forced to walk home, in an advanced state of pregnancy. She miscarries. Her father asserts that she has killed him, and when he forgives her she has already gone mad. She dies, and her lover, who has returned, is in some danger of going mad and expiring too. His father is sorry.

5) "Sir Egbert": Sir Egbert is in England looking for his missing friend Conrad and Conrad's fiancée Bertha. He shelters with some Knights Templar who point out Cundolph's Tower, where are said to sleep an enchanted couple; five knights have died attempting to rescue them. Egbert decides to try, though without guessing that they are the couple he seeks. He meets Matilda, sister of one of the dead knights. In the tower he finds a series of dangerous illusions. A corpse with a sword locks him in a vault, but he breaks out. He sees Hell Mouth but disperses it by invoking Heaven and leaping in. He is lured to a well by Conrad's voice, but God sends lightning to show the brink just in time. He is almost lured out of a tower door by a counterfeit Matilda. At last he penetrates illusory flame to free Conrad and Bertha. De Weldon, the villain who owns the tower, turns out to be Conrad's uncle. He dies in agonies, seeing demons. Conrad explains that he and Bertha were lured to a cave and drank something just before they went to sleep. They have not aged in six years. Egbert wins Matilda.

44: Edridge, Rebecca   THE HIGHEST CASTLE AND THE LOWEST
    CAVE, OR, EVENTS OF THE DAYS WHICH ARE GONE   3 vols.
    London: George B. Whittaker, 1825

This novel, which begins rather innocently with the passionate Matilda de Montgomery giving her consent to Richard de
St. Evremond, winner of a tournament, and which has much to
say about the evils of war, settles down by the third volume
into remarkably lurid villainy. Matilda, married to St.
Evremond and mother of a son, is shaken by the unexpected
birth of a little brother, Jocelyn. Jocelyn's arrival means
that she and her son will not inherit and causes her father
to lose all interest in her. Her bitterness and jealousy,
which lead her to villainy, are perceived by the other villain of the story, the confessor Austin, whose own life has
been embittered by the discovery of his aristocratic origins
and by his perpetual scheming to regain what he sees as his
property. Austin encourages her most sinister desires — he
will blackmail her later — until he has persuaded her to
kill her baby brother. She first makes friends with the
infant lest it cry when she carries it off, then drugs the
nurse and with Austin carries the child to a particularly
dark and loathsome cave on the premises. There they leave
it, Austin having pushed her hand down on its chest to crush
it. After this Matilda is melancholy and stupified with
guilt. At last she falls into lunacy and dies. Austin's
punishment is to be isolated in a monastery and kept on the
verge of starvation.

45: FATAL VOWS, OR, THE FALSE MONK. A ROMANCE   28 pp. Lon-
    don: Thomas Tegg, 1810

Count Savani, owner of Savani Castle, has two dissimilar
sons, Montavole (bad) and Alberto (good). Montavole, who
has left home young, makes an appointment to talk to a man
who has saved him from robbers. The man calls himself Rinaldo and swears Montavole to friendship; if Montavole de-
faults, the Sword will ruin his family and kill his son,
if he has any. Rinaldo was preceded at the interview by
a female specter who told Montavole to "beware of holy St.
Peter's Day." After their father's death the brothers both
marry. Montavole and Leonora have a son. Alberto's wife
dies in childbirth (as does the child) after her husband
disappears during a walk, leaving behind no evidence but a
bloody cloak and a sword.
    Twenty years pass. Leonora is nursed on her deathbed by
an orphan girl named Miranda, who loves and is loved by Alphonso, the son of the house. He is obliged to marry, in
order to save his father from debt, a woman named Cassandra,

but Cassandra accidentally drinks poison and dies. Miranda is persecuted by a monk named Roderigo. She makes friends with Alonzo, a cottage boy who has been deranged for ten years as the result of falling downstairs. At the end of the story Alonzo is killed by Montavole's ruffians but proves to be Montavole's own son. Someone swapped babies. Alphonso is Alberto's son, and Alberto is not dead after all. Alphonso and Miranda marry, and Rinaldo is executed.

46: Fletcher, Grenville   ROSALVIVA, OR, THE DEMON DWARF. A ROMANCE   3 vols. London: Longman, 1824

Leontini loves Viola di Morini, but she marries someone else. On the rebound he becomes involved with Rosalviva, who suffers from vanity but appears at first to have some good qualities. She abandons Leontini for his friend the Conte Golfieri. Golfieri and Rosalviva are two of a kind. We discover that Golfieri assassinated Rosalviva's father, which is awkward as Rosalviva has made a vow to avenge her father's death. She overlooks the vow for the sake of her love, though a priest assures her that she will be damned if she does not keep her promise. Leontini, who plans to take revenge for Rosalviva's infidelity, is imprisoned by Golfieri.

Golfieri takes Rosalviva to see the fun of Leontini's execution, but their victim somehow escapes. Romantic complications develop as Golfieri's adoptive father insists that he marry a woman named Francesca, and the priest Vivaldi (who is also Leontini's father) pressures Rosalviva about her vow. Golfieri solves the latter problem by strangling Vivaldi. Rosalviva deliberately chooses the love of Golfieri rather than the love of God, but because the marriage with Francesca does indeed take place, she fears that she will only be Golfieri's mistress. Therefore she tries to blackmail him into killing his wife.

At this point a character known as the Demon Dwarf appears and reminds Golfieri of his first murder; he claims kinship with Leontini. He and Rosalviva become associates and at last he consents to kill Francesca and move her body to Rosalviva's own vaults so she can enjoy the sight of it, but on condition that Rosalviva belong to him. Rosalviva hopes to win back Golfieri, but he has repented and is mourning his wife; this makes Rosalviva so angry that she decides to lock him up with the decaying body of his wife and hang him later. Suddenly the Dwarf reveals that he is really Leontini and that Francesca is not dead. Rosalviva, stunned and terrified, commits suicide. Leontini marries his first love, Viola.

47: Fox, Joseph, Jr.   SANTA-MARIA, OR, THE MYSTERIOUS PREG-
       NANCY. A ROMANCE.   3 vols. London: G. Kearsley, 1797

On the morning of her wedding to Prince Rinaldo, Santa-Maria
is found apparently dead in her bed. At her funeral she revives and reports a dream of being raped by their kinsman
and enemy Contarini. The wedding is next delayed by Rinaldo's illness, and before the event takes place Santa-Maria
is discovered to be pregnant. She asserts her chastity but
is not widely believed. Her mother thinks it best to send
her off in pilgrim's garb lest her father kill her. She is
taken in (we discover later) by some peasants who find her
in labor, and she is delivered of a premature and stillborn
child, after which she acquires a shepherd's costume and
vows never to reveal her sex until the mystery of her pregnancy is solved. Twice she stays with families, under different aliases, but is forced to move on when impressionable
young ladies are smitten with her beauty and press for marriage. She leaves behind with each girl a piece of her
mother's jewelry as a token of affection. At last she saves
a starving recluse in a ragged monk's habit and lives with
him for a month until he dies. Father Conrad has told her
that after his death she should look behind some mysterious
black hangings, but she is afraid to do it alone, for she
thinks she may find a corpse. So she recruits a passing
cavalier, who finds for her a chest of money and a manuscript that makes him too angry at Father Conrad to give
him a decent burial. He tells Santa-Maria that she may read
it later and takes her to a cottage where she will be safe.
     Meanwhile, Count Rudolph, Santa-Maria's father, is tak-
ing retributive measures. Suspecting her mother's complic-
ity in the escape, he makes her sleep in a separate room.
He sends assassins to murder the Prince and his guardian
Manfredi. He wants revenge against the person he reasonably
presumes has ruined his daughter, and, further, he is in
line to inherit from the Prince, which he needs to do if he
is to make a good showing with troops for the Viceroy. Word
comes that the Prince and Manfredi are missing — it seems to
him extraordinarily fast work — but when Count Rudolph arrives to investigate, he finds the treasure missing too and
suspects that the assassins have cheated him. The castle
shows signs of being haunted, so Rudolph gives it to D'Ar-
cos, his kinsman, in ostensible gratitude for a gift of
money.
     When Rudolph comes back from the wars, D'Arcos has giv-
en up trying to live with the haunting, and Rudolph decides
to move into the castle with his wife. They have had no
word from Santa-Maria. On their way to the castle, however,
they come across the girls with whom Santa-Maria has left

jewelry and discover a number of inns that are decorated
with sketches of Prince Rinaldo. Rudolph finds the castle
disquieting. It, too, has pictures of Rinaldo and Santa-
Maria. Suddenly Rudolph is brought to trial for the murders
of Rinaldo and Manfredi, whom he now suspects to be alive.
While he is waiting to be sentenced he stabs himself. A
number of interesting facts are uncovered on the occasion
of the trial. Santa-Maria's brother Ferdinand (who was also
the helpful cavalier), heretofore supposed dead, accuses
Contarini, who has himself been Rudolph's accuser, of murder, sacrilege, and incest. Father Conrad's manuscript has
revealed that he drugged Santa-Maria with a substance previously proved effective on high-principled nuns and let
Contarini rape her. Contarini is beheaded, Santa-Maria marries her Prince, who is not dead after all, and brother Ferdinand marries one of the girls who had been misguidedly in
love with his sister.

48: Gaspey, Thomas   THE MYSTERY, OR, FORTY YEARS AGO. A
    NOVEL   3 vols. London: Longman, Hurst, Rees, Orme, and
    Brown, 1820

Charles Harley, a naval officer, comes back to see his old
benefactor Sir George Henderson. Sir George's two daughters, "the playful Caroline" and "the pensive Amelia," were
Charles's childhood companions. Caroline is already married
but Amelia is not, and Charles fancies that Sir George may
intend her for him. Both Charles and Amelia come to like
the notion, but when Charles, after some colorful but irrel-
evant adventures with mobs and imprisonment, asks Sir George
for her hand, he is given a flat negative which hurts his
pride and drives him away from the house. Having received
a commission — Sir George arranged it — and an unexpected
inheritance, he leaves for Africa and subsequently is believed to be drowned.
    In fact Charles manages to reach shore but is pursued by
a lion into the jungle, where he is lost for two months before finding some friendly natives with whom to settle down.
He stays for several months, making friends and inculcating
useful skills, but with the advent of a new and hostile
chief he decides to go home. He is encumbered by a female
servant/companion who insistently comes along, intent upon
marrying him, until partway through their journey a tiger
resolves the difficulty by eating her. In one native village he finds Smithers, an English missionary with a long
beard, "dead blue eyes," and two long teeth like "the prongs
of a toasting fork." His sinister appearance notwithstanding, Smithers is a gentle old man, so high-principled as to

be somewhat useless as a companion in adventures. He dies
and leaves Charles his Bible and papers.

Though both Amelia and Sir George have been exceedingly
woeful at the rumor of Charles's death, she is still forbidden to him after their joyful reunion because, as he now
admits, Sir George suspects that Charles is Amelia's half-
brother, his own son, fruit of an impulsive moment with his
wife's visiting cousin Frederica. Charles moves sadly into
the new house which the undertaker Shovelem has procured for
him and prepares to live alone. He is visited by a happy
Sir George, who has discovered, thanks to Smithers's papers
which Charles himself brought home, that Charles is not
after all his son. The relieved lovers marry at once.

It is worth noting, though they are impossible to fit
into the summary, that long and frequent passages of the
novel are devoted to conversation and even informal debate
on such topics as society, economics, and marriage.

49: Godwin, William   FLEETWOOD, OR, THE NEW MAN OF FEELING
      3 vols. London: R. Phillips, 1805

Casimir Fleetwood, the protagonist and narrator, says that
the story is a record of his errors. He is an only child,
raised in an isolated part of Wales by his widowed father
and a capable tutor. Sensitive to the beauties of nature,
he is given to reverie and daydreaming. (Later he believes
that daydreaming leads to despotism because the dreamer's
control of events is absolute.) "Positive, assuming, and
self-conceited" is his description of his youthful character. At Oxford he takes up worldliness and permits the development of his passions, though he is relatively kind to
beleaguered Freshmen, including one who kills himself after
being persuaded to read aloud his verse tragedy about the
hygienic problems of the Augean stables.

After Oxford, Fleetwood travels on the continent and has
love affairs with two promiscuous and unsuitable women. In
Switzerland he finds his father's friend and foster brother
William Ruffigny, at whose house Fleetwood learns that his
father has died in Wales and goes home to mourn. Ruffigny
manages to save him from a third love affair, but the reformed Fleetwood is cynical and misanthropic.

Fortyish now and devoured with ennui, Fleetwood travels
restlessly and longs for a real friend. One day he hears of
a man named Macneil, a friend of Rousseau's, and wrangles a
meeting. The Macneils and their three charming daughters
lead a rather private existence because of a misguided
elopement in Mrs. Macneil's early life, but they take Fleetwood into their family circle. Macneil tries to convince

him that he should marry and start a family, though, knowing
Fleetwood's disposition, he is a little daunted to see him
looking with partiality at Mary, the youngest of the daughters. At last all the Macneils except Mary, who stayed in
England to visit a friend, are shipwrecked and die on their
way to Italy. From a combination of oversight on Macneil's
part and skullduggery on the part of a Genoese banker, Mary
is left penniless. Only the economic challenge of her situation keeps her from pining away. She marries Fleetwood,
who has been her only consolation through her troubles, and
prepares for a happy ending.

Alas, Fleetwood is ill suited to marriage. Mary annoys
him by usurping his favorite spots in the family home, by
wishing to socialize, and by raising other innocent con-
flicts of interest. He picks quarrels and becomes jealous;
she pines. When he takes her to Bath for her health they
become involved with two of Fleetwood's kinsmen, Gifford and
Kenrick. They are the sons of a loose but engaging woman
whose shenanigans led to the illegitimizing of Gifford, her
elder boy, who has been an accomplished villain since his
childhood. He persuades Fleetwood, through a complicated
intrigue of circumstantial evidence, forgeries, and so on,
that Kenrick and Mary are in love and that all the world
gossips about them. Fleetwood accuses Mary and, half insane, dashes off to the continent, leaving orders to have
Mary evicted penniless and divorced, and their baby declared
illegitimate. His lunacy climaxes on his wedding anniversary, when for celebration he has waxwork figures made of
Mary and Kenrick, dresses them in suitable clothing, plays
their favorite tune on a barrel organ, and at last, imagin-
ing that he sees them move, tears them to pieces. When he
recovers from the illness which this scene precipitates he
goes to Paris to meet Gifford but on the way suffers from
an attempted assassination. When he recovers, his life is
turned upside down, for he learns that Kenrick has rescued
him and that the villain Gifford is in the Bastille. Scarborough, the old neighbor who has taken him in, explains
that the apparently incriminating exchanges between Kenrick
and Mary had to do with his own daughter Louisa, who wishes
to marry Kenrick despite her father's despotical intervention on behalf of the ugly, imbecilic, and effeminate Lord
Lindsey. Kenrick at last wins Scarborough over. Fleetwood
sees the error of his ways and gives up nearly all his fortune to Mary and the baby (which incidentally looks unmis-
takably like him), planning to retire to the Pyrenees. At
the end, however, Mary unexpectedly forgives him and they
are reunited. Kenrick marries Louisa and Gifford is executed.

50: Godwin, William   ST. LEON. A TALE OF THE SIXTEENTH
    CENTURY   4 vols. London: G. G. and J. Robinson, 1799

St. Leon is trained to be honorable and upright. Orphaned
at eighteen, he fights for Francis I and is knighted, but
acquires one disastrous vice — gaming. He marries Marguerite Louise Isabeau de Damville; her father hopes her goodness will reform St. Leon before he is ruined. It almost
does, but when he takes his son to college in Paris, St.
Leon begins to game again and loses all his fortune. While
he is temporarily insane from shock and guilt, his wife settles affairs and moves the family to a cheap Swiss cottage.
During a famine the neighbors drive them away and they go
through a period of near starvation, selling their clothes
to buy food.

After things are a bit better, an old beggar comes to
stay in their summer house. He appears to be some kind of
Wanderer. In exchange for refuge from the Inquisition he
offers St. Leon two secrets which are not to be told to anyone else, including Marguerite. St. Leon is torn between
marital loyalty and desire to know the secrets. He chooses
the latter and is given instructions for the Philosopher's
Stone and the Elixir of Life. The old man dies. St. Leon
manufactures money and buys a big house, but his marriage
has sustained a blow. Furthermore, because he is unable to
explain where his money comes from, people suspect that he
has killed and robbed the old man. Charles, the son, leaves
his family in order to preserve his honor; worse, St. Leon's
wife guesses his secret and says that he has killed her,
adding a few remarks about what low creatures alchemists
are. He is jailed on suspicion but bribes his way out.
A mob burns his house and kills Hector, his faithful friend
and servant. Marguerite dies, and he gives his daughters
into the care of a friend.

Next the Inquisition seizes him. He is to be burned after twelve years' imprisonment. So much for endless life,
he thinks. But he escapes on his way to the stake, mixes
the elixir, drops thirty years, and eludes capture. So that
they may inherit, he tells his daughters that their father
is dead; they are nice girls but recover from their grief
too quickly to please him. He tries being a philanthropist,
whereupon his friend Bethlem Gabor, a confirmed misanthrope,
is so annoyed by his do-gooding that he locks him in a dungeon, finally, however, giving him a key so that he can
escape during a siege by the Austrians. St. Leon's son
Charles proves to be the Austrian commander, but their warm
friendship (Charles treats him like a younger brother) is
destroyed by a misunderstanding about Charles's girlfriend.
Worse, Charles finds out that St. Leon used to feed infidels

and implacably holds this against him. St. Leon refuses to
duel with his son and flees. Thirty years later he writes
his memoirs, with no good news of his own. He ends by list-
ing his son's virtues and being glad of his happiness.

51: Godwin, William   THINGS AS THEY ARE, OR, THE ADVENTURES
    OF CALEB WILLIAMS   3 vols. London: B. Crosby, 1794

Caleb Williams, who has been brought up to be honest, is employed as secretary/librarian to Mr. Falkland. Williams is
young (only eighteen), greatly admires his employer, and is
by nature obsessively curious. His employer, sometimes re-
clusive and unsmiling, sometimes outright frenzied, is said
to be a mere ruin of the man he once was. Falkland's story,
as Williams is told it by a third party, accounts for his
melancholy: he was once accused of murder. The victim was a
squire named Tyrrel, a man of rough passions and no breed-
ing. Tyrrel and Falkland fell into a kind of social rivalry
in which Falkland's sophistication outshone Tyrrel's wealth.
Growing jealousy of his rival turned Tyrrel savage toward
his dependent cousin Emily, who admired Falkland. At her
refusal to marry a particularly uncouth farmer named Grimes,
to whom he had perversely betrothed her, he had her imprisoned for debt and thus precipitated her death. Knowing himself despised by the whole town and goaded by Falkland's
reproach at a public gathering, Tyrrel got drunk, came back
to the gathering, and knocked Falkland down. Falkland was
wild with humiliation and Tyrrel was later found dead in the
street. A poor farmer and his son, whom Tyrrel had formerly
persecuted and Falkland tried to help, were convicted of the
murder and executed, but the change in Falkland's character
began then.
     It occurs to Williams that his employer may in fact be
guilty. He finds himself unable to leave murder and related
topics out of his conversation and watches Falkland closely.
The relationship becomes tense and embarrassing. Then one
day Falkland finds Williams breaking into a trunk of his.
After that he swears his secretary to silence and admits to
the murder of Tyrrel, but he asserts that Williams has sold
himself for the information. Soon Williams, chafing at the
closeness of Falkland's supervision and at the prospect of
never being free, runs away. Falkland pursues and accuses
him of robbery. When Williams escapes from prison he falls
in with some bandits who refrain from turning him in for the
bounty Falkland has put on his head, but leaves them after
the woman of the house tries to kill him with a cleaver.
He attempts to sail to Ireland disguised as a beggar but is
taken off the ship, suspected of some crime committed by an
Irishman. He wears various disguises, keeps moving, writes

for a living. Always he is hunted and execrated. When at last he is captured he decides to reveal Falkland's guilt. Regretting this decision when Falkland, clearly a broken man, enters the courtroom, Williams makes a long speech in which he blames himself and praises Falkland's virtues. Falkland, uttering reciprocal sentiments, falls into his arms and dies three days later.

52: Green, Sarah   DECEPTION   3 vols. London: Sherwood, Neely, and Jones, 1813

Maisuna Cleveland, an East Indian heiress, is traveling in England, accompanied by her parrot, when the coach overturns and the passengers are taken into the house of hospitable Sir William Coats. There Maisuna first meets Mr. Jefferson, to whom she is instantly attracted. He is poor, being inclined to indolence and extravagance, but she has a secret nocturnal meeting with him all the same, during which he warns her against the villainy of Mrs. Bruce and the confessor Jocelyn. Nevertheless she goes to stay with Mrs. Bruce and meets some interesting people, most of whom get her into trouble. Miss Meredith, whose suicide Maisuna prevents, is deeply involved in gaming and constantly requires large sums of money, which Maisuna wheedles from Mr. Mortimer, her guardian; as a result he supposes Maisuna herself to be gaming or at least indefensibly extravagant. This misunderstanding is cleared up when Mortimer is dying and the two young ladies rush to his bedside. Maisuna comes of age and receives her inheritance — her first act is to give Mr. Jefferson ten thousand anonymous pounds — and Miss Meredith reforms and marries a clergyman, so the financial difficulties are over. But the social ones are just beginning.

Mr. Berresford, whom Maisuna has earlier declined to marry despite her guardian's endorsement, is an intimate of Mrs. Bruce's house (her bastard son, we discover later) and still bent on marriage. Toward this end he has Maisuna kidnapped from a masquerade and locked up. Jocelyn attempts to arrange a Roman Catholic ceremony, but Maisuna (though she has had some Roman inclinations, her mother having been a Catholic) informs him that she is a Protestant and that he is false and idolatrous, whereupon Jocelyn suggests that Berresford rape her. She escapes at night in her petticoat with a handkerchief tied around her head and is at last reunited with Mr. Jefferson, with whom she exchanges vows of love. After a somewhat anticlimactic incident in which, instructed by a maternal note, she searches the house for "the talisman of Tippoo Saib, Sultan of the East" (her father), she and Jefferson, who is after all a nobleman and a good match, settle down to a happy marriage.

53: Green, William Child   ABBOT OF MONTSERRAT, OR, THE POOL
    OF BLOOD. A ROMANCE   2 vols. London: A. K. Newman, 1826

Fernandez and Isabel, who have eloped in search of a cooperative priest to marry them, spend the night in the monastery
of Montserrat. Isabel's father has opposed the marriage
because of an ancient boundary dispute with Fernandez's father, who disappeared after losing the lawsuit. Fernandez's
mother had been carried off by bandits some years earlier.
(It is bandit country, in fact. The monastery pays protection money to Roldan, formidable chief of the local bandit
troop.) At the monastery Fernandez discovers that a dying
monk is his missing father, so the marriage receives a parental blessing after all.

    Also at the monastery is a malcontent monk named Obando.
He is accosted on several occasions by a demon who exudes
yellow light and tries to corrupt him. At last he bargains
away his soul in return for finding his long-lost brother,
possession of aforementioned Isabel, and the post of Abbot.
He discovers that Roldan is his brother. Roldan captures
Isabel for him but forbids him to rape her, and she will not
give in. Fernandez and others in the company whom Roldan
also captures are released by Roldan's ex-mistress, who
proves to be Fernandez's missing mother.

    Though Obando becomes abbot by murdering his predeces-
sor, his new position fails to make him happy. His crimes
finally bring the bandits against the monastery from one
side, the Inquisition from the other. Just then the demon
carries him away through the roof, leaving the two forces to
fight it out. (The bandits lose.) Obando repents in midair
and is dropped back into the holocaust, where monks promise
to pray for him, so perhaps his soul is not lost. The lovers marry and Fernandez's mother comes to live with them.

54: Green, William Child   THE ALGERINES, OR, THE TWINS OF
    NAPLES   3 vols. London: A. K. Newman, 1832

Vicenza is the father of twin girls, who were born under unfortunate circumstances. Jealous at the attention paid his
wife by a man named Castelli, he gave his rival a crippling
wound and moved his wife to Naples. When she died in childbirth, partly as a result of travel and emotional upheaval,
he gave the elder twin, Alphonsine, to a convent in expiation. He has raised Victoria himself and is outraged to
discover when she grows up that she has a secret romantic
relationship with Castelli's son Caesario. He is informed
of this by Zacherelli, a servant turned bandit. Vicenza removes his daughter to Naples, but Caesario finds this out
and follows. Disillusioned with Victoria, Vincenza begins

visiting Alphonsine in the convent and wondering whether he has incarcerated the wrong twin. When Caesario gets into Victoria's room with a rope ladder, he is sure of it and persuades the abbess to trade daughters, since Alphonsine has not yet taken her vows.

Also in Naples is the Algerine Abdallah, whose father was Aghar Hussein and whose mother a captured army wife who later ran away (and later yet, we discover, became the abbess mentioned above). Looking for a woman to marry, Abdallah spends some time sending notes of introduction to Victoria. He believes himself particularly eligible because of an arrangement he made at home with a demon called Himmalay, who is visible only on mountains; it permits him to grant prolongation of life to three people of his choice. When Caesario is wounded by Zacherelli, Abdallah finds him and nurses him, and they become friends. One night when Abdallah is drunk — he is unaccustomed to alcohol — he responds to the delirious and apparently terminal mumbles of Caesario ("Save me") by giving him one of his charmed lives. Caesario recovers and Abdallah learns that he is competing for Victoria but behaves gallantly. Vicenza is so angry at Caesario's recovery that he stabs Zacherelli for incompetence, and Zacherelli extorts the second of Abdallah's charmed lives by having his bandits hold the Algerine over the edge of a precipice.

Meanwhile Vicenza has secretly swapped daughters, and Alphonsine is having what she regards as an exciting time in the seclusion of the family home. But she is a little confused by the young men — Caesario and Lioni, the latter a rejected suitor of Victoria's — who, mistaking her for Victoria, come to her balcony and say passionate and heartbroken things; her previous training has not equipped her to deal with this situation. She rather prefers Lioni, who is more polite. Hoping it will cure her father's depression over Victoria, she persuades him to take her to Palermo, but on the way they are captured by Zacherelli and his bandits, who have secured Caesario as well. They want a ransom for Caesario but plan to kill Vicenza and give Alphonsine to one of the younger bandits. Rather than pay the ransom, Caesario's father goes to the Viceroy and asks for soldiers. Abdallah, who has found his old friend Haly and bought him from a planter, comes to visit just in time to join the rescue party. When, in the fracas at the bandit's quarters, Abdallah comes face to face with Zacherelli, the bandit assumes that stabbing such a magical man would be futile; Haly is so pleased that he gives Zacherelli a turban to disguise his escape. He is especially pleased since he himself was Himmalay, playing a joke on his friend, and he has been feeling sorry.

At the convent, Victoria has politely but firmly declined to take her vows. She is delighted when Caesario arrives with a note from the now reconciled Vicenza, asking
for her release. Lioni finds that he is very fond of Alphonsine. And when Abdallah discovers in the abbess Rosalie
his runaway mother, he converts and marries Victoria's convent friend Ebba, who had been driven to the religious life
by unrequited love for Lioni. Zacherelli comes once to beg
for money to leave Sicily. Vicenza and Castelli never learn
to like each other despite the marriage of their children.

55: Green, William Child   ALIBEG THE TEMPTER. A TALE WILD
     AND WONDERFUL   4 vols. London: A. K. Newman, 1831

Alhamet, who is bored with his desert home, is lured away
by a mysterious and satanic stranger named Alibeg, despite
foreboding dreams of falling off precipices. They make a
pact, unspecified. There follow for Alhamet a series of
episodes, fragments of lives, which are always interrupted
by disaster. 1) As Gialdini, in Sicily, he is in love with
a beautiful girl named Seraphina, whose father disapproves.
He suffers capture by pirates and undergoes various other
difficulties. At one point he is befriended by an erstwhile
fortune-teller named Geronime. After changing his name to
Lorenzo during a sojourn in the Azores, Gialdini/Alhamet
finds Geronime again, but she is struck by lightning and
dies after redirecting him to Sicily. On the way he finds
her yet again (alias De Rolphe), commanding another pirate
ship. De Rolphe, who makes Lorenzo feel vaguely uncomfort-
able, finally offers him his dearest wish, i.e., to see Seraphina, and thereupon torments him with the sight of her
corpse. 2) Alhamet makes his next appearance as Ozembo, a
young hunter in Patagonia. He is happily betrothed to Ora,
but a mysterious stranger, a European named Falkland, appears and then reappears after being shot with arrows and
drowning. After an enemy attack, Ozembo and Ora and the
latter's old father escape; Falkland, now called Ogloo, is
still with them. Ozembo tries to kill him but Ogloo will
not die. Ora is drowned, her father dies, and their tribe
soon forget Ozembo and Ogloo, who have disappeared. 3) In
Russia a foreigner named Lovinski (alias Alhamet/Gialdini/
Lorenzo/Ozembo) loves Agatha, a noblewoman. She reciprocates and refuses a suitor whom her parents prefer. A servant, Nicolas, murdered by Lovinski for his inefficiency in
delivering messages, reappears and is said to be somewhat
changed. Agatha wrongly believes Lovinski to have suffo-
cated while hiding in her trunk, and Nicolas demands her
person as the price of burying him secretly. When she commits suicide he makes no attempt to stop her, tells Lovinski

that it is his revenge, and disappears without leaving tracks in the snow. 4) In Cornwall, as Edward Penrose, Alhamet is rescued in a storm and becomes involved with Amelia whose brother is supposed to have died in the same storm. But the brother returns, changed for the worse, and makes considerable mischief — gets his "father" to kill his "sister," etc. He intimates to Penrose that he is not who he seems to be. 5) In Circassia Alhamet is called Cassimir and has a family. He is happy until a Tartar enemy (Hassaraic) refuses to stay dead and enters a compact against him with a jealous rival. The latter soon regrets the association, as Hassaraic is somehow unnerving. Nevertheless they attack and nearly everyone is killed except Cassimir, who disappears, and Hassaraic. 6) Suddenly back in the desert, Alhamet as an unrecognized Wanderer hears from his sister that their parents died of grief over him. He is caught in a simoon and drowns from a rudderless boat in the Red Sea. He is buried by strangers.

56: Green, William Child   THE PROPHECY OF DUNCANNON, OR,
    THE DWARF AND THE SEER. A CALEDONIAN LEGEND   1 vol.
    London: Joseph Emans, 1824

Lorrimond, Laird of Glenwark, is about to marry Margaret, daughter of the dwarf Sir Andrew Draulincourt. Rosilda Dinwoodie (whose woodcutter father raised Lorrimond as a foundling until his own father acknowledged him) has for some time been in love with him but is trying to behave. Shortly before the wedding the seer Duncannon arrives and warns, not for the first time, that the marriage is improper and shame will result from it. Lorrimond, who vows not to marry until he has vanquished his enemies, swims to St. Serf's island to confront the seer. As his new sword, a jeweled gift from Dinwoodie, would be awkward for swimming, he leaves it with Rosilda for safekeeping; she decides to place it on the sand where he can find it on his return, but the miser Ralph Linnecombe finds it first and takes it home.
    On the island Lorrimond discovers a beautiful girl named Mora and promptly falls in love. He returns to the island often but he is not for some time permitted to meet the seer or to know whether the seer is Mora's father. Margaret is wondering what has become of Lorrimond and is feeling angry and jilted. At this point her ex-suitor Richard Cadwaller comes to town with a friend, Edward Allandale. They stay at the castle, and Cadwaller, who is both ambitious and too fond of Margaret to hold a grudge, works his way back into her affections. They decide to elope. Allandale has been courting Rosilda, who is under great parental pressure to marry. Even Sir Andrew pushes her on Allandale's behalf,

and she is too confused to refuse, but she decides to run
away on the eve of her wedding.

On that evening several important things happen simultaneously: Allandale, needing money for a hasty wedding,
borrows from the miser, who later is so upset at his own
prodigality that he murders Allandale with Lorrimond's jeweled sword and drops it by the body; Cadwaller and Margaret,
just stepping into their chaise to elope, hear Allandale's
dying voice but are unable to find him in the fog; Lorrimond
is allowed to meet with the seer Duncannon, who tells him a
long tale of intrigue and baby-swapping, proving that Margaret is his sister and Mora is the true heiress of Draulincourt. Duncannon was a friend and former vassal of Lorrimond's father, promoted for his services. He thinks it
best that Lorrimond and Mora marry and leave Margaret alone,
since the confusion of identity is not her fault.

When Lorrimond gets back to the mainland he is imprisoned for Allandale's murder. He does not protest, for he
supposes that Rosilda still had his sword and must have done
it, and he is gallant. Margaret comes with the keys and
lets him out, but he insists on returning for his trial.
When he reaches the island, Duncannon tells him that Mora
is missing with the boat and has apparently gone to look for
him. The night is fearfully stormy, and Mora is drowned.
Thanks to Rosilda, who has seen evidence in the miser's cottage, and to several minor characters who come and testify,
Lorrimond is acquitted and the miser convicted. He marries
Rosilda with the demonstrated approval of Mora's ghost.
Duncannon disappears and is seen only once again, on the
couple's twelfth anniversary, when he makes an appearance
as an elderly minstrel.

57: Green, William Child   THE WOODLAND FAMILY, OR, THE SONS
    OF ERROR AND DAUGHTERS OF SIMPLICITY. A DOMESTIC TALE
    1 vol. London: Joseph Emans, 1824

Emily, Caroline, and Ethelia are sisters. Emily, her father's favorite, is innocent, beautiful, unassuming, and
shorter than her sisters. Mr. Arthur Sunderland sees Emily
and admires her sentiments. He is so upright that the two
men of fashion — Captain Frederic Mountdale, an atheist, and
Mr. Alfred Clairfort, something of a fop — who pursue and
plan to seduce Caroline and Ethelia respectively, think that
he is a Quaker. Nevertheless Sunderland and Emily meet,
lose their heads, and are ruined. Caroline and Ethelia are
ruined too, for despite Emily's advice to the contrary they
elope with their suitors only to find themselves mere mistresses. Sunderland promises to reclaim Emily's sisters and
makes her promise to keep his name a secret until he gives

her permission to tell it. An awkward promise, for while he is away Emily's pregnancy becomes noticeable to her parents; her mother dies and her father calls Emily a matricide.

Meanwhile, Caroline and Ethelia's men have gone abroad; Ethelia would like to go home but Caroline is too proud, so they go into the world and come under the protection of Mrs. Montague, who periodically bewails old sins. Ethelia, having fortuitously reunited Mrs. Montague with an old beggar woman who is her long-lost mother, goes home herself at last, coincidentally arriving just in time for her own mother's funeral. News of their mother's death softens Caroline to repentance, and Sunderland comes back to throw himself at Emily's feet and announce that he is the Marquis of Grandeville and wishes to marry her. Mountdale and Clairfort come too, penitent, and throw themselves at Caroline's and Ethelia's feet respectively. Other miscellaneous relationships are accounted for, and the three sisters marry their lovers.

58: Grosse, Karl   THE DAGGER   1 vol. London: Verner and
    Hood, 1795

The Baron St**, who is attractive and knows it, is married by his family to Albertina of F**. She is not only beautiful but intelligent and virtuous; she loves the Baron very much because it is her duty to do so, and tries to make him cultivate his mind and character. Although a fairly willing pupil, he is not a ready one and, when he is appointed ambassador, goes to court unprepared to deal with knavery and temptation. There are three ruthless and contending parties at court — the Prince's, the Princess's, and Julia's. Julia is the Prince's mistress. The Baron and Julia promptly fall in love, and he, being young and ardent, becomes conspicuously foolish. Meanwhile Albertina is doing her best to keep her husband out of trouble. She even goes to see Julia, and the two women like each other so much that Julia, who is tiring of the Baron anyway, promises to give him up. The Baron, beside himself with rage and loss, impulsively poisons Albertina's lemonade, but then he and Albertina, overcome respectively with guilt and nobility, each try to drink the mixture and break the glass in the struggle. After that he leaves Julia for a while, only to be taken up by the Princess, who has been waiting for her chance. Later Julia tries to stab the Baron, an attempt that leads not to his death but to their reconciliation. Just as she is giving him a hair ring as a pledge of love, a hand reaches down and takes it; the hand is Albertina's and she puts the ring on her finger, saying that she wants to be included in the bond of their love. There is hugging all around, and the others greatly admire her.

The Baron, out of sentimentality, has kept the dagger
with which Julia tried to kill him; Julia, however, wants it
back, it having been a gift to her from the Prince, who may
ask where it is. When the Baron brings it back to Julia,
hidden in his bosom, her dog (not for the first time) bites
him, and in bending over to deal with the attack he accidentally stabs himself in the stomach. The Prince now being
better informed about Julia's affairs than is healthy for
her, she decides to emigrate. The Baron refuses to go with
her, so she uses the dagger to force him into a carriage and
abduct him. At dawn Albertina, who waited up all night after she heard her husband go out, goes to Julia's rooms and
finds them empty of all save confusion and the Baron's hat.
Albertina stays faithful, dangles the Prince, who is now
pursuing her, and hopes to recover the Baron. He is in fact
becoming very bored indeed in his rural hideaway, and Julia
in consequence is once again becoming dangerous. One day a
hermit (Albertina in disguise) prevents Julia from stabbing
him, whereupon she stabs herself and dies asking forgiveness. She has left Albertina her whole estate. The reunited couple leave court life and go home, where the Baron
learns to find happiness in tranquillity.

59: Grosse, Karl   HORRID MYSTERIES. A STORY   4 vols. Lon-
    don: William Lane, 1796

Because the events in this novel are dominated and manipulated by a secret society called the Confederates, it is
full of surprising and unexplained incidents, delusions,
spirits, mysterious documents, losses and resurrections, and
is difficult indeed to render lucid. The following summary
deals with only the more comprehendible events; the novel is
much more complicated.
    Carlos is told by his friend Count S-- a strange tale of
having been captured by white phantoms and accused of illicit relations with a woman he does not know, called Francisca. Count S-- was at last released and sworn to a year's
secrecy, but Francisca was thrown into a pit. Carlos himself is warned, in a vision, about invisible spies. Later
the Count returns and tries to assassinate his friend but
is stopped by a Superior Being; he does not appear to recall
the incident afterward. Carlos marries a girl named Elmira,
who also warns him that unknown hands direct things in
Spain. Elmira is killed mysteriously just after the wedding. After Elmira's death Carlos meets Don Pedro, who
is said to have killed his wife Francisca and her lover.
One night when they are dining together Francisca arrives,
alive, and begs forgiveness. Later still she confesses that
she loves Carlos, and vanishes, to reappear at intervals

throughout the novel. Meanwhile, Carlos has reluctantly joined a secret society on the understanding that the "brothers" will find Elmira's murderer, and he spends a voluptuous day with a girl called Rosalia, who is affiliated with the society and, as it turns out, eager to ruin him. Elmira appears again and suggests that she and Carlos elope, which they do despite the warning of a kind of spiritual mentor, the Genius Amanuel. Elmira is shot as they drive away and dies. After complicated wanderings and some brushes with the Confederates, Carlos finds Elmira alive in Switzerland. She knows nothing of the second episode and says she was drugged the first time, not dead. They have a brief but happy marriage; then she and their son fall sick and die. This time she really is dead.

Carlos and Count S--, in Paris, find a girl, Caroline, whom they both like; Carlos asks her to choose between them and she chooses the Count. Carlos marries Adelheid Baroness of V--, with whom Count S-- subsequently falls in love. At about this time the Genius Amanuel fights with Carlos's faithful servant Alfonso, who, dying of the wound received, confesses that he is Carlos's uncle and the head of the Confederates. Carlos has problems with women, finding it necessary to shoot a friend who is discovered making love to his wife and having to cope with the advances of the Count's wife, Caroline. At the end, however, the Count and Carlos are saved from bandits by their two wives, who, wearing male attire, attack the assassins from behind. The couples are reconciled.

60: Hamilton, Ann Mary   THE FOREST OF ST. BERNARDO
     4 vols. London: J. Hughes, 1806

Emma Roberts has been sent to a French convent by her father as retribution for her refusal to marry his friend Sir William Maynard. Sir William was especially helpful when General Roberts, after his wife's death, fell in with a whore and took up gaming. But as the novel begins Sir William is sorry that he has caused Emma trouble and effects a reconciliation with Henry Millward, whom she loves. General Roberts removes Emma from the convent, along with her orphaned friend Fanny Edwards. Near the newlywed Emma and Henry's estate lives Father Edmund the hermit, who is doing penance for having left his monastery to elope with a nun; she died during the escape while giving birth to his baby, who also died. Emma and Henry also meet someone who knew an Edwards in India — Fanny's late Uncle Charles, as it turns out, who has left Fanny £10,000.

By the second volume Emma and Henry have two children, Edward and Matilda, and are given a third, Juliana, by Alon-

za Vaena. Most of the subsequent excitement is Juliana's or
Alonza's. Alonza does not wish Juliana to know her family
history, which involves his secret marriage. Alonza marries
a second time and the son of that marriage is assassinated.
Like all the rest of the villainy, this assassination was
perpetrated by Gusman (Alonza's cousin) and Triphosa (a
woman Alonza once refused to marry). Family affairs reach
a crisis when Juliana is kidnapped and her father is discovered to be missing. Gusman and Triphosa have Juliana in a
castle; they wish her to become Roman Catholic and to marry
their feeble son. Though they try to act friendly, Juliana
is not deceived, for she has found her father's ring — diamond, with a hidden miniature of her mother — under a tree
and suspects that he was murdered there. And she is quite
right. Further, Gusman wishes to rape her, and Triphosa
wants to kill her afterward. When Juliana's friends arrive
to rescue her they find her father's unburied body, but she
is gone, safely escaped to the protection of a good priest.
Gusman and Triphosa are to be executed; Juliana marries Edward; and Matilda marries Charles, who with his poor but
aristocratic mother was earlier taken into Emma and Henry's
family.

61: Hamilton, Ann Mary   MONTALVA, OR, ANNALS OF GUILT
    2 vols. London: N. L. Pannier, 1811

Stephano Montalva and Ferdinando D'Rosorio, whose parents
are friends, grow up together. D'Rosorio is good, Montalva
bad. Montalva is a seducer of girls, a borrower of money,
a faithless friend. He loves Valeria but will not marry her
because she is poor. Instead, he seduces her with promises
of marriage and after the birth of their daughter puts Valeria in a convent and the child out to nurse. Mother and
child die. Jealous of D'Rosorio's child and money, Montalva
poisons him and acquires both. He tires of the child and
hires a man to help drug it and spirit it away, pretending
that it is dead. The accomplice later dies.
    Montalva, in Spain, begins to notice other people doing
kind deeds and starts to feel wicked and sorry. He finds a
girl (Ellen Dudley) who still loves the seducer who deserted
her, and he supports and lives with her. When she has a
child and leaves Montalva, he goes after her and invites her
back even though he learns that the child is not his, but
she refuses to come. He has begun to do other mildly good
deeds and to feel new emotions, like pity. He finds in a
convent a girl he believes to be D'Rosorio's child, the one
whom he drugged and cheated of her inheritance; she does not
want to stay cloistered. A demon disguised as a minstrel
tempts him to kill her and avoid the rack of the Inquisi-

tion, then disappears in blue flames. As Montalva approaches the girl's bed with a dagger, the ghost of Valeria informs him that it is his own child Isobel, who did not die but was kidnapped in infancy. Montalva dies in agonies of remorse. Isobel marries her lover and they found a monastery with D'Rosorio's money.

62: Harley, Mrs. PRIORY OF ST. BERNARD. AN OLD ENGLISH
      TALE   2 vols. London: William Lane, 1789

In the time of Henry II a new Lord Raby comes into his estate, which includes the Priory of St. Bernard. A villain named Manston (his uncle, it appears) manages to take away his property despite the efforts of a woman who turns out to be Raby's mother, and Raby hides himself in a peasant cottage. Raby, when he earlier encountered his mother in the priory, did not recognize her because during his infancy his father had deserted his wife and two daughters; he put them in the priory for safekeeping during wartime and failed to reclaim them, but he kept his infant son with him. Family relationships of all sorts are tremendously complicated. Edmund, who is supposedly Manston's son but who is in sympathy with Raby and his sisters, is informed that he is really the son of a hermit, formerly his tutor, the real Earl of Manston. The false Manston, hereinafter called De Courcy, has gone, according to the hermit, to Palestine in order to produce some heroics which might make the king authorize his marriage to Raby's sister Laura. Raby and his other sister, Maud, lead an army on a crusade, and Edmund's sister (or perhaps foster sister) Julia simply runs away, having been too much courted by a profligate. All these disappearances frustrate the efforts of Edmund and his real father to bring about any good in the private sector, but they join the army and fight well for King Richard.

At the Battle of Joppa, De Courcy brings to King Richard an old Saracen named Abudah and his daughter Zoraide. Abudah, however, admits that Zoraide is really "Christian Elmira"; simultaneously the king looks at her and recognizes her as his "lost Berengeria," his wife. Raby also loves her but she is sacrificed to a marriage with King Seofrid of Cyprus, who will keep the peace of Christendom on no other condition. Her unhappy life is ended prematurely when she throws herself into a fight between Raby and Seofrid and is accidentally stabbed by the latter. More identities are revealed as Lucius, a page acquired by Raby and Maud, proves to be the runaway Julia, who was called Eleonora during her childhood in Wales. She was at that period raised by a woman called Alice, whose real name is Emma and whose real relationship to Julia is maternal. "Lucius" has confessed her identity during a decline brought about by frustrated love for Raby, but Raby consents to marry her and thereby cures her. Edmund and Laura marry as well, and Maud goes into a nunnery of which the abbess is Alice/Emma. The king takes away De Courcy's ill-gotten gains and banishes him from court. The real Earl of Manston at the end of the novel dies blessing all the appropriate people.

63: Helme, Elizabeth   DUNCAN AND PEGGY. A SCOTTISH TALE
    2 vols. London: J. Bell, 1794

Duncan, who will someday be chief of the Campbells, is living with his uncle the Colonel. He defends Peggy, about whose poverty the other children are cruel, and the Colonel educates her and makes a settlement on her. Duncan and Peggy fall in love, to his parents' considerable disapproval; he proposes before going into the army. Peggy and the Colonel go to London and stay with Lady Beugle, Duncan's aunt, who tries to find a man for Peggy so that her own daughter Eleanor can have Duncan. Peggy is unshaken in her loyalty to Duncan, despite the honorable advances of a nice old man who tries to give her a diamond necklace, and the attractions of Lady Beugle's son Wilmot. After the Colonel learns from Peggy's foster grandmother that the girl was born of a passing Jacobite who died in childbirth, he is opposed for political reasons to her marrying Duncan. Some years earlier the old woman's only son, Alan Grant, carrying a miniature portrait, went to hunt for Peggy's real family and never came back; but suddenly he appears, having survived slavery, dungeons, and Cherokees, to announce that Peggy is the Colonel's granddaughter. Duncan's engagement to Peggy is now acceptable. After some additional trouble (e.g., Peggy is arrested for shooting out the front teeth of a woman who earlier abducted her), the novel ends happily and Peggy's father is discovered alive.

64: Helme, Elizabeth   THE FARMER OF INGLEWOOD FOREST. A
    NOVEL   4 vols. London: William Lane, 1796

As the novel begins, Farmer Godwin has a good life with his wife and three children, William, Edwin, and Emma. William and Edwin are courting the daughters of a neighboring family, Fanny and Agnes Bernard. This rural idyll is interrupted by a coaching accident that brings the widowed Mrs. Delmar and her unhappily married brother Mr. Whitmore, both in their twenties, to stay with the Godwins. Whitmore is a libertine and begins a flirtation with Emma. When he goes back to London he takes Edwin, the more ambitious of the brothers, to place as a clerk. In the wicked city Edwin's principles deteriorate rather rapidly: he reads novels, drinks, games, and is seduced by a girl named Sophy. Mrs. Delmar finds him attractive enough to marry and makes him a socially plausible husband by buying him a commission in the army. Edwin is silent about his marriage when he goes home to the farm, the more so since he finds himself still drawn to Agnes. When he returns to London he takes his sister Emma with him. The swiftness of her moral decline makes Edwin's look leisurely. When Whitmore needs to flee to France after a duel he persuades Emma to go with him. Apparently with some notion of retaliation, Edwin sleeps with Mrs. Whitmore. He has, as well, contrived to ruin Agnes. At last William comes to London to inquire after Emma's welfare; there he learns of his brother's marriage and his sister's ruin and finds Edwin himself lolling about with Mrs. Whitmore. In the subsequent familial distress Mrs. Godwin has convulsions and dies.

The pregnant and intermittently lunatic Agnes is removed, with Fanny in attendance, to a house belonging to Mrs. Palmer, the benevolent lady of the local manor. Agnes's baby is christened Anna Palmer and given to Fanny to bring home and nurse, for Fanny was pregnant too but miscarried from the stress of Agnes's delivery. The baby is to be given to her godmother after her infancy. Edwin arrives unexpectedly and secretly, just in time to raise a coffin lid and see the corpse of Agnes holding the corpse of Fanny's baby, though Edwin naturally supposes the dead child to be his own. He suffers from some resultant lunacy but ultimately goes to France, where he finds Emma, who is guilty but prosperous. He duels and kills Whitmore, which so angers Emma that she refuses his protection and instead goes away with a man named Hartford.

Years pass. Anna Palmer is thirteen, William and Fanny's son Reuben is fourteen, and his two siblings Edward and Agnes rather younger. The children begin one at a time to travel to London under the protection of adults. Reuben and William see Emma at the theater but are unable to find her afterward. (Later William and Fanny find her nearly frozen outside their house. She has been a prostitute and has come home to die penitent. She reports that Edwin is alive, rich, and wicked.) Both Edward and Anna, on their turns to travel, become friends with Editha Fitzmorris, an excellent young woman though the child of a libertine father. Mrs. Palmer permits Anna to visit Editha, whereupon the girl falls prey to the complicated schemes of Editha's father, who turns out to be Edwin. He drugs Anna and is about to rape her when he sees on her finger a ring that he had given Agnes and had last seen on her finger in her coffin. This deters him temporarily, but he persuades himself that he is

the victim of a coincidence. (This is not his first accidental brush with incest. He very nearly had Emma during
her career of prostitution, but was prevented by his own
drunkenness and a warning dream of hers.) Anna is preserved
for a while by the canny stubbornness of a black female servant whose freedom Editha had negotiated, but at last he
assaults the elderly servant and carries Anna off by force.
William and Reuben arrive just in time. Edwin shoots himself. Editha and her brother are taken into the Godwin family, and their generation intermarry in suitable ways.

65: Helme, Elizabeth   ST. MARGARET'S CAVE, OR, THE NUN'S
    STORY. AN ANCIENT LEGEND   4 vols. London: Earle and
    Hemet, 1801

The frame tale takes place in the early seventeenth century
near Bremen, when the widowed Baroness De Warminstroct enters the Convent of St. Mary and gives the abbess some family papers to read. The story which they contain, and which
took place a century earlier, is the matter of the novel.
    St. Margaret's Cave and the adjacent ruins of an old
chapel are said to be haunted. They are near Castle Fitzwalter in Northumberland. Young Fitzwalter meets in Germany
a nobleman named De Hoffman. The pair do good service
against Richard at Bosworth Field. Fitzwalter is supposed
to extricate his father from debt by marrying Edith, his father's ward and the daughter of his creditor. Unfortunately
Fitzwalter loves his father's other ward, Blanch Stanley,
the penniless daughter of an old friend. Blanch and Fitzwalter elope to Germany and stay with De Hoffman, where
Blanch dies in childbirth. The infant Margaret is raised
by Fitzwalter and Edith, whom he finally consents to marry.
Edith is not unkind to Margaret but appears to disapprove
of the affection between her and her half-sister Isabel.
At one point Fitzwalter brings home a semilunatic friend
Austin, who escapes from his host's ministrations to don a
Franciscan habit and become a kind of hermit. Later, when
Fitzwalter dies, Austin becomes an important emotional support for Margaret, whose stepmother is content to raise her
but denies her any legal rights. When Edith remarries (Lord
De Launcy, whom nobody likes), she and her husband and Isa-
bel go away for three years, leaving Margaret behind.
    Subsequent adventures belong to the younger generation.
Isabel has kept up an affectionate correspondence with her
sister and persuades a virtuous abbess to offer Margaret
sanctuary. The abbess is the aunt of Ferdinand de Hoffman
(also second generation), who loves Isabel. A boy named
Leopold Sternheim arrives bearing papers that testify to
Margaret's legitimacy; he is a friend of Ferdinand's, os-

tensibly a peasant's son, but Ferdinand's father is curious-
ly upset at the sound of his name. When the De Launcys come
back and lock Margaret in, Leopold assumes blackface and the
role of Cuthbert, a minstrel, so that he and Austin may rescue her. She and her old nurse Alice survive a storm at sea
in the course of her escape. Meanwhile the elder De Hoffman, increasingly distraught, sends a hired assassin to dis-
patch Leopold, but the assassin accidentally stabs Ferdinand
(who does in fact look remarkably like Leopold) and in his
excitement admits who sent him. The elder De Hoffman apologizes, confesses secrets that we are not told at the time,
and dies. We soon discover that Austin is his elder brother
and has a lurid tale of his own: he had a mistress who
tricked him into false suspicions about his wife's fidelity
and led him accidentally to stab their infant in an attempt
to kill a supposed lover, really his own sister Clarice.
After that his wife and Clarice both took the veil and Fitzwalter brought Austin to England. Leopold is really Austin's son and consequently the real De Hoffman heir. He and
Margaret are in love. Isabel, who loves Ferdinand (and vice
versa) refuses to marry her stepbrother De Launcy or to forget Margaret's claim to their father's estate. When Margaret's case comes to court, Lady de Launcy relinquishes
all except that portion of Fitzwalter's estate to which she
is honestly entitled and later relinquishes even that. Margaret and Leopold are married, as are Isabel and Ferdinand,
and they all live to old age and die peacefully.

66: Hogg, James   THE PRIVATE MEMOIRS AND CONFESSIONS OF A
    JUSTIFIED SINNER   1 vol. London: Longman, Hurst, Rees,
    Orme, Brown, and Green, 1824

The novel is composed of two narratives, the editor's and
the sinner's. The events overlap.
    Part I: George Colwan, who likes a good time, marries
an intolerant Presbyterian woman. She and her spiritual ad-
viser, Robert Wringham, espouse a particularly vicious species of Calvinism and see most of the world as unregenerate.
Against a good deal of resistance Colwan manages to father
a son, whom he raises himself. Mrs. Colwan's second child
is adopted by, named after, and probably sired by Wringham
the minister, to whom Mrs. Colwan flees after a brief and
intolerable marriage. Young Robert Wringham is taught to
hate his half-brother and, when they meet as young men in
Edinburgh, contrives to follow and torment him unbearably.
Two particularly dramatic instances stand out. In the
first, Robert, black garbed and sinister, haunts George at
a game of tennis, mocking the casual profanity of the play-
ers and getting underfoot until his nose is bloodied. He

continues to pursue George and his friends about the court
and finally into town, dripping blood and self-righteous-
ness. The second incident takes place at Arthur's Seat,
where George has gone in hopes of getting away from his re-
lentless brother; some condition of sun and mist produces
an optical illusion that projects the face of the pursuing
Robert (just then creeping up behind him to push him over
the edge), magnified twenty times, onto the empty air before
him. George, Jr., is finally murdered under somewhat mysterious circumstances, and a friend of his is accused of the
murder. Years later his father's housekeeper/mistress and a
crony of hers get evidence that Robert Wringham, Jr., is the
murderer, but the young man disappears before they can bring
him to justice.

Part II: This time the story is told from young Wringham's point of view, which is largely self-satisfied and
nasty. On the day his adoptive father gets word from God
that Robert, Jr., is one of the Elect, the boy falls in with
a mysterious companion who looks just like him and calls
himself Gil-Martin. The reader soon perceives that Gil-
Martin is Satan, but Robert avoids the knowledge for a long
time. Under the tutelage of his new friend, Robert is
strengthened in the most pernicious points of doctrine and
persuaded to commit an impressive series of murders, having
appointed himself a scourge of God. He is certainly responsible for the murder of a kind old clergyman who has tried
to save him from impending damnation and guilty of at least
intending to murder his brother. Worse, he is thought to
have murdered his mother, but Gil-Martin, being a shape-
changer, may be responsible for any number of atrocities at-
tributed to Robert. Robert's anxiety grows as his control
diminishes; he is apparently subject to long periods of am-
nesia, after which he awakens to find more horrors perpetrated in his name (or perhaps, after all, by himself). At
last he undertakes a futile and nightmarish flight from Gil-
Martin, during which he himself is suspected of being demonic. In the end he gives up and Gil-Martin apparently
persuades him to commit suicide. Hogg asserts at the end
of the narrative that the memoirs were found in the grave
of a remarkably preserved suicide with a hay rope around his
neck.

67: Hogg, James   THE THREE PERILS OF MAN, OR, WAR, WOMEN,
    AND WITCHCRAFT. A BORDER ROMANCE   3 vols. London: Long-
    man, Hurst, Rees, Orme, and Brown, 1822

This novel divides rather neatly into two separate but connected plots, one of which deals with witchcraft and is of
interest to the Gothicist. The other, which deals with war

and women, concerns the siege of Roxburg castle. Robert II, king of Scotland, has offered his daughter to the man who can recapture the castle for him, and Douglas decides to try. Princess Margaret and Lady Jane Howard, who wish to help their respective sides, find themselves at the same cottage, both dressed as boys. Margaret suspects and captures Lady Jane for Douglas. Musgrave throws himself off the battlements of Roxburg. Later the Scots get into the castle disguised as cows; the English are hungry. The war-and-women plot involves various jealousies and rivalries between Princess Margaret and Lady Jane.

As for witchcraft, one of the gentlemen involved in the siege sends a delegation to solicit a prediction from his kinsman, Michael Scott the wizard. The wizard is not hospitable; he puts them all in a cell, except Charley, with whom he occupies himself upstairs. The others escape by overpowering the seneschal. They put a stray witch in the cell in their place and rescue Charley, sending away some imps with prayers and curses. Michael Scott is amused and gives them all a magic dinner which sometimes disappears and sometimes simply does not fill. The Friar in the delegation is the Primate of Douay, a master chemist who is invariably persecuted as a necromancer; supposing him to be a fellow wizard, Scott challenges him to a contest. The Friar uses gunpowder and blows up the seneschal; meanwhile the imps are off dividing a mountain for their master. Scott does a lot of magic and is good at illusion. He gives a dinner with the devil (a particularly interesting Satan, with molten insides) in attendance and gets Tam to sell his soul for three years' fat bacon. Witches are disguised as beautiful girls, monsters as lovers for the witches, and at last the men are turned into bulls, for Scott has succeeded in arousing their bestiality. The Friar releases them by removing scrolls from their noses. Finally the devil and Michael Scott have a battle, with the former's forces of fire and earth against the latter's forces of air and water. They conjure up polar spirits and fiery dragons. Scott is killed but dies with some dignity and his eyes open. His magic rod is buried with him.

68: Holcroft, Thomas   ANNA ST. IVES. A NOVEL   7 vols. London: Shepperson and Reynolds, 1792

In this epistolary novel, Anna Wendbourne St. Ives travels to the continent, where she hopes she may meet Coke Clifton, the brother of her best friend, Louisa. Although both families have engaged in surreptitious matchmaking toward this end, Louisa has some misgivings that her brother may be a libertine. Further, Anna admires Frank Henley, the son of her father's comic but slightly sinister steward Abimelech, but is nervous about class difference. Anna is, however, sufficiently impressed by Frank's character and charity to take him along to France. Tensions between Henley and Clifton are complicated by Henley's twice saving Clifton's life. Clifton adores Anna and proposes to her but becomes increasingly incensed and desperate at learning of the matchmaking, at Anna's and Frank's attempts to reform him, at the catholicity of Anna's kindness. His marriage is delayed by his mother's insistence on a large dowry, which Abimelech despotically refuses to produce for his employer unless his own son Frank is to be the bridegroom.

The result of Clifton's anger is his decision to mask and play the hypocrite, to pretend reform and plot seduction. When he sees that Anna and Frank now plan to marry, and to Serve and Improve society, he decides to kidnap them both. Clifton proposes to rape Anna as an act of dominance but he encounters problems. On his first attempt she mashes his arm in the door, and on a subsequent occasion she simply talks him out of it. Clifton plans to kill himself after he accomplishes the rape (if he ever does) and has really repented but feels compelled to keep on as he has begun. He is not enjoying his project. Anna escapes over a wall and persuades Clifton to save Frank, who is about to be murdered by his jailer. Clifton is wounded and prefers death to benevolent nursing but is finally won round to goodness and recovery.

69: Holford, Margaret   WARBECK OF WOLFSTEÏN   3 vols. London: Rodwell and Martin, 1820

Baron Wilhelm of Marchfeldt is sent home from the wars to his sister Louisa. He is dying, not of wounds but of grief for a fiancée three years dead. In the army he had made a true friend, Casimir Vallensteïn, and a sinister acquaintance, Warbeck of Wolfsteïn; the two seem to be particular enemies. Wilhelm would like his sister to marry Vallensteïn, though Wolfsteïn has disconcerted him by seeing and admiring her picture. After Wilhelm's death a miniature of an unknown man is discovered among his possessions. Louisa, who has been warned against Wolfsteïn, fears (and knows deep down) that it is he, but convinces herself that it is Vallensteïn; a somehow potent object, the picture has a sinister effect on her nerves and disposition as she becomes attached to it. On a stormy night the original of the picture arrives, claiming to be Vallensteïn and to have been attacked. The reader is aware from a few incongruous speeches and bursts of temper that it is Wolfsteïn. An old servant identifies him just in time to prevent a hasty marriage.

Louisa goes to the court at Vienna, where she is cruel
to Casimir, who is trying to effect his father's political
reinstatement. He pines, though pursued by the Princess
Stolberg. Meanwhile Wolfsteïn arrives and pursues Louisa,
who, though fearful, is still attracted to him. When he
pretends religious conversion and repentance, even to wearing a hair shirt, she succumbs and, in spite of Stolberg's
sincere efforts to warn her, marries him. At once his mask
is put by and all his previous plots are revealed. He
tries, for his sadistic pleasure, to make her weep; he abandons her servant to the wolves; he throws her priest's religious books into a torrent. She is almost too discouraged
to care but not too depressed to convert to Christianity
numbers of the troops and banditti in her husband's castle.
Casimir is brought to the castle a prisoner. He and Louisa
are both death-obsessed. Wolfsteïn begins to be depressed
and wishes someone loved him. Soon he is taking opium and
training a feeble-minded child to blow up the castle. Finally the Inquisition closes in on him, so he gives the
child orders to set off the gunpowder, and all except the
virtuous principals are blown to perdition. The survivors,
including servants, pair off into appropriate marriages.

70: Huish, Robert   THE BROTHERS, OR, THE CASTLE OF NIOLO.
    A ROMANCE   2 vols. London: William Emans, 1820

Frederic and Leopold Lindamore are brothers; the Castle of
Niolo, on Lake Geneva, is their father's. Frederic is home-
loving and good, but Leopold is a real terror — kills people, destroys altars, rapes nuns. After Frederic loses his
wife in a boating accident, he raises his daughter Adeline
with the help of Mademoiselle Schlaffenhausen, who is supposed to be a tutor but, rumor has it, pays more attention
to the father than to the daughter. When Adeline is about
sixteen her uncle Leopold suddenly ceases decimating Europe
and comes home to Niolo, pretending to be reformed and
pleading his way into his father's favor. He brings with
him his friend Ortano, who decides that he wants Adeline;
Leopold encourages him, as he wishes Ortano to assassinate
Frederic. While Adeline and her father are on a trip (during which she falls in love with Adolphus Rosenheim) the
villains attack them and Frederic is dragged away and taken
to Sazzano, a maimed outcast who lives in a ruined castle.
Lindamore père is subsequently at Leopold's mercy.
    Meanwhile Adolphus Rosenheim, visiting Adeline, sees
something so terrible in the family vault that he leaves the
castle without a word. He overhears a conversation between
the villains and asks a friendly abbess to protect Adeline.
Leopold demands that Adeline marry Ortano and makes a ter-

rible threat — he will kill Adolphus, after informing him
that Adeline could have saved him.   In the midst of her
forced wedding to Ortano a voice cries "Never," and Adolphus
appears; Anselm, the monk who was supposed to poison him,
discovered that they were brothers.   Adolphus is promptly
dragged off to the Western Turret.   Villano, an in-law of
Frederic's who has been all along engaged in the pursuit of
justice, discovers that Frederic still lives, and together
they try to find out what Leopold has done to his father —
buried him alive, they fear.   They find only stones in his
coffin and are informed later that Adolphus's brother Anselm
was supposed to poison the old man with sacramental wine but
persuaded the abbot to keep him a prisoner instead.   The
villains burn a convent in hopes of smoking Adeline out, but
although they enjoy raping the nuns who run out of the burning building they miss their principal prey.   At last Ortano
stabs Leopold in mistake for Adolphus.   The villain is buried without coffin or marker.   Ortano commits suicide.   Adeline and Adolphus marry.   Anselm, thoroughly reformed, becomes abbot of Arienheim, and Mademoiselle Schlaffenhausen
goes into a convent.

71: Huish, Robert   FITZALLAN   2 vols. London: Thomas
    Kelly, 1832

Hector Fitzallan is the son of an unusual union.   His mother
and father eloped and had six weeks together in a cottage
before Henry's parents arrived and made their son marry
someone else.   After the new wife's death, Henry tried to
marry Hector's mother again but, refused, he set out for
America and apparently died.   These circumstances account
for some of the more improbable incidents in Hector's life.
On his way home from university, on his birthday, he is kidnapped and drugged; he awakens in a room containing his
mother's portrait, and his host identifies himself as his
father's twin brother, who just wants an avuncular visit.
After this Hector receives an assortment of notes and warnings pertinent to or purportedly from his father.   His mother says that the notes are from an imposter.

     Besides these adventures there are excitements of a more
ordinary sort.   Hector falls in love with Amelia Fortescue,
whom the Earl her father intends for a silly snob named Sir
Henry Montfort.   The dangerous Adeline Gordon, who is "in
heart a fiend" but is capable of great emotional heights,
falls in love with Hector.   She is friends with the libertine William Monckton, who has seduced and abandoned Maria
Arnfeld.   Maria's father, Major Arnfeld, wanders the roads
like a lunatic, raving of hell and serpents and looking for
her seducer.   When Hector helps Maria, that and other inno-

cent actions are partly misunderstood, and wholly misrepresented, by his enemies, so that his reputation is blackened. Though Amelia faints at hearing the gossip, she does not lose faith in Hector and much prefers him to Sir Henry. Difficulties and dangers multiply — Amelia is kidnapped by a hag and rescued by Major Arnfeld; the Major stabs Hector; Henry is arrested for abducting and possibly killing Maria; Adeline tries to seduce Hector (who is the only man she has ever loved) and revolves the notion of killing Amelia. Finally, though warned by the Earl not to go near Lord Dufresne's house (Dufresne is the father of William Monckton), Hector lurks on the premises partly in hopes of seeing Amelia, who is visiting there, and partly because he suspects that Dufresne is the uncle who once kidnapped him. He is greatly surprised to see Amelia with his mother in the conservatory and to learn that his mother is Lady Dufresne. Monckton sees Amelia and Hector together at the door and over dinner alludes in veiled terms to their meeting. This so incenses Amelia that she tells all she knows about Maria's seduction and the Major's misdirected wounding of Hector — a real conversation-stopper. Monckton rushes out in pursuit of Hector but is discovered and shot by the Major, who afterward kills himself. Lady Dufresne admits that Dufresne is Hector's father. Hector marries Amelia. When Maria hears about the murder of Monckton and her father's suicide, she goes mad and dies. Adeline goes to France to be a nun and dies of consumption.

72: Huish, Robert   THE RED BARN. A TALE, FOUNDED ON FACT
     1 vol. London: Knight and Lacey, 1828

The Red Barn is a fictitious account, with appendixes, of the Polstead murder, which was first reported in the *London Times* of April 22, 1828. A young woman named Maria Marten, having been promised marriage by William Corder, whose child she had already borne, went in male attire to meet him at the Red Barn. After some time during which her parents received letters penned exclusively by their purported son-in-law, her mother dreamed that the girl was dead and buried in the barn. When the floorboards were taken up the family discovered Maria's decomposing body. Corder, when apprehended, was running a female boarding school with a wife for whom he had advertised in the papers; he was convicted and hanged.

Huish says that in his novel he proposes to exhibit the fatal results of loose habits. The names are thinly disguised — Marten is given its alternative spelling, Martin, and William Corder becomes William Barnard. The bulk of the novel takes place before the murder and deals with the principal characters' previous relationships, but Barnard is apprehended before the end.

73: THE IDIOT HEIRESS. A NOVEL   2 vols. London: Lane, Newman, 1805

Leonard Willmot goes home with his friend Viscount Haverford, who is to be married to Lady Azelia, an orphaned cousin who lives with the family. "The idiot heiress" is Haverford's irreverent way of describing his future wife. Azelia is only fifteen and is not an idiot but might properly be described as simple. Ignorance, deliberately maintained by the family, is her principal difficulty; her artless behavior is reminiscent of the country misses from Restoration comedy. Leonard, who dislikes the family's treatment of Azelia, begins to educate her in secret, with the accidental effect that she loves him and is determined to marry no one else. (Her cousin Lady Jane would like to have him as well, but is herself pursued by their lecherous chaplain Skeffington, who consequently becomes jealous of Leonard.) Azelia's background is clarified by a manuscript given to Leonard by Mrs. Bentley, a Quaker woman whose daughter he rescues from drowning. Azelia's parents were not married when she was born — her father had deluded her mother with a bogus ceremony — but they later legitimized her. When they died, Haverford's widowed father took Azelia to raise with Haverford and Lady Jane.

After Leonard is called to the bedside of a dying uncle, Azelia overhears plans to have her committed. She runs away to London, believing in her simplicity that she can easily find Leonard and that he will marry her. There she stays for some time with a lower-class woman whom she met in the coach to London, but eventually she takes a job as a servant.

Because her family has advertised her as a lunatic, she needs to stay out of sight. After going into service she holds a series of jobs, all of them unsatisfactory in different ways, including one with a troupe of comedians. (It is not coincidental that she carries around with her a favorite copy of *Rasselas*.) At last she is taken in by friends of her mother, discovers that Leonard is already spoken for, and is proposed to by Sir Lucius Amamore, the son of her hostess. She accepts conditionally, wishing first to establish her paternal rights. This is accomplished through an initially unpromising encounter: Skeffington kidnaps her to a madhouse, and the madhouse keeper proves to be her maternal grandmother. Therefore she is released, identified, and marries Sir Lucius. Skeffington is banished. Lady Jane drinks herself to death.

74: Ireland, William Henry   THE ABBESS. A ROMANCE   4 vols.
   London: Earle and Hemet, 1799

Maddalena Rosa, daughter of the Duca Bertocci, is a convent
boarder at Santa-Maria del Nova at Florence. There she is
seen and loved by the Conte Marcello Porta, a young man who
has come to observe a religious ceremony and have a look at
the nuns. He in turn is watched by the grim Padre Ubaldo,
who demands a midnight meeting. After some interruptions
and delays Ubaldo exacts from Marcello a vow of silence
about the identity of the woman whom he will be taken to
see. The young man persuades himself that he is going to
Maddalena, but, after an exchange of declarations with a
veiled seductress in a sensuous convent hideaway, he discovers that his partner is the abbess herself, Vittoria Bracciano. Altogether unscrupulous, malicious, and licentious,
she is friends only with Beatrice, a nun who was put into
the convent after the mysterious and sinister disappearance
of a man who had rejected her. Because Marcello perceives
the abbess to be bloodthirsty and jealous, he is obliged to
dissemble his surprise in order to protect Maddalena. At
their next meeting the abbess drugs his wine and seduces
him.

     In the meantime, Maddalena's dearest convent friend Mar-
ietta has died, leaving Maddalena a gold crucifix and a suggestion that her spirit may hover nearby at midnight. Grief
and distraction lead Maddalena to sleepwalk to the room in
which Marietta had been laid out, a room into which Marcello
blunders as he leaves the scene of his seduction. Ubaldo
and the abbess discover the pair together and begin to plot
their destruction. Accusing her of letting a man into the
convent, the abbess evicts Maddalena and persuades Bertocci
to send his daughter to a certain family castle where the
conspirators know that they will have access to her.

     Marcello follows Maddalena to the castle, whence they
are both removed by the Inquisition at the end of the second
volume. Maddalena's father follows in a bootless attempt to
see his daughter and is extricated from the prisons of the
Inquisition by a mysterious youth who had earlier tried to
kill him. The youth is Don Giuseppe Cazini, an innately
virtuous young man who was educated by his natural father to
vice and has promised to take revenge on Bertocci for a purported wrong against his family. In fact, he is Bertocci's
own son, Maddalena's twin brother who was said to have died
in infancy. He has been raised by Ubaldo's brother, one of
the story's principal villains. The accusations that Ubaldo
and the abbess have brought against Marcello and Maddalena
could all be dissolved by the breaking of Marcello's promise
of silence, but both of them so value the integrity of his

word that they survive torture and threats of torture without breaking. Thanks to a sudden confession from the abbess's confederate Beatrice, accusations are brought in turn
against the accusers, who at last betray themselves. Retribution is lurid and just — burning, lifelong penitence and
flagellation, murder in the midst of trial. The attachment
of Marcello and Maddalena is sanctioned by parental consent.

75: Ireland, William Henry   GONDEZ, THE MONK. A ROMANCE OF
    THE THIRTEENTH CENTURY   4 vols. London: W. Earle and
    J. W. Hucklebridge, 1805

Huberto Avinzo, born in Italy, was brought to Scotland by a
man named Alzarro and was subsequently taken in by the family of Sir Alan Macdonald. He survived with Macdonald's
wife a siege by the English and was taken with her to a
prison in London, where he grew up in a dungeon. When his
foster mother died, Huberto managed to escape from his prison and followed a stray dog to a ruined castle where he
found two bare-breasted hags surrounded by mangled and decaying snakes; although they did some magic at his request,
they were unable to tell him what had happened to Alzarro.
As the novel begins, Huberto has joined the Scottish army in
support of Robert Bruce. More of his history will be revealed in an Italian subplot which, if I have read it properly, seems to drop a generation back with perfect sangfroid
and little or no warning.
    Huberto, along with some other soldiers and Robert Bruce
himself, takes refuge in a monastery, St. Columba's, of
which Gondez is abbot. Gondez, who is a cadaverous color
and has an unusually wide mouth, looks bad and mean and
crafty. And so he is. Rather horrid things go on in the
monastery. For one thing, it is haunted by a nasty specter
called the Little Red Woman; she wears a red mantle and is
scourged with hissing snakes. While Huberto is in the monastery a crucifix bleeds three drops of blood (which subsequently disappear) onto his hand, and a hag outside the
window shrills, "Blood!" Two monks (or one monk twice) say
"Murder and Treason" into Huberto's ear. Further, a woman
whom Huberto sees at the altar, and with whom he falls instantly and reciprocally in love, warns him to flee the monastery. She herself, she mysteriously says, is involved in
working retribution. Huberto warns the king and they all
escape just in time to avoid some English soldiers who would
have killed them. For this good work Huberto is made a
knight and Lord of Scotland's Isles. Later, on his way back
to the monastery to find out more about the woman he met at
the altar, Huberto encounters more supernatural phenomena,

notably the Tall White Man, who haunts Jura, and a specter
on skeletal horseback who is pacified by kissing Huberto's
gold crucifix. At the monastery he finds the monk John of
Dunbar, earlier Gondez's closest friend and confidant,
chained to a ring in a subterranean pavement with food in
sight but deliberately out of reach. Huberto rescues him,
and he in turn, after his recovery from Gondez's cruelties,
helps Huberto to discover the woman. She is locked in a
dungeon, as is her emaciated brother. Her name is Ronilda,
and her father was the Laird of Finlagen Castle on the island of Ila; he was also the specter earlier put to rest by
Huberto's crucifix. Gondez was trying to seduce Ronilda by
threatening to torture and kill her brother unless she co-
operated. Huberto and Ronilda take Gondez's crimes before
the king; the Inquisition wants Gondez too, for heresy,
parricide, and murder. At last he breaks down under torture
and confesses some things that need to be clarified by the
subplot, as follows.

The young Duca Martini Gonzari goes to Rome to see his
uncle, the Cardinal Nicolo Gonzari. The Cardinal is depraved, ambitious, and scheming — besides wanting to be Pope
(not in itself a sign of depravity), he wants to secure the
inheritance of his nephew, whom he hates. The Duca is too
innocent to fathom him but has a more astute friend, Count
Ferdinando Ozimo. When Ozimo is called home by his mother's
illness, the Duca accompanies him partway, during which
journey he is hidden from desperadoes by a woman named Valenza, with whom he falls in love. Back at Rome again he
cultivates Valenza's father and avoids a loathsome companion
thrust upon him by his uncle — the toady Giovanni Maldachini, small and ugly and full of passions repugnant to
right-thinking young men. He succeeds in marrying Valenza
privately, with her father's consent, but when Ozimo comes
back after his mother's death he finds that the Duca, Valenza, and Valenza's father the Marquis have all disappeared or
come to sad ends. Giovanni has been involved; at any rate,
the Marquis died of poison the same night he took Giovanni
into his house. Ruffians have carried off Valenza, and the
Duca has disappeared on his way to Rome. Ozimo assumes a
disguise as a religious mendicant and searches for his
friends through eight months. At last he is addressed by a
marble figure on top of a tomb (the wicked Cardinal's) and
given, by a nun, some jewels, several letters, and a baby in
a basket. The baby is the Duca Gonzari's child. Furthermore, the baby is Huberto of the principal plot, and it is
Ozimo who, calling himself Alzarro, takes him to Scotland.
Some years later, after imprisonment by the Inquisition,
Ozimo is so tired and discouraged that he goes into a monas-

tery — Gondez's monastery, where he helps Huberto without recognizing him.

As for Gondez, we have already seen him as Giovanni. He was the child of the Cardinal and a dissolute abbess and was raised in an especially depraved convent. He and the Cardinal were responsible for all the attacks, abductions, and so on; he himself poisoned the Cardinal, for they both wanted the Gonzari estates and the Duca's wife Valenza. She died after the birth of her child and lay unburied for six days, after which Gondez locked the Duca in with her body and offered him poison to drink. Comforted by her spirit, which told him that he would join her before dawn, he drank it and died. Gondez is condemned to die by slow fire, and Huberto becomes the Duca Gonzari. He prepares to marry Ronilda. (Two other couples, not crucial to the plot, whose nuptials have been delayed by English-Scots animosity, now find their ways clear as well.) The night before his wedding two witches appear at Huberto's bedside, apparently wishing him well; they wave their "ebon crutches" and disappear. At the wedding itself the spirits of Ronilda's parents appear and dispense a blessing.

76: Ireland, William Henry   RIMAULDO, OR, THE CASTLE OF
    BADAJOS   4 vols. London: T. N. Longman and G. Rees,
    1800

The Condè Don Rimauldo is leaving his ancestral home, the Castillio del Lara, to go to court. Being a sensitive young man who will spend much of the novel in contemplation of God and Nature, Rimauldo is hesitant and emotional about leaving. His father, made of sterner stuff, is annoyed at his weakness. On his way to the king, Rimauldo acquires Cesario, a peasant who is mourning a dead wife; later, when Cesario saves him from assassination at an inn, Rimauldo promotes him to secretary. At court there is a man — the Marques Diego de Badajos, sixty, gloomy, and proud — for whom Rimauldo conceives an instant antipathy, and who seems to be watching him. Further acquaintance suggests that Badajos is in cahoots with a sinister monk, Sebastiano, who is known to the local peasants as Father Benito. Rimauldo hears them talking about Constanza, a beautiful and mysterious woman with whom he is increasingly in love. She seems to be troubled, sorrowful, and somewhat inaccessible; once when he goes in secret to watch her pray he sees before she arrives a phantom who looks as Constanza would if she were dead and bloodied. The relationship is further complicated by angry letters from his father, who says first that he has spies watching for unauthorized relationships and, later,

that Constanza is a whore (he has been misinformed) and that
Cesario should be killed for his part in their meetings.
In fact, Rimauldo's father is raving and talking of filicide
despite the soothing attempted by Rimauldo's mother, who finally takes to her bed from sheer strain. Sebastiano tries
to stab Rimauldo — Cesario prevents it — and carries Constanza away. Rimauldo has no sooner rescued her than his
own father takes her away from him and carries her off
again, this time to be locked up in the Castillio del Lara
en route to another convent. Rimauldo wheedles a nocturnal
meeting with his mother, who still loves him but will not
tell him about Constanza. Rimauldo's father throws him out
of the castle but is beginning to be impressed by Constanza's goodness and to wonder if he has been mistaken. It
turns out that Constanza is not, as we were led to believe,
Sebastiano's child, but has a pedigree sufficient to recon-
cile Rimauldo's parents to her as a daughter-in-law.
    Cesario, too, discovers that he has noble blood. Al-
though raised by robbers who accidentally retained him in
the excitement of assaults and hostages, he is the proper
heir to the Montalvan estates. When he is imprisoned by
Badajos he finds a manuscript and some mementos which in-
criminate his jailer. Badajos killed the brother of his own
unwilling wife, supposing him to be not brother but lover,
after which some confusion and transportation of infants
ensued. Cesario and Badajos are both horrified at the increasing likelihood that they are father and son. At last
Cesario recovers from the melancholy into which the idea has
thrown him and becomes the new Duca di Montalvan, Badajos
having killed himself.

77: Isaacs, Mrs.   ARIEL, OR, THE INVISIBLE MONITOR
    4 vols. London: William Lane, 1801

Rosaline, a foundling raised in a good family, keeps hearing
a mysterious voice which is followed by soft music; at first
it says amorous things but later it sustains her in her various difficulties with utterances like "Virtue is its own
protector, and innocence is ever the peculiar care of the
Deity." After some initial uneasiness she learns to trust
it. Her invisible monitor calls himself Ariel. Rosaline,
evidently too attractive for her own good, has a great deal
of trouble with importunate suitors: she is frightened by
the advances of her foster brother Adolphus, though he is
a good man and she apparently loves him; she is desired by
both a count and a marquis, who stab each other; and she
falls into the hands of a baron who locks her in a dungeon
to force her marriage to a confederate of his. Ariel, who

has earlier admitted his corporeality, leads her out of
the Baron's dungeon. He has been in love with Rosaline all
along. However, revelations of identity prove Rosaline to
be the long-lost daughter of Baron St. Alvars, and as Ariel
is really Bertrand St. Alvars they are too closely related
for marriage, so he hands her over to Adolphus. The story
is embellished by concealed doors, familiar-looking minia-
tures, and a madwoman who dresses in white and sits singing
and praying on a tomb. All moans and other mysterious
noises are accounted for in the end.

78: Jamieson, Frances   THE HOUSE OF RAVENSPUR. A ROMANCE
    4 vols. London: G. and W. B. Whittaker, 1822

The Earl of Ravenspur's younger brother Lord Henry is inferior (though cunning) and therefore jealous. The brothers
go to Italy for a royal wedding — the son of Edward III is
marrying Victorine — and there meet the bride's friend Angelina Frescati, who wants the Earl but is willing to settle
for marriage to Lord Henry. Victorine also wants the Earl
and later appears to have pined to death; at any rate she
dies, warning Ravenspur to beware his brother. Ravenspur is
by that time married to his real love, Lady Geraldine Fitzhugh. Lord Henry makes trouble for his brother, at first
relatively minor trouble like competing against him at a
tournament (the motto on Henry's shield is "My time will
come"), and later serious trouble, like undermining the
king's trust in him until he is arrested for treason and
sent into exile, leaving Henry to become Earl. Geraldine
is pregnant at the time; her old father dies of grief. The
servant Jacques remains faithful, and Clod the fool, though
Clod now works for Henry.

   Henry and Angelina have a son, Harry, who is a brat,
"spoiled and riotous." His foster sister, a foundling named
Gertrude, when she grows up prefers a convent to marrying
him, for the convent is at worst merely boring. In the convent she sees the ghosts of both Ravenspur and Geraldine,
and it is thought when she disappears that the ghosts have
carried her off, but in fact she has been abducted by Father Rupert. By this time the reader has begun to suspect
that Ravenspur and Geraldine are alive and back in the country, as is indeed the case. Gertrude is aided to some degree in her difficulties by Lord Edward Saltoun, who marries
her at the end. The Ravenspurs' adventures are recounted at
length. There are complications of villainy and kidnapping
and some dealing with the Inquisition, but at last Henry admits that Gertrude is the daughter of the rightful earl, and
the novel ends with the establishment of justice.

79: Kahlert, Karl Friedrich   THE NECROMANCER, OR, THE TALE
    OF THE BLACK FOREST   2 vols. London: William Lane, 1794

Herman tells his friend Hellfried about a strange experience. Once he stayed at an inn where his money and watch
were somehow removed from his person. A mysterious stranger
returned the watch, an action that upset the ghost of Herman's mother. The ghost appeared a second time, conjured up
by the stranger; at its appearance Herman suddenly found
himself in a speeding carriage with Something snoring beside
him. The carriage overturned and a nobleman rescued him.
    Hellfried believes him, having had a strange experience
himself. He tells of a wicked nobleman who used villagers
as hounds (and sometimes prey) for hunting and so was condemned to ghostly hunting every night. Hellfried was pres-
sured by the example of his friends' bravado into spending
the night in the nobleman's uninhabited castle, where he indeed saw the ghosts. A mysterious old man later raised the
nobleman's ghost and that of his lady (still maritally incompatible) and locked the young men in the vault.
    A document from one of Hellfried's friends tells yet an-
other story. A soldier who was one of the ghost-seeing company above tries to find out more and made friends with a
man called "The Austrian." The latter knew a military man
named Volkert who dabbled in necromancy, and once, though
forbidden by his general to play with the occult, conjured
a live man, nearly killing him in the process. Volkert was
frightened by that one himself. The narrator and the Austrian went back to the town of the ghostly hunt. There they
discovered the "ghosts" to be bandits. But a Father Francis
raised a different ghost for them, and the Austrian recog-
nized the priest as Volkert. At the end Volkert was exposed
as having been in league with the robbers.

80: Kelly, Isabella   THE ABBEY OF SAINT ASAPH. A NOVEL
    3 vols. London: William Lane, 1795

After Sir Malcolm Douglas is killed in battle, Lady Douglas
raises their children (Elinor and Lionel) by herself. She
also takes in and educates Jennet Aprieu, whom she found in
a cottage. Jennet and Lionel fall in love at once, though
they are only children. Later Lionel brings home a Harrow
friend, Clement Montague, who forms an attachment to Elinor.
Clement's younger brother Henry also loves her but defers to
his elders. Clement and Elinor marry and have a daughter;
suddenly Clement announces that he was twenty, not twenty-
one, when they married, so the union is not legal. Further,
he declines to be married again, saying that this way it
will be easier if they tire of each other. Elinor leaves

him and goes into service, only to discover that her mistress is, in a different sense, Clement's mistress. Lionel
feels that Elinor has dishonored him. He also stabs a man
whom he finds with Jennet, though Jennet in fact has not
permitted anything untoward to happen.

Jennet's family has inherited a little farm near the
Abbey of St. Asaph, where the ostensibly supernatural goings-on of the story take place. On one occasion a ghost
in the abbey ruins wraps Jennet in its long arms and she
faints. On another occasion she is locked in a vault with
open coffins and sees a skeleton with glowing eyes shake
itself. (Uncanny phenomena are explained at the end; e.g.,
there was a rat inside the skull.) Jennet discovers in the
midst of her wedding to Lionel that her real father is Sir
Edred, who has survived fraternal usurpation and attempted
murder. Elinor has been imprisoned for debt at Clement's
instigation, but they are reconciled at last and Clement is
revealed to have been of age after all. Clement's brother
Henry marries a suitable young woman by whom Jennet was earlier employed.

81: Kelly, Isabella   MADELINE, OR, THE CASTLE OF MONTGOM-
    ERY. A NOVEL   3 vols. London: William Lane, 1794

This novel deals with the lives and loves of three generations, with principal emphasis on the middle one. The only
hints of the macabre are the reputation of part of the castle as haunted and a girl's dream about the fiery death and
ascension of her parents. In the first generation, Archibald Montgomery wishes to marry Madeline Clifford, whose father is pushing her to marry old Lord Rutland and £15,000
per annum. When she considers running away, Archibald offers to protect her; three months later they marry, apparently with no sin or cohabitation in the interval. Two of
their children, Ellen and Madeline, live to adulthood; Ellen
is the more beautiful. The philanthropic Montgomery family
establishes an old-age asylum and a little charity school.

Two other local families, the Clevelands and the Primroses, are pertinent to the love interest. Sir Joseph
Cleveland has three daughters and an illegitimate son; the
Primroses, who are Quakers, have a son (Josiah) and a daughter (Miriam). (When Ellen and Madeline do a performance of
The Provoked Husband for their parents' wedding anniversary
— a tactless choice? — Miriam is not allowed to participate.) Young Mr. Cleveland proposes to Madeline and propositions Miriam. Josiah Primrose proposes to Madeline too;
she does love him but feels that her affection is sisterly
and she certainly does not wish to become a Quaker. Miriam
is admired by a young man named Glanville.

Through some involvement with Sir Joseph Cleveland, who
commits suicide at about this time, Madeline and Ellen's father is arrested for debt as the family are sitting around
reading *Night Thoughts*. Ellen craftily saves the family
portraits from a Mr. Solomon by offering instead her mother's jewels, by which she means the aged pensioners and the
alms-school children. (Mr. Solomon does not take them.)
Madeline is sent to her maternal aunt, who is cold and rude.
After supporting herself for a while with her fancy work and
preserving her honor, she is at last protected by her uncle
and makes a happy marriage. Ellen, on the other hand, marries unhappily, for her husband is too indulgent and she becomes quite useless. Ellen's husband brings Madeline their
baby Frederick to nurse; Madeline's husband and sister are
both outraged when she matter-of-factly sits down and does
it — an indecent display, they think. Miriam has married
Glanville, and when his first wife, thought dead, arrives
suddenly, he kills himself. Miriam dies in childbirth.
The novel goes on long enough to marry the children in
Frederick's generation.

82: Lamb, Caroline   ADA REIS. A TALE   3 vols. London:
    J. Murray, 1823

Ada Reis is an unscrupulous but handsome adventurer who
kills and betrays to satisfy greed and ambition. One of his
victims is the woman he loves, murdered in a fit of jealousy, so he raises their love-child Fiormonda alone. He becomes allied with the sinister Jew Kabkarra, who is clearly
delighted by Ada Reis's evil deeds. The plot is principally
concerned with Kabkarra's attempts to turn Fiormonda's depth
of thought and feeling to evil. He gives her gifts and in-
stalls his mother, Shaffou Paca, as preceptress. His efforts are opposed by a good spirit named Zevahir, who sings,
lectures, and also gives gifts to Fiormonda. The evil in
Fiormonda grows — wild anger, love of luxury — and Kabkarra
appears from time to time in various forms. At last a game
between good and evil is played on a magic chessboard; evil
having won, Kabkarra says Fiormonda belongs to him and takes
her, Ada Reis, and the old woman off on a ship, the latter
two bound like sacks. They go to South America, where they
live like royalty. En route they rescue Count Condulmar, to
whom Fiormonda becomes attached. Condulmar indulges her and
looks fiendish at times, and she loves him. But she doubts
that he is her true friend, as Zehavir was. She begins to
feel somehow sad and guilty and besmirched. Condulmar is
increasingly unkind to her and at last he deserts her, singing a song about the impossibility of restoring her innocence.

The Lima earthquake takes place on the day and hour that were earlier predicted by a ghost for Ada Reis's doom. Fiormonda shows signs of repentance. Ada Reis is washed off to an Indian isle and made king of a tribe which practices human sacrifice; this bores him. He is caught by a huge spider, which is Kabkarra, and transported to new territory to hear a lecture: it seems that Kabkarra's mother mated with a demon and later turned into Niagara Falls; Kabkarra explains his possession of Condulmar and others, and his fight for Fiormonda. He persuades Ada Reis to drink poison and go to hell; Ada finds with disgust that Kabkarra is only a servant there. Or is this hell? Perhaps it is a sort of waiting room for Judgment. Ada Reis finds Fiormonda and Condulmar in unhappy majesty at a banquet. They all want a second chance. Given it, they find themselves alive again but all fall into their old errors except Fiormonda, who repents. This time the others are doomed forever, and forever fall into an abyss. Fiormonda is baptized and does good works, but after her death poisonous plants grow on her grave.

83: Lamb, Caroline   GLENARVON   3 vols. London: J. Murray, 1916

Lady Margaret Delaval is upset by the birth of a nephew, for she had expected her son Buchanan to inherit from her brother the Duke of Altamonte. Margaret, who is headstrong, passionate, and ruthless, persuades her current admirer Viviani to kill the baby; afterward she comes to dislike him and he goes away hating her. The murdered infant's mother pines away and dies, leaving her daughter Calantha in Ireland to mature under the influence of her bad Aunt Margaret and a good aunt named Lady Seymour. Calantha is indulged and admired, and although basically sound of principle she suffers from romanticism, excess of sensibility, and a remarkable childishness. By nearly dying of an emotionally induced fever she persuades her father to permit her marriage to Henry Mowbray, Earl of Avondale, though she was intended for her cousin Buchanan. Despite initial tantrums and hysteria at leaving her father's house, she readily adjusts to the atmosphere of Modern Philosophy which she finds in her husband's household. Later in London she falls into what novels call the vortex of fashionable dissipation. She has a good time making bad friends and is given as a gift a little boy named Zerbellini, who makes a fascinating page, but she feels that her life has gone downhill since the first stages of passion with Avondale. Upon her return to Ireland, she is ripe for a new interest.

In Ireland she finds Glenarvon, a glamorous young fire-

brand who writes revolutionary documents and causes a lot
of local political trouble. He is faithless, false, and
crafty, but enormously interesting. He is followed about
by packs of young ladies who wear green ribbons and recruit.
Extreme cases like his former mistress Elinor St. Clare
carry harps as well. Calantha and Glenarvon begin a long
and passionate relationship which is consummated only by
some kind of impious oath of faithfulness. Calantha is not
deterred by the sight of former mistresses dying or desperate, or even by Glenarvon's own assertions that he will en-
slave her and that he is a walking hell. Although she is
kept technically chaste by her principles and is prevented
from running away to London with him by the sickbed summons
of Mrs. Seymour, the good aunt, she finds that her reputation is ruined and her friends alienated. Glenarvon, in
London, has lost interest in her and has shown her letters
to his friends. Her husband speaks kindly but insists on a
marital separation. She pursues him, falls ill, and dies in
his arms.

Zerbellini the page is discovered to be Calantha's little brother and the heir of Avondale. Due to a highly complicated background of double-crossings and multiple kidnappings, the boy is not dead after all. In the course of
the revelations Margaret is stabbed at her own request by
one of her confederates.

Glenarvon is becoming unpopular and slightly mad. Elinor curses him and stirs up the local troops to burn his estate. She is wounded and deliberately rides her horse over
a cliff. Glenarvon escapes with the British fleet but falls
ill and begins to see spirits, the most complicated of which
is a phantom ship with black sails and white-faced crew,
carrying a giant friar and incense and guns. He jumps
overboard and hears a voice from below telling him that he
should cry out from the lower pits and urge people to repent.

84: Lamb, Caroline   GRAHAM HAMILTON   2 vols. London:
    Henry Colburn, 1822

Graham Hamilton, somewhere in the New World, discusses
with an acquaintance the sources of misery. He asserts
that weakness and feebleness of will cause more pain to the
possessor than decisive vice. He offers his own story as
proof.

Graham is raised by his father in the country, where he
falls in love, as a child, with his cousin Gertrude. Gertrude is a steadying influence on Graham, who is dreamy and
not amenable to discipline. A wealthy uncle in London, much
taken with some of Graham's poetry which was sent him with

the annual grouse, offers to take the boy to the city and
ultimately make him his heir. Although something of a miser, the uncle is generous with Graham and does not protest
very much at his frivolous life-style. Home for a holiday,
Graham exchanges declarations of love with Gertrude, but
upon returning to London falls in with the beautiful Lady
Orville.

Lady Orville is only marginally respectable — chaste,
but extravagant and given to fast company. Moncrief, whom
Lady Orville jilted to marry money, still loves her and
takes some pains to protect her reputation. Although Graham
would like to be discreet and does not really misbehave, his
boyish passion for her begins to cause talk. Lady Orville's
extravagances are forcing her to retire to the country, so
she plans an unusually lavish farewell-to-society party,
wishing to make a spectacular finish. Just then Graham
hears from his uncle that cousin Gertrude may be given to a
local farmer, but that the family will first come to town to
discuss the situation. Immersed in the process of regaining
his cousin, whom he finds he still loves, Graham ignores
Lady Orville's notes for several days. When he goes to her
last extravaganza, he finds that her husband is leaving her
and taking their child. Had Graham come when she asked him,
he might have explained their relationship and cleared up
the scandal for which she is being punished. He embraces
her with remorse and is caught at it. Meanwhile the sher-
iff's officers are carrying away the furniture. Losing his
head in all this excitement, Graham offers a warrant of attorney, pledging that he will pay her debts and save her.
But the uncle, who is on Gertrude's side, refuses to supply
the money, and Graham is jailed. He worries and falls ill.
When his family takes him home, he finds that Gertrude has
heard a more colorful version of the story, in which Graham
is said to have shot himself; in consequence she has burst
a blood vessel and is dying. Ultimately the rest of the
family dies too. Lady Orville is living a poor and charitable life. Graham explains to his acquaintance that he has
no ties and no prospects and is waiting for death, hoping
only to expiate his crimes.

85: Lathom, Francis   ASTONISHMENT!!! A ROMANCE OF A CENTURY
     AGO   2 vols. London: T. N. Longman and O. Rees, 1802

Claudio is brought up by the Di Bartelma family as a foundling. (He came to them with a bracelet, and a note saying
that he must never ask who he is.) On his fifteenth birthday he meets a pilgrim who is interested in his bracelet but
who makes no comment. The Marchese di Bartelma's friend,
the Count di Ponta, has a son, Lodovico, who is in college

with Claudio; Lodovico is a bit wild, but Claudio is a good
influence and they are friends. One day an old monk takes
Claudio to a seductive woman, Viola, in her hidden and sensuous apartment. When in the midst of an embrace she discovers his bracelet, she faints. Claudio is told to leave
her alone in future, as she is under the protection of the
Inquisition. Zelia, Viola's attendant, is attracted to
Claudio, who receives notes saying what a good wife she
will make him. Claudio spends a vacation with Lodovico and
rather likes his sister Valeria, home from convent school.
These normal activities are interspersed with symbolic
dreams on Claudio's part and warnings from mysterious monks
and pilgrims to beware Di Ponta. Claudio is kidnapped by
Zelia and forced to marry her.

Mysterious relationships are finally made clear when the
pilgrim and Di Ponta are accidentally brought together. The
pilgrim is Claudio's true father. He once tried to murder
Di Ponta for having an affair with his wife but accidentally
killed his wife instead. At any rate, he thought he killed
her. As it turns out, Viola is really his wife Horatia,
which accounts for her earlier alarm at the sight of Claudio's bracelet. Rudolpho, the man she really loved, preceded
Claudio's father and sired Valeria, who is not Lodovico's
sister after all but was only brought up by Horatia/Viola's
friend. So it is just as well Claudio did not marry her.
Zelia is, by an earlier indiscretion, the daughter of the
monk who succeeded the pilgrim as Horatia/Viola's man.
Claudio's sister Fulvia is discovered too; she is the girl
Lodovico has been drunkenly pursuing about the estate. She
was brought up in Florence and called Nina. Viola, since
her monk has been unable to support her, has been the Grand
Inquisitor's kept woman and has whored on the side, which is
what she was doing when Claudio was first introduced to her.
During the revelation she stabs Di Ponta. She repents to
some degree. The monk goes into a monastery. Valeria goes
back to the convent, which she liked anyway. Claudio learns
to get along with Zelia, who really does love him.

86: Lathom, Francis   ITALIAN MYSTERIES, OR, MORE SECRETS
     THAN ONE. A ROMANCE   3 vols. London: A. K. Newman, 1820

Valeria Urbino's father is a physician in Venice; he has
raised a friendless orphan, Paulina, as her sister. Her
mother and brother are dead, the latter having been killed
in a duel. One night when Urbino goes out on a sick call he
is kidnapped by some people who want him to bleed a woman to
death. When he refuses he is told to leave Venice on threat
of death. Consequently the family departs for the Castello
della Torvida, which belonged to Valeria's mother and is

erroneously supposed to be haunted. At the castle, Valeria
receives a message from Julio, to whom she was once attracted at a masked ball, and meets him at a recluse's hut. The
recluse turns out to be Julio himself, who tells Valeria the
story of his life. He was left an infant at a monastery,
equipped with a cameo brooch which he was supposed to wear
upon reaching puberty, and a note telling him to be careful
whom he marries because he has a sister somewhere. One
night after he was grown he was taken to meet a beautiful
woman, who, seeing his brooch, shrieked and fainted and sent
him away. He found upon awakening from a drugged sleep that
she had hung a miniature around his neck, with an accompanying note that suggested she was his mother. A couple
of years later an acquaintance invited him to see the dis-
section of a beautiful courtesan. It was the same woman.
Feeling that his mother had been dishonored, he challenged
and killed the man who invited him. His victim turns out
to have been Valeria's brother.

Paulina, meanwhile, is kidnapped by Alberto de Valdetti,
who gives her a marriage contract to sign. She receives as
much support as possible from the kidnapper's nephew Vincentio, who also loves her, and from Lipardo, the majordomo.
Under increasing pressure from her captor, she reluctantly
consents to a secret wedding to Vincentio. This escape is
cut off by the mid-wedding arrival of Valdetti, who attacks
his nephew. The servant tears open Paulina's dress to reveal two scars near her neck. Valdetti faints. Small wonder, for these wounds, we are later informed, were inflicted
by Valdetti himself on his infant niece whom he accidentally
nicked in the process of stabbing her mother, who was his
sister-in-law and a woman he once loved himself. Other relationships are revealed and clarified. A pilgrim arrives
and admits that he is Claudio Valdetti, the real marchese,
the elder of twin brothers. Further, he is father to both
Julio and Paulina, who have never suspected that they are
siblings. (Paulina had been left to her foster father by
a woman whom he treated for a stab-wound. The woman was
Claudio's wife Camilla.) Claudio had gone into hiding after
being falsely accused of his wife's murder. In fact she was
not murdered, though her brother-in-law did his best; nor
was she the dissected courtesan on the operating table.
That was her sister Antonia; Julio misunderstood the note.
Camilla herself, who is alive and a nun, arrives to complete
the reunion. Vincentio is identified as the son of Lipardo,
Claudio's dearest friend. He and Paulina evidently consider
themselves married, despite the interruption of the ceremony. Julio and Valeria feel that it would not be right for
them to marry, since he has killed her brother, so he goes
into a monastery and she is happy in having done her duty.

87: Lathom, Francis   THE MIDNIGHT BELL. A GERMAN STORY,
      FOUNDED ON INCIDENTS IN REAL LIFE   3 vols. London:
      H. D. Symonds, 1798

Alphonsus is sent away from home under bizarre circumstances: his father has been murdered; his mother has made
him swear to kill the murderer, whom she supposes to be the
dead man's brother Frederick; but she subsequently appears
covered with blood and orders her son to fly forever "as he
values life and heaven." Having joined the army, Alphonsus
hears the story of his comrade Arieno's sister Lauretta, who
loved Alphonsus's uncle Frederick but was deceived by her
family into a different marriage. Later Alphonsus falls in
love with Lauretta's daughter Lauretta and they are married.
She is kidnapped, still weak from childbirth, by a spoiled
and covetous young man named Theodore D'Aignon and is locked
up in a turret, whence she is released by a fortuitous bolt
of lightning which breaks away the wall and permits her to
fall out. She is taken in by a hermit who dies the same
night, but not before telling his own unrelated tale. Theodore catches Lauretta a second time, but she is rescued by
her father (one of the abductors), who recognizes her mother's pearls and crucifix. He too had been tricked into the
marriage which produced her. He has been imprisoned in the
Bastille as an Italian spy and has escaped by feigning
death.
      Alphonsus takes Lauretta back to his family castle, con-
cerning which there now flourish local superstitions about
bells that toll at midnight. Expeditions discover monks,
coffins, and a flagellant mother's accusing "ghost." At
last a priest unravels the mystery: Alphonsus père was given
to marital jealousy and persuaded his brother to test his
wife's fidelity by making advances to her. Also, he pretended to die. These ruses led to a moment of confusion
when he came to his wife, who thought that he was Frederick
and killed him. She realized too late that the vow ex-
tracted from her son would catch him between matricide and
perjury. The church promises to find a loophole for Alphonsus, his mother goes into a convent and dies, and the others
are restored to happiness.

88: Lathom, Francis   THE MYSTERIOUS FREEBOOTER, OR, THE
      DAYS OF QUEEN BESS. A ROMANCE   4 vols. London: Lane,
      Newman, 1806

William de Mowbray's daughter Rosalind (whose name was chosen by her godmother Queen Elizabeth I) has suffered from
parental tyranny. Though her dying mother made De Mowbray
promise that Rosalind could marry according to her heart,

he refused to sanction her preference for Edward, a peasant
boy with whom she had grown up, and tried to make her marry
Lord Rufus. Further, he had Edward imprisoned in Flanders,
but Rosalind was secretly married to Edward already and was
pregnant. Her father spirited the baby away, told her that
it had died, and hoped that it had — at the hands of his
confederate.

Rosalind is living with her father as the novel begins;
he is warden of the borders and is about to be attacked by
moss-troopers, led by Allanrod. He is warned of the attack
by Donald, a former moss-trooper whose sister Allanrod has
raped and whose father he has killed. Allanrod captures De
Mowbray and wishes to marry Rosalind. A forced wedding is
prevented, however, by the advent of Edward, in black armor,
who has escaped from imprisonment. (The story of his escape
occupies several chapters.) Lord Rufus has offered earlier
to save Rosalind from marriage to Allanrod, but this shows
extraordinary duplicity, for we discover at the end of the
novel that Rufus and Allanrod are the same man. He is also
the real father of Edward and kills himself after these revelations of identity. The reader has earlier been exposed
to a manuscript account of his villainy, written by Eloise,
who turns out to have been Edward's mother. A brother is
identified as well. Further, Edward and Rosalind discover
that their baby is not after all dead and recover it.

89: Lathom, Francis   MYSTERY. A NOVEL   2 vols. London:
    H. D. Symonds, 1800

Charles Melford is in love with Margaretta, but both their
fathers die before he can get permission to marry her.
Leaving her in the friendly care of a Mrs. Wallace, he travels to Italy. There he meets the Marchese di Marvaldi, with
his wife Laura and his daughter Paulina. The Marchese offers Charles his daughter, but Charles refuses because of
Margaretta. Paulina's mother is a greater hazard to his fidelity; Laura pursues and seduces him and later follows him
out of town, asserting that she has left her husband forever. She disappears for a while, but he discovers her lying on a street in Rome and takes her back to England, where
he finds that Margaretta and Mrs. Wallace's son are in love.
Distressed and wishing not to get in Margaretta's way, he
marries Laura, who has by that time announced that her husband is dead. Immediately Laura takes him back to Venice,
and there is the Marchese with his wife Laura and his daughter Paulina — a happy but disconcerting family group. So
who is the woman Charles has married? Laura's twin sister
Antonia, as it turns out.

Years earlier, Antonia explains, the Marchese, confused
about the twins, briefly and accidentally courted Antonia,
who was so incensed at his marriage to Laura instead of to
her that she followed them to the altar and there vowed to
take revenge on her sister and brother-in-law. This she
has done by disgracing the family with a bastard child
and by marrying someone as eligible as the Marchese (i.e.,
Charles); having made these revelations she completes her
revenge by stabbing the Marchese, after which she poisons
herself. Charles discovers that Margaretta is Antonia's
illegitimate daughter by the father of one of his friends.
Having been married to her mother, Charles would certainly
be forbidden by the church to marry Margaretta, so he re-
signs himself to her marrying the Wallace boy.

90: Lathom, Francis   THE UNKNOWN, OR, THE NORTHERN GALLERY.
    A ROMANCE   3 vols. London: Lane, Newman, and Co., 1808

Eleonora is Bishop Hugh Latimer's daughter, or so we suppose. She has formed a secret acquaintance with an unknown
man in some kind of mysterious trouble and fears that an unidentified body found on the premises may be his. When she
goes in secret to look at the corpse she is frightened away
by a mysterious figure and a sharp noise of clapping. She
finds a note from someone anonymous who informs her that
the sound of three claps will announce his presence. Later,
when her father goes to the tower and she asks who will protect her, she hears the claps again. The reader is expected
to believe, as Eleonora does, that the Unknown is the man
with whom she is already acquainted. In fact, though evidence changes from pro to con and back again, her acquaintance is apparently Percival Godolphin, who helped to put
Lady Jane Grey on the throne. Eleonora's grandmother dies
not long after Latimer goes to the tower, so Eleonora is
sent for protection to Lady Blunt and Sir Sigismund, whose
family includes three young men: Sir Hildebrand, surly and
tyrannical; Valentine, said to be insane and kept in a
tower; Lord Henry Fitzroy, illegitimate son of Henry VIII
and Sir Sigismund's former wife.
    Sir Hildebrand, whose proposal Eleonora has refused,
wishes to kill his elder brother Valentine. When he tries,
Eleonora throws herself between them and is stabbed in the
shoulder. Believing her to be in love with Valentine, Sir
Sigismund warns her that the young man is her brother: he
was so eager for an heir that he kidnapped little Valentine
from the Latimers and, when his own son was subsequently
born, declared his purloined heir insane; this seemed the
best solution to an awkward situation. Eleonora intends in
fact to marry Henry Fitzroy, but his spectral mother cancels

the wedding by appearing to Henry and announcing that he and
Eleonora are siblings. At about the same time, Sir Hildebrand attacks Henry's castle, where Edward VI is purportedly
hidden, in the course of which he blows up his own mother
with a shell. (Actually, the refugee is not Edward VI; Henry has been imposed upon.) The information from the ghost
of Henry's mother was accurate; she is the ghost of Eleonora's mother as well, and Sir Sigismund is Eleonora's father. Eleonora was somehow given to the Latimers to replace
the kidnapped Valentine. Godolphin, Eleonora's Unknown, is
guilty of various crimes including joining a band of robbers
and poisoning his wife. Valentine is released and marries
Eleonora.

91: Lathy, Thomas Pike   THE INVISIBLE ENEMY, OR, THE MINES
    OF WIELITSKA. A POLISH LEGENDARY ROMANCE   4 vols. Lon-
    don: Lane, Newman, 1806

The interest in this novel lies less in the events than in
the skill and anonymity of the villain who masterminds them.
Leopold is raised as a peasant because his title and property have been usurped by Lafranco. He recovers his title and
marries Rhodiska, whom Lafranco also desires. Their married
life is marked by extraordinary persecutions. A letter
tells Leopold that Rhodiska is unfaithful. They find a body
hidden in a trunk in their house. Their crops are burned
and their animals killed. Their son is kidnapped. They go
into exile, whereupon they stop hearing from their friends,
at least one of whom turns out to be in a dungeon. They do
receive a letter from their persecutor, however, saying that
all their friends are false. When they recover their son,
their daughter is kidnapped. At last they are all bundled
into a coach and taken to Lafranco, the perpetrator. (The
bandits who convey them to Lafranco try to create the illusion of a ferry by paddling in containers of water and singing.) Lafranco tries to seduce both Rhodiska and her daughter by offering to release the men in their family, but they
resist. At last the villain is defeated and the novel ends
in appropriate weddings and executions.

92: Lee, Sophia   THE RECESS, OR, A TALE OF OTHER TIMES
    3 vols. London, T. Cadell, 1783-1785

Matilda and Elinor are brought up in a stony recess, for-
merly a convent, by Mrs. Marlow, who admits that she is not
their mother. The recess is on the estate of their uncle
Lord Scroope, and they are attended by another uncle, Father
Anthony, a Roman Catholic priest. Mrs. Marlow and Father
Anthony were once married but right after the wedding found

out that they were brother and sister. The girls are really
the twin daughters of Mary Queen of Scots by Lady Scroope's
brother Norfolk; Matilda resembles her royal mother.

When the girls are old enough, Matilda falls in love
with Leicester, whom they found in trouble and hid in the
recess. They marry and keep it secret. This causes some
awkwardness, as Sir Philip Sidney falls in love with Matilda
and Rose Cecil wants Leicester, to whom Queen Elizabeth proposes as well. The couple flee to the recess but are there
captured by an arrogant and unscrupulous ex-soldier who once
tried to threaten them into giving him Elinor; instead they
shanghaied him onto Drake's ship for a long voyage. Now
he is home and eager for revenge. They escape, thanks to
a miraculous burst of lightning which shows them the right
door, and Leicester smashes their captor's head. Rose
Cecil, who lives in the house formerly occupied by Uncle
Scroope, helps them get away to France and comes with them.
This leaves Elinor unprotected in Elizabeth's court. When
the Queen hears of Leicester's departure, she hits Elinor
with a book and knocks her out, consequently discovering
the identifying papers she wears, which precipitate Mary's
execution. Soldiers coming to arrest Matilda and Leicester
accidentally kill the latter. Matilda finally escapes to
further tribulations — slave uprisings in Jamaica, rheumatic
fever, imprisonment. At last she returns to England to find
Elinor insane and to learn her story.

Elinor and Essex were in love but delayed marrying.
Elinor was forced by Burleigh to sign a document denying her
parentage in return for his tearing up the order for Queen
Mary's execution. And she is obliged to marry another man
to save Essex's head. This is only the beginning of her
trouble. She has spells of partial insanity, loses her
reputation, is denied by her brother King James, is wounded
in a skirmish in Ireland, is shipwrecked. All this time
she is trying to rejoin Essex. Before they manage much time
together he is condemned to die and she goes mad. After Matilda comes home, Elinor sits in the snow too long one day,
catches a fever, and dies in front of Essex's picture. For
a while it looks as though Matilda's fortunes are changing,
for James seems disposed to recognize her. But it comes to
nothing, her daughter Mary is poisoned, and Matilda declines
and writes these memoirs for a friend.

93: Legge, F.   THE SPECTRE CHIEF, OR, THE BLOOD-STAINED
    BANNER. AN ANCIENT ROMANCE   24 pp. London: J. Bailey,
    c.1800

When wicked Rosalviva finds that his father is on the opposite side of a territorial dispute, he orders him murdered

by the servant Barbaro. Then he accuses his good brother
Marcellus of the murder and takes Marcellus's sweetheart
Angelia. He is prevented from raping Angelia by seeing the
ghost of his father beside the bed, which is curious because
his father is not dead after all. In fact, he is so full of
vigor that he kills Barbaro with an ax and hangs him up to
rot, then shuts Rosalviva up in the tower with his body.
Marcellus and Angelia marry. The father goes to a monastery.
  With THE SPECTRE CHIEF is bound BARON FITZALLAN.
The hero is called home to the bedside of a dying guardian
but is captured en route and put in a dungeon by his enemy
Baron Fitzallan. He dreams while imprisoned that his wife
is being stabbed and is calling for help. A ghost (the
ghost of his father, as he later discovers) lets him out
of the dungeon and gives him a dagger with which to take
vengeance. Fitzallan confesses that he killed the hero's
father and has captured his wife because he lusts after her.
He dies of stab wounds, seeing demons.

94: Leigh, Sir Samuel Egerton   MUNSTER ABBEY. A ROMANCE,
    INTERSPERSED WITH REFLECTIONS ON VIRTUE AND MORALITY
    3 vols. Edinburgh: W. Creech, 1797

Mr. Belford, who owns Munster Abbey on the River Ex, marries
Miss Melville. They have a daughter Aurelia. Mr. Belford
has also an apparently incorrigible brother Charles, who was
born during a terrible storm. Despite Belford's support and
encouragement, Charles has twice robbed his brother's house,
once even stealing a diamond studded miniature of their
mother, which he later penitently returned. Charles is
about the only dark spot in a peculiarly sunny novel, and
by the time Aurelia is grown the family discovers that
Charles has a good job at Leghorn and is virtuous and prosperous. Aurelia turns down several eligible suitors but
falls in love (at first sight) with Lord Altamont, and he
with her. At one point after their engagement Aurelia goes
with her family to meet Altamont at Dover and, when he does
not arrive, becomes ill from fear that he may be dead; but
he is merely delayed. Altamont and Aurelia marry and have
children, Charles marries a Miss Draper, Belford founds two
academies, and everything turns out well.

95: Leland, Thomas   LONGSWORD, EARL OF SALISBURY. AN HIS-
    TORICAL ROMANCE   2 vols. London: W. Johnston, 1762

Sir Randolph, retired knight, is surprised to discover that
a pilgrim with a big sword whom he sees disembark from a
small boat is his old general, the Earl of Salisbury. The

Earl is accompanied by a younger pilgrim who is introduced as the daughter of his friend and former enemy Les Roches. Salisbury, who is the illegitimate son of Henry II, wants nothing more than peace and retirement with his wife Ela. He has had an exhausting time since Sir Randolph last saw him, having been shipwrecked in France, where he made friends with Les Roches and where they both suffered the persecutions of the jealous and vindictive Count Mal-leon. There have been escapes, betrayals, kidnappings, and misunderstandings, and at last Les Roches has disappeared; his daughter Jacqueline and the Earl still hope to find him. Jacqueline is also separated from the young man whom she loves and who helped her when she was kidnapped for politico-military reasons by his father, Count Chauvigny.

Sir Randolph reluctantly tells the Earl that his castle has been taken by Raymond, nephew to the king's favorite. Raymond would like to have Ela as well. He and his villainous friends try to make her marry him by threatening to harm her child, and she falls gravely ill from shock and strain. Her forced wedding to Raymond is interrupted by the announcement of Salisbury's impending arrival, though he does not actually come to the castle for some time. He has been incorrectly informed that his wife has married Raymond and has gone to demand his rights from the king. This gives the villains time to quarrel among themselves and, after an abortive attempt to poison the Earl, they come to bad ends. Les Roches, whose sudden arrival caused the Earl to drop his poisoned cup, is reunited with his daughter, young Chauvigny arrives to fight for justice, and marriages are made and resumed.

96: Lewis, Matthew   THE BRAVO OF VENICE   1 vol. London:
    J. F. Hughes, 1805

Count Rosalvo, banished by an enemy, is starving in Venice. He hires himself out under the name of Abellino to a band of assassins, to whom he proves himself by beating them all in a test of strength. He is extraordinarily ugly, with only one eye and a big mouth, but this appearance is merely a disguise. His first assignment is to murder the Doge's niece Rosabella. Instead he kisses Rosabella and murders his chief; the murder is part of his plan to kill the other bravos and be the only one in Venice, thus acquiring all the business and discovering which villains employ assassins. At this time a handsome stranger, Flodoardo, comes to the Doge and offers to destroy all the bravos. He and Rosabella immediately fall in love. The discerning reader comes to suspect that Count Rosalvo is managing yet another alias. The difficulties of wearing two hats climax when Flodoardo is promised Rosabella on condition of his capturing Abellino. At a large dinner party, to which a number of conspirators against the Doge have been invited, he manages an approximation of this feat by a quick exit and change of costume. The guests are understandably angry. However, Rosabella pleads for him, and he satisfies the Doge by identifying the conspirators and restoring several important statesmen he was supposed to have killed in his capacity as bravo. As he managed really to kill his enemy the Prince, who was courting Rosabella too, the story ends happily for him.

97: Lewis, Matthew   FEUDAL TYRANTS, OR, THE COUNTS OF
      CARLSHEIM AND SARGANS. A ROMANCE. TAKEN FROM THE GERMAN
      4 vols. London: J. F. Hughes, 1806

Feudal Tyrants is a tremendously complicated novel because it contains so many manuscript memoirs of people who actually have some connection with the plot line as well as elaborate stories of their own. In the frame story, Elizabeth, the Widowed Countess of Torrenburg, corresponds with her old teacher Conrad, who is abbot of Cloister-Curwald. Conrad wants money for two girls called Constantia and Ida, the Damsels of Werdenberg, but although Elizabeth wishes to do the right thing she cannot rid herself of some resentment over Ida's theft of Henry Montfort, the man she loved. The Damsels' manuscript, the fourth to engage our attention, makes clear that the apparent theft was misunderstood. Ida and Elizabeth were friends, and Ida's intentions were good, but she discovered at Elizabeth and Henry's wedding that Henry was also Erwin Melthal, a man to whom she had been unofficially espoused and whom she believed to have died in battle. Equally surprised to find that Ida was not, as he had supposed, dead, Henry fainted. When he recovered he dashed off to find Ida, with no explanations. The sisters have various difficulties including captivity by robbers, but at last they manage to retire to a cottage. When Elizabeth hears the whole story she repents her hostility and gives them Torrenburg. Ida marries Henry, Constantia marries an old friend, and Elizabeth takes the veil as she had been planning to do.

Early in the novel Elizabeth has in her possession the memoirs of Urania Venosta, who was sent to live with her Uncle Leopold lest by her beauty she outshine the Emperor's daughters. She marries Ethelbert Carlsheim, who has proved himself valiant in trouble but turns out to be rather unscrupulous and vicious, a circumstance especially awkward since he apparently has some claim to Leopold's holdings. After Urania comes to the aid of some monks whom he has

imprisoned, Ethelbert locks her up in shabby Castle Raven-
stein. There she discovers Edith Mayfield, also a prisoner,
whose child Ludolf she had helped to deliver under emergency conditions. The two women are permitted to correspond.
When the castle catches fire they lower three-year-old Ludolf down the wall and send him for help, which he in fact
procures. Urania's Uncle Leopold is in love with Edith; his
apparently lunatic wife, Lucretia, also imprisoned in the
castle, conveniently dies, making a new marriage possible.
Leopold's son Donat becomes a menace after the marriage, for
he arrives in the neighborhood bent upon avenging his mother. Donat's sister (Adelaide, the Lady of the Beacon-Tower)
warns Urania to be wary of Donat and of his terrible wife
Mellusina, and later manages to have her released from a
second imprisonment, this one in the Castle of Sargans.

Adelaide's memoirs follow next. Leopold's wife Lucretia
was her mother; when Lucretia produced twins she hid the
extra one (Adelaide) for safety's sake. Later she decided
not to identify Adelaide lest Donat, to whom she had become
particularly attached, should have to share his inheritance. Adelaide later marries the best of Donat's libertine
friends, a man who assassinates the Emperor and is consequently tortured and killed. Adelaide spends the rest of
her life in a convent.

Yet another tale concerns Donat's twin daughters, Emmeline and Amalberga. Emmeline is ashamed of her wicked relatives and steals out with her friend Amabel to visit Urania
in her convent cell. Her sister Amalberga has mysteriously
disappeared. Later she reappears, disappears again, and is
at last rescued by her lover, who marries her. As for Emmeline, she is renounced by her father, falls in love with
Herman of Werdenberg, and escapes going to a convent so corrupt that the nuns do not even cut their hair. Herman despises Emmeline because of her father, but when he rescues
her, unrecognizably pale and wasted from a dungeon, he falls
in love without suspecting her identity. She discreetly
marries him first and tells him afterward. Other imprisonments and rescues have to do with Emmeline's friend Amabel
and Donat's new wife Helen. Barring some casualties along
the way, most of the good triumph and the wicked come to
suitably unhappy ends.

98: Lewis, Matthew   THE ISLE OF DEVILS. AN HISTORICAL
    TALE, FOUNDED ON AN ANECDOTE IN THE ANNALS OF PORTUGAL
    40 pp. Kingston, Jamaica: Privately printed at the
    Advertiser office, 1827

Irza is shipwrecked and washes ashore on the Isle of Devils.
She earlier admired it from a distance but was told that the

place was evil, a spot where the damned congregate. Upon
her arrival she is attacked and bitten by horrible dwarves
but is rescued by the Demon King. Smitten by her beauty,
he kneels to her and leads her to his cave. Although he is
huge, black, hairy, and terrifying, he behaves like a gentleman and Irza is able to tolerate him. At some point the
chastity of their relationship breaks down and Irza produces
an infant, the image of his father, about whom she has very
ambivalent feelings. After a period of insanity, the result of seeing her demon lover beat out the brains of her
human lover who has tried to rescue her, she has a second
child who looks altogether normal and upon whom she dotes.
When more rescuers arrive and force her to go with them —
she objects to leaving her younger child, whom its father
has kept with him as a sort of hostage — the Demon King retaliates by flinging the human child into the ocean. Then,
wild with grief, he flings himself and the demon child into
the ocean as well. The tale is in verse.

99: Lewis, Matthew G.   THE MONK. A ROMANCE   3 vols.
    London: J. Bell, 1796

The monk Ambrosio, whose piety and eloquence are the admi-
ration of all Madrid, falls prey to temptation through his
lust, pride, and inexperience. His ruin, the process of
which constitutes the primary business of the novel, is effected by a demon in the guise of a beautiful woman, Matilda. Matilda, further disguised as a male novice, persuades
Ambrosio to let her remain in the monastery by appealing to
his lechery and to his gratitude, the latter provoked by her
apparently saving his life at the expense of her own, having
sucked the poison from a snakebite. She heals herself by
sorcery. This is an example of the web of seduction, deception, and recourse to the demonic which ends in Ambrosio's
damnation. Matilda introduces him to the intoxications of
"the syren's luxurious couch," and, when he tires of her,
encourages his desire for Antonia, an innocent who resorts
to him as confessor and whom we ultimately discover to be
his long-lost sister. Not even the aid of sorcery turns Ambrosio into a facile seducer; he finally murders Antonia's
(and hence, his own) mother, drugs the girl, and rapes and
kills her in the monastic charnel house. His crimes discovered, he escapes the cells of the Inquisition by signing a
Satanic pact, whereupon Lucifer transports him to a mountain
and, flying up with him, drops him down the side of it to
die in slow agonies.
    The subplot deals with the obstacles to love and the fi-
nal reunion of Agnes and Raymond. Two incidents stand out.
First, Raymond, supposing himself to be eloping with Agnes

disguised as the legendary ghost of a Bleeding Nun, accidentally elopes with the real ghost and calls on the Wandering
Jew to undo the match. Second, Agnes is confined to a convent (sister institution to Ambrosio's) and, discovered by
Ambrosio to be pregnant, is locked by the prioress in the
charnel house to have her child and to watch it die and de-
cay. She is rescued on the night of Antonia's rape, a convent fire, and the destruction of the wicked prioress.

100: Lewis, Matthew   ROMANTIC TALES   4 vols. London: Long-
    man, Hurst, Rees, and Orme, 1808

Summaries of the prose tales follow. I have not taken notes
on the eight poems.
    "Mistrust; or Blanche and Osbright." Osbright of Frank-
heim and Blanche of Orrenberg suffer the effects of a long
train of hostility and misunderstanding between their
houses. Indeed, Blanche herself mistrusts the house of
Frankheim and falls in love with Osbright only because she
does not know who he is, but that is a later part of the
story. As the tale begins, Osbright has come back from the
wars just in time to see the funeral of his little brother
Jocelyn, who his father is wrongly convinced was murdered
by the Orrenbergs. To compound the apparent outrage, one
of Jocelyn's fingers is missing. The reader, however, comes
to suspect that the Orrenbergs are not such a villainous
crew; the vassals are hotheaded, and Blanche has imbibed
some wrong notions from her suspicious mother, Ulrica, but
Blanche's father is a good man and still loyal to Frankheim,
with whom he was once on friendly terms. The Orrenberg vassals, by the way, believe the Frankheims to have murdered
Philip, Blanche's little brother.
    Complications multiply. An insolent herald from Frank-
heim who comes to accuse Orrenberg of murder is killed by
Orrenberg's vassals. Later a Sir Ottokar, who is both
friend to Orrenberg and kinsman by marriage to Frankheim,
goes to Frankheim for diplomatic purposes and is murdered
at Frankheim's orders. Meanwhile some difficulties of a
more personal sort are distracting Osbright. His young half
brother Eugene (son of Frankheim and a nun), who dislikes
him from jealousy, has also fallen in love with Blanche despite the unsuitability of his station. When Eugene sees
Osbright and Blanche together he goes mad; because he wishes
Blanche to kill him he chases her with a sword, an action
that is understandably misconstrued by Ottokar, who stabs
Eugene, though not fatally. Eugene's insanity persists and
his father becomes increasingly unbalanced from guilt and
rage. Frankheim decides to kidnap Blanche, who, having been

forewarned of this, puts on Osbright's armor as a disguise.
In consequence she is captured by her own father's men.
Osbright, who has walked out of their retreat in Blanche's
clothing, is assassinated by his father's hirelings. Frankheim kills himself in remorse. Blanche pines for a few
years and dies, Eugene wanders off to the Holy Land and disappears, and the two mothers go into a convent, where they
raise a monument to their children: "Here rest the Victims
of Mistrust."

And what of Jocelyn's missing finger? And who really
killed him? One stormy night Osbright is stranded in the
forest and enters a hut, where he finds his little brother's
finger boiling in a cauldron. Observing that "there seems
to be something improper going on here," he elicits from the
young lady who tends the cauldron the information that Jocelyn died defending himself from a wolf with his dagger. The
girl found him too late to save him and was later sent back
by her grandmother to procure his finger (nearly severed in
the struggle) for its value in magical potions.

"The Anaconda." Everard Brooks returns from India
wealthy, only to discover that rumor (rumor propagated by
the aunt of the girl he loves) accuses him of having killed
in India a fiancée named Anne O'Connor; all the most grisly
details of his clubbing her to death are common property.
He tells the real story, which is not about Anne O'Connor
but about an anaconda that trapped his employer, Mr. Seafield, in a summer pavilion. Brooks at last devised a
scheme for stupifying the snake by letting it eat a cow, and
then killing it. The stratagem came too late for Seafield
who soon died from the suffocating effects of the anaconda's
offensive breath. But Seafield wanted Brooks to marry his
widow and left them the property jointly, so when the widow
grieved herself to death, Brooks became a rich man. With
the mystery dissolved Brooks marries his English sweetheart.

"The Four Facardins." I shall not describe this rather
fantastic and convoluted piece in detail, but it involves
four men, each of whom is named Facardin and has his own activities. The adventures have a fairy-tale tone at times,
being stocked with giants, witches, curious costumes, and so
on. The tone, too, can be un-Gothically frivolous: "...have
you really reached the age of one-and-twenty without having
once been turned into a blue bear or a china tea-pot?"

"My Uncle's Garret Window." The narrator has a tele-
scope through which he watches the family next door as if
he were at a play. He keeps notes on their domestic sorrows
and joys and misunderstandings. Their drama turns out well
and the narrator decides to make friends with one of them.

101: Lewis, Matthew   TALES OF TERROR. WITH AN INTRODUCTORY
      DIALOGUE   149 pp. London: J. Bell, 1801

Including the introductory dialogue there are twenty tales,
all of them in verse. An oddly assorted group, they include
a comic poem about the ghost of a twenty-two-year-old cook
who returns to haunt her faithless lover, and a version of
Little Red Riding Hood, as well as more predictably heroic,
sentimental, and quasi-mythic poems. The tales include such
excitements as poisoning, fratricide, shape-changing, seduction, corpse-kissing, shipwreck, suicide, exorcism, remorse,
and attempted infanticide. The disconcerting moral at the
end of "The Wolf-King; or Little Red-riding-hood" typifies
the crudity and grimness of many of the verses — "Get not to
bed with grandmummie,/ Lest she a ravenous wolf should be!"
(See Montague Summers's *A Gothic Bibliography* for a detailed
discussion of why the attribution to Lewis must be false.)

102: Lewis, Matthew   THE WOOD DAEMON, OR, "THE CLOCK HAS
      STRUCK"   34 pp. London: J. Scales, c.1807   (The story
      exists not only in the dramatic version but also as a
      chapbook.)

Una is warned in a vision to save the child Leolyn from
the Wood Daemon, who is said to drink a child's blood every
year. Count Hardyknute, whom Una considers marrying for
social reasons, has secretly pledged the Daemon an annual
victim in return for wealth and good looks. He always kills
children because they can die innocent. Leolyn is the true
heir to Hardyknute's place and title, and for years has been
sheltered by Una's aunt; he is tongue-tied but is supposed
to recover when he is ten. Hardyknute snatches Leolyn,
stands on a bed, pulls a string, and sinks into the "fatal
cavern." Aided by the ghosts of Leolyn's parents, Una du-
plicates the bed maneuver and joins them in the cavern. If
Hardyknute does not sacrifice either Leolyn or Una to the
Daemon by one o'clock he will be the Daemon's slave forever.
Una delays the sacrifice by asking to pray, and Leolyn
pushes the clock ahead, whereupon the Wood Daemon carries
off Hardyknute. Una embraces the peasant boy to whom she
was engaged before she was distracted by her ambition to
marry into the aristocracy.

103: Lucas, Charles   GWELYGORDD, OR, THE CHILD OF SIN.
      A TALE OF WELSH ORIGIN   3 vols. London: A. K. Newman,
      1820

Lucy Charmont was born in Newgate and chosen from the Philanthropic Charity by Admiral Maurice, who gave her to his

sister Lady Apreuth. Her new foster sisters named her Charmont after the brother in Otway's *Orphan* and have grown to
be very fond of her, for she is sensible, beautiful, and
loyal. She receives a number of proposals despite her
shocking parentage but turns them all down. She would like
to marry Lord Atheling but is worried about her lower-class
background, so refuses him until she learns that family upsets have stripped him of his title and that he is going to
the East Indies. Thereupon she dons male clothing and arrives at the dock asking to go along. The couple marry, and
Lucas makes the point that Lucy has not, as is the way of
heroines, suddenly acquired upper-class parents to facili-
tate the marriage; virtue, Lucas says, is pedigree enough.
    There are two amusing minor plots. The first involves
Mr. James Howell, a tenant's son who was educated by Lady
Apreuth and has turned Methodist preacher. Lucy has to ask
him not to proselytize Lady Apreuth's servants. At last his
zeal leads him to marry Miss Sally Coral, a beautiful fish
seller, for he wishes to convert a wicked wife, and Sally
swears magnificently. It is a keen disappointment for him
to discover that she is really virtuous, and that she is
shocked at his expecting her to swear at home. The other
plot, brief but fascinating, is provided by Dr. Wardine,
whom Atheling meets in his travels. Wardine says that
Frankenstein is a true story, with some of the particulars
altered. In Ingolstadt Wardine met Henry Clerval, a servant
of Victor Frankenstein's, from whom he learned how to make
some easy money. Clerval said that his master was experi-
menting with the creation of life but was clearly afraid of
succeeding; if Wardine would put on suitable clothes, lie
down in the laboratory, and "come to life," he could subsequently extort money from the frightened scientist. Wardine
did this but finally revealed the whole plot to Frankenstein, who wrote it up, altering the real circumstances to
their more dramatic fictitious counterparts, and published
it under the name of Mary Shelley.

104: Lucas, Charles   THE INFERNAL QUIXOTE. A TALE OF THE
      DAY   4 vols. London: W. Lane, 1801

Lucas is opposed to Modern Philosophy and especially to the
theories of Godwin. The novel, with a preface allegedly by
Satan, recounts the infamous career of Marauder, a man who
embraces these pernicious doctrines. Marauder poisons the
mind of a girl named Emily with Godwin's views of marriage
and persuades her to elope without benefit of clergy. Wilson Wilson, on the other hand, is conspicuously religious
and good, and Emily's sister Fanny is good; they like each

other. Wilson, though a carpenter's son, is a trustee of
Marauder's estate and tells him that he is not the true
heir, which leads to a certain amount of legal machination
on Marauder's part. Marauder challenges Wilson to a duel,
but Wilson is against dueling on principle and makes the
man who carries the challenge read tracts and scripture.
Meanwhile, Marauder, who is involved in an Irish uprising,
is getting into lengthy discussions of religion and Modern
Philosophy, and Emily is weeping and tiring of being a mistress. Hearing that Wilson and Fanny plan to marry, Marauder decides to kidnap and seduce the latter. Wilson rescues
her. Marauder at last goes berserk and jumps off a cliff.

105: Mackenzie, Anna Maria   THE DANISH MASSACRE. AN HIS-
     TORICAL FACT   2 vols. London: William Lane, 1791

Edrie Streou, the wicked and treacherous Duke of Mercia, is
dying in a cave as the novel begins. He is discovered by a
man whose son and grandson he has killed, and who, lost in
the fog, happens to hear his groans. The Duke leaves some
papers which provide the material of the story, though it is
not told from his point of view. King Ethelred is somehow
controlled by Mercia, who is behind the scheme of slaughter-
ing Danes in quantity. Princess Elfrida at one point reluctantly consents to marry Mercia on the condition that he
stop persecuting a Danish family (that of her friend Athela)
to whom he is particularly cruel. Athela's agony is principal to the story and reaches a peak when she goes to Ethelred about her husband's death, and Mercia murders her children in front of both her and the king. Finally the only
important survivor in this grim novel is Elfrida, who is
consoled for her troubles by finding a good man and making
a happy marriage.

106: Mackenzie, Anna Maria   THE IRISH GUARDIAN, OR, ERRORS
     OF ECCENTRICITY   3 vols. London: Longman, Hurst, Rees,
     and Orme, 1809

Mackenzie's preface makes a statement in favor of virtue in
novels, citing those of Dr. Moore and Mr. Dallas as good examples, and assures the reader that in the novel at hand all
the errors of the Irish Guardian's conduct arise from his
goodness of heart.
     The Irish Guardian is Captain Derrick, who some years
before the story begins found a female infant in Portugal;
its family was being tortured to death for political reasons
and it was to be executed with the others. Derrick presented the baby, Almeria, to his married sister to raise and
later taught the little girl to think of him as an uncle.

As the novel opens she is grown up and in love with Frederico de Lima. She and Captain Derrick (both in masculine clothing) have just survived a shipwreck together. Their affairs are complicated by those of Frederico, a man much persecuted — drugged, straight-jacketed, and imprisoned in Portugal, where much of the story takes place. At one point, incited by the villain Polygon, the Inquisition arrests Almeria and accuses her of being contracted in marriage to her own brother. Investigation shows that the charge is based on a statement of Derrick's; he hotly asserts that he said Almeria and Frederico "loved like brother and sister," not that they were. (Presumably his unlucky statement is one of the errors arising from his goodness of heart.) After further complications the couple are aided by Count de Lima, who has appeared in several guises during the story — Favorita the hermit, a Spanish officer, an Inquisitor. Lost relatives are discovered, e.g., a sister for Almeria, and justice prevails.

107: Maturin, Charles Robert   THE ALBIGENSES. A ROMANCE
     4 vols. London: Hurst, Robinson, 1824

Religious wars and persecutions are central to this novel. Sir Paladour, whose background is mysterious even to him, exterminates heretics and fights Raymond of Toulouse. He loves Isabelle of Courtenaye. At her family's castle both a minstrel and a phantomlike woman suggest that Paladour is the true heir to Courtenaye. The woman turns out to be Marie de Mortemar, who had supposedly been executed earlier for heresy. (At the time, she had cursed the Lord of Courtenaye, saying that a fiery arrow would level his towers.) The company at the castle also tell of the returning dead and of how a Courtenaye ancestress married a werewolf by mistake.

Meanwhile, Armirald, a sympathetic boy knight, is trying to reason the heretic Albigenses into good behavior and is falling in love with Genevieve, one of the heretics. In a confrontation between crusaders and Albigenses the latter win, and as a result several things happen: Isabelle is snatched away by a black knight and put in a stronghold on a cliff; her old governess is put in a pit with a chained wolf; Sir Paladour is captured and finds a lycanthrope (who later bites him and gets thrown downstairs in retaliation) howling around his room. He discovers Isabelle's whereabouts by leading the lycanthrope to talk about lambs. Also as a result of the conflict Genevieve nurses Armirald, who is wounded, and begins to like him. Her people banish her for helping the enemy and she tries to get to Toulouse. On the way she saves the Queen from assassination. When she is kidnapped later, she shows the Queen's ring and is treated well. Some nobles, however, burn her house over her for refusing the Dauphin. Meanwhile Isabelle escapes with Paladour, but the latter is stabbed by Marie de Mortemar. Marie tells him that all his family were killed as heretics by the Lord of Courtenaye. She also tells him to kill his last enemy, Isabelle; this so upsets the couple that they commit double suicide.

Paladour discovers that Raymond of Toulouse is his father and Armirald his little brother. The Lord of Courtenaye is burned to death when some occult paraphernalia catch fire. Marie de Mortemar poisons some sacramental wine, which kills the wicked Bishop of Toulouse and causes communicants to die in droves. She jumps out a window to her death. Heroes and heroines rescue one another from their miscellaneous predicaments.

108: Maturin, Charles Robert   FATAL REVENGE, OR, THE
     FAMILY OF MONTORIO. A ROMANCE   3 vols. London:
     Longman, Hurst, Rees, and Orme, 1807

Ippolito and Annibal are the two eldest sons of the Count of Montorio. They are close to each other but dissimilar; Ippolito is fond of luxury and high living, while Annibal is inclined to stay at home and muse. The sinister confessor Schemoli works hard during the course of the novel to convince the brothers that he has supernatural power and that they must obey him and kill their father. His devices are complex and ingenious and provide the principal business of the novel. His approach with Annibal is to pass himself off as a specter who requires, indeed demands, aid and obedience. He impresses Ippolito chiefly with his omnipresence and consequent inescapability. Both young men are persuaded that they are predestined to be parricides and at last perform the deed. Schemoli, however, has made a miscalculation which requires explanation. He was Orazio, the former count of Montorio. His wicked brother led him to kill a man supposed to be his wife's lover. Orazio killed the man with relish and in front of his wife, who died of shock, cursing him. He later discovered that his brother's hints had been misleading and so he fled, leaving behind his two boys. When he comes back to take vengeance on his brother, he fails to recognize Annibal and Ippolito as his own sons and makes them murderers. They go into the army and are pardoned. Orazio dies of a broken blood vessel.

109: Maturin, Charles Robert   MELMOTH THE WANDERER. A TALE
      4 vols. Edinburgh: Constable; London: Hurst & Robinson,
      1820

Melmoth lived his natural life in the late seventeenth century but because he dabbled in the occult has been condemned
to wander for 150 years, trying to persuade someone to
change places with him. His quest has been fruitless. When
the frame story takes place, his 150 years are at an end and
he comes home to Ireland to die. His story is pieced together from a series of manuscripts and recitations which
provide extraordinarily complicated tales within tales.

     First, young John Melmoth inherits the Wanderer's house
from his miser uncle. There he finds a disturbing portrait
and a manuscript. The manuscript, badly damaged, tells in
fragments the story of

     1) *Stanton* who becomes interested in the mysterious Mel-
moth and pursues and investigates him. His obsession results in his being put into a madhouse. Melmoth comes there
to offer him his bargain. Stanton's manuscript includes a
fragment of story about some Spaniards, told to him by a
woman in an inn.

     2) Later, John Melmoth is told a very long story by a
Spaniard. The *Spaniard's Story,* autobiographical, is the
account of a man who, forced to be a monk, ill treated at
his monastery, betrayed in an escape attempt, and taken by
the Inquisition, is offered Melmoth the Wanderer's bargain.
He escapes burning and is taken in by a Jew, who sets him
to copying a manuscript, as follows:

     3) *Tale of the Indians.* Melmoth has a long relationship
with Immalee, who is an altogether innocent and beautiful
child of nature. He loves her so much that he intends to
leave her alone, and she loves him. His resolves weaken,
and after she goes to live with her Spanish family he secretly marries her and fathers a child. He is at his most
human in these passages. But the Inquisition takes her,
and he once again offers his bargain. She refuses him
though she still loves him. Earlier in this story, Immalee's father hears

     4) *The Tale of Guzman's Family.* Money that should have
gone to this family was left to the church. Starving, they
turn hostile toward one another. Melmoth makes his offer
to the father, but the father tries to kill all his family
instead of accepting. Finally the will is proved false
and the family can eat again, so Melmoth fails to strike
a bargain.

     5) Also, Melmoth himself tells Immalee's father a story,
The Lovers' Tale. This is a historical tale about the Mor-
timers. Two cousins love each other, but the girl is left

at the altar with no explanation. It seems that an ambitious parent has lied to the boy and said that the pair are brother and sister. He becomes imbecile and she takes care of him for the rest of his life. She too repulses Melmoth's offer.

Melmoth at the end of the story dreams of falling into hell and of all the people who refused his bargain rising past him and leaving him. In the morning he is mysteriously and ominously gone.

110: Maturin, Charles Robert   THE MILESIAN CHIEF. A ROMANCE
     4 vols. London: Henry Colburn, 1812

Armida, heroine of this piece, is unusually interesting.
She is even more effortlessly talented and intelligent than the average Gothic heroine, but she is given to posing and loses her confidence when not sufficiently admired. Her great regret as the novel opens is that she does not feel love; no wonder, for she is courted chiefly by a sinister boor named Wandesford. When she and her father move from Italy to Ireland she meets a highly romantic and impoverished cousin, Connal, who is involved in revolutionary activity out of loyalty to his demented grandfather. He saves her life several times and they fall in love, which provides them with mutually satisfying scenes of misunderstanding and reconciliation. Ultimately Connal kills Wandesford, who has come to Ireland and continued to make trouble, but not until Armida has taken poison; it is slow-acting poison, for she has time to follow him, as a bride, to his political execution and die across his body.

Partway through the story a heretofore hidden wife of Armida's father arrives with a son. The son and Connal's younger brother Desmond fall in love, to Desmond's horror.
But the son, Endymion, turns out to be a girl, whose real name is Ines. Ines goes mad and raves like a Shakespearean lunatic over the body of her lover, who is executed with his brother. The novel as a whole is full of specters, funeral bards, drownings, and Celtic gloom.

111: Maturin, Charles Robert   THE WILD IRISH BOY   3 vols.
     London: Longman, Hurst, Rees, and Orme, 1808

Ormsby Bethel knows little or nothing of his own family until a letter from his natural father arrives with instructions for his education. When he goes to visit, he finds his father's household unpleasant despite the presence of his sister Sybilla, for the father is bad tempered and ill, and there is a fierce governess, Miss Percival. The governess, he learns at a ball some years later, is his father's

mistress and mother to him and to Sybilla. In the aftermath
of the revelation Ormsby's father is killed in a duel that
Ormsby ought, perhaps, to have fought himself. He is next
taken up by his uncle, an old Irish chieftain whom he has
rescued from a strangler, and goes to London for a season of
high life. Indeed his life there is so high that his uncle
is imprisoned for his debts. The uncle is cross about this
but recovers from his pique and arranges a surprise for
Ormsby — a marriage to Athanasia Montolieu. Ormsby's pleasure is somewhat qualified by his being in love with Athanasia's mother, Lady Montrevors. However, he marries Athanasia and things seem to be going well. The pair are fond
of each other and they inherit a fortune from Ormsby's
uncle.

Further complications arise in London. Machinations
against Ormsby are undertaken by his cousin Deloraine, who
wants to ruin him, and Lady Delphina, who wants to buy him
when his price goes down. Ormsby falls deeper and deeper
into debt from gaming and finds himself in a labyrinth of
scandal, bribes, hush-money, loans, and so on, the result of
his having been seen with Lady Delphina under compromising
circumstances. Athanasia is very kind to him and is glad to
leave London, having herself narrowly avoided an affair with
Deloraine. Meanwhile, Lady Montrevors's husband, who has
long wanted to be rid of her, plans to divorce her for the
affair that he believes her to be having with Ormsby. Fortunately for her he dies and his wife is unexpectedly restored to the only man she ever loved. This gentleman has
appeared in various disguises throughout the story and is
now revealed to be Ormsby's real father and the younger
brother of Ormsby's supposed father; Miss Percival, Ormsby's
mother, apparently had a busy girlhood. So, despite a number of other complications not mentioned here, the good end
happily.

112: Meeke, Mary   COUNT ST. BLANCHARD, OR, THE PREJUDICED
      JUDGE. A NOVEL   3 vols. London: William Lane, 1795

The prejudiced judge is the President De Ransal, and the
description is somewhat misleading. His general reputation
for impartiality is excellent, but he does harbor a temporary prejudice against the hero of the story, Dubois, because of a long-standing animosity to Dubois's purported
father. As a young man the President married secretly,
against his father's wishes, a lovely young woman named
Eugenia, whose proper fortune had been usurped. When she
was eight months pregnant, his father sent him out of town
on prolonged legal business, after which he was abducted and
detained for six weeks. Home at last, he found that his

wife had disappeared and that Eugenia's great uncle had been
led by a crafty servant to suspect him of dishonoring and
murdering her. Eugenia had in fact been abducted by her
father-in-law on her way to Mass but could not be discovered
in any of the convents to which her grieving husband ap-
pealed. Finally after the death of his father he received
a letter from an abbess, asking for his wife's board money,
then in arrears. When he recovered Eugenia, she reported
that their son at six weeks old had been taken away from
her. She feared that he was dead. The couple, reunited
for sixteen years, have been unable to find their child, but
because of a servant's tale they have come to believe that
Dubois's father, an old apothecary who calls himself Rhubarbin, knows more about the child than he will tell — hence
the prejudice.

Dubois, the hero, has been friends since childhood with
the Marquis D'Elcour, an excellent young nobleman who makes
no distinction between Dubois's social standing and his own.
Dubois is trained as a physician, rather against his inclination, but is enabled by his learning and good sense to save
the life of Adelaide, the Marquis's beautiful sister, with
whom he falls in love. Adelaide understands and fears the
class prejudice of her father, who she believes will have
Dubois locked up if he discovers that they are in love. Two
years later she is obliged to run away to an abbey in order
to avoid a forced marriage to a man so impeccably eligible
that she can invent no objection to him. On the way she
is robbed and tied to a tree by her own footman, but she
is rescued by Dubois, who suddenly reappears from Italy.
Near the convent to which Dubois is conducting her they are
arrested by soldiers in the employ of Adelaide's father.
Dubois is jailed and badly treated, while Adelaide is sent
to a Parisian convent run by a grudge-holding woman who was
jealous of Adelaide's mother. The servant who robbed Adelaide lied about an elopement between his mistress and Dubois, and her irate father fully intends to see Dubois hang.
To this purpose he attempts to prejudice the President, who
is to be Dubois's judge.

The President begins to find Dubois more convincing than
Adelaide's father but plays tough for a while in hopes of
frightening information from Rhubarbin. He discovers by
this ruse that Dubois is his own lost son. Rhubarbin, who
had just lost his own infant, without whom he could not control his elderly wife's estate after her death, found the
infant Dubois providentially left on a doorstep. Dubois is
identified by the indelible heart painted on his arm with
foundling-hospital ink. But when the President and Rhubarbin (who has been forgiven) go to the prison to see Dubois
they find him dangerously ill. He is moved to a better cell

from which he unwisely tries to escape with a fellow con-
vict. He soon collapses and sends a note to Rhubarbin, after which he is installed in a nearby house belonging to the
President. When he is slightly recovered he is introduced
to his new parents and his new title — Count St. Blanchard.
Dubois's own small estate is made over to a deserving female
cousin, who is advised to marry Rhubarbin and is quite willing to do so. Adelaide's father is browbeaten into reasonable behavior and permits Dubois to marry his daughter.

113: Meeke, Mary   MIDNIGHT WEDDINGS. A NOVEL   3 vols.
      London: William Lane, 1802

Edmund Browning, son of a squire who married his cook, is
mean, stubborn, and stupid, but does well as a cadet in the
East Indies and comes home a nabob at thirty. Edmund and
his crochety spinster sister Penelope lord it over their
brother Thomas, who rose to secretary and married (gossip
says) a formerly kept woman. Edmund marries Penelope's paid
companion, is made Baron Vilmore, and has a son who is clever, proud, handsome, and essentially noble, though not from
principle. On the eve of his son's parentally arranged marriage to Leonora M'Dougall, Edmund falls ill and, dying,
confesses that his son is not really his. His own son died
of a tantrum at an early age and he kidnapped this boy,
whose real name is Octavius, as a replacement. So Octavius,
whose fiancée breaks the engagement upon hearing Edmund's
confession, finds himself out in the world hunting for his
real parents. A French Minister sees his birthmark and after some mysterious arrangements introduces him to his real
father; Octavius is the illegitimate son of Louis XV and is
made Duke de Valentinois.
    Leonora is sorry now that she broke her engagement. At
a masked ball that Octavius also attends she elopes with and
marries someone whom she supposes to be him. (This seems to
be one of the midnight weddings of the title; I cannot account for the plural.) The groom is really a crafty valet;
Leonora and her family are furious and blame the episode on
Octavius, whom they consequently arranged to have pushed out
of a boat in hopes of drowning him. He is rescued by fishermen and lives to discover that his mother is Lady Trelawn-
ey, to learn that a girl to whom he has been attracted is
really his sister, and to be married by the king's arrangement to a fascinating woman whom he met at the masked ball
which undid Leonora.

114: Meeke, Mary   "THERE IS A SECRET, FIND IT OUT!"
        4 vols. London: Lane, Newman, 1808

The secret is pertinent to the parentage of Frank Yates, the
hero. He has been raised by the Wheelers; his foster father
is a junior clerk and his foster mother an erstwhile house-
keeper/nurse to the Haslemere family. They are a rather unappealing pair, the mother especially, who still wheedles
the Haslemeres' patronage for her own ill-bred son John and
daughter Caroline. Frank is purportedly the natural child
of her brother but he looks more like a Haslemere, which
causes rumors and domestic suspicions. Since he can sing,
he is admitted to the Westminster Choir School and taken
under the special care of the choirmaster Corse, who trains
him for a musical career. He is a vast success on the
stage. In the meantime Caroline, who has dislocated a hip
and become a cripple, is trying hard to find a husband.
Her family try both Frank and his friend Kempthorne (John
threatens the latter melodramatically with the prospect of
his sister's "grimly ghost") but to no avail. As the Wheeler fortunes decline, Frank's rise: he inherits from Corse
and again from Corse's cousin, keeps a carriage, associates
with the Countess of Bayfield, and becomes friends with the
elder Haslemere, who speculates that Frank may be an indiscretion of his son's. Frank injures himself in rescuing
a widowed Mrs. Archer from a coach accident and decides
to give up his career for the sake of his health, but he
no longer needs the income and he wins Mrs. Archer's hand,
so the accident is on the whole a happy one.
    Caroline and John Wheeler have married respectively a
Mr. Eastwood (a villain who absconds with all he can get and
causes John to be arrested for forgery) and a Miss Atwood
(formerly a kept woman). The Wheelers' troubles are aggravated by the Haslemere son's dying revelation that Frank is
his late sister's child, product of a private marriage to
the Earl of Merioneth. This makes Frank Lord Caerleon and
the Wheelers, whose blackmailing and lying have for years
deprived Frank of his rights, the objects of enormous outrage among the knowledgeable. Poor old Wheeler, who was
largely manipulated by his wife, weeps and repents, and
indeed always loved Frank more than his own son, so people
hope that he and Caroline will not suffer unduly; for Mrs.
Wheeler, public opinion favors the workhouse at least, and
it considers with equanimity the prospect that John may
hang. John is acquitted, however — Mrs. Wheeler tells her
husband too abruptly and kills him — and gets a job in the
dustheap business, fighting pigs for scavenge. Caroline is
taken in by a family friend. Mrs. Wheeler sets up a chand-
ler's and green-grocer's shop but takes to drink, breaks a

leg, and dies.   Frank and Mrs. Archer marry and continue to
prosper.

115: Meeke, Mary   THE VEILED PROTECTRESS, OR, THE MYSTERI-
      OUS MOTHER. A NOVEL   5 vols. London: A. K. Newman,
      1819

Pemberton tells his wife that their marriage is not valid,
that he is already married to someone else, and that Pemberton is not his real name.   He leaves her two thousand pounds
and an apologetic note.   She decides not to tell their
three-year-old son, and in order to maintain his respecta-
bility she calls him Henry Pembroke and sends him to live
with a friend who calls herself Mrs. Wilson.   Four months
later Henry is told that his mother has died.   The reader
soon surmises that she has not, but is the new and heavily
veiled companion of Mrs. Jane Meredith, a blind woman.   The
three women — Mrs. Wilson, Mrs. Jane Meredith, and Henry's
mother — form a kind of secret committee devoted to Henry's
welfare.   They send the boy away to school, where he is
kindly treated and where his mother comes to see him from
time to time.   He calls this mysterious woman his Veiled
Protectress and apparently believes her to be Mrs. Meredith.
While Henry is still a boy both Mrs. Wilson and Mrs. Meredith die, and he is given into the guardianship of Sir Herbert Charleville, a pleasant man with a new wife.   Henry has
a number of adventures in his boyhood, but the one with the
farthest-reaching effect is his rescue of Anna Farnham from
her drunken foster father.   Some years later, after he has
embarked upon a military career, he discovers that Anna is
the daughter of his Colonel and marries her.   The major revelation, however, is that his mother is not only alive but
is the wife of Charleville, his guardian.

116: THE MIDNIGHT GROAN, OR, THE SPECTRE OF THE CHAPEL
      36 pp. London: T. and R. Hughes, 1808

Horatio has left home after being informed that Miranda,
whom he loves, is his sister.   Sheltering from a storm in a
convenient but ruined castle, he sees a ghost that leads him
to a diamond ring and a putrefying female corpse.   He finds
himself locked in.   When he escapes he discovers a secret
assembly of men, Miranda's natural father presiding, who
are dipping daggers into a bowl of blood.   He is told that
he must join their assembly or die by torture.   Meanwhile
Miranda has been sought and nearly acquired by several
(sequential) men who are willing to marry her by force.
She escapes all her difficulties by various means, however,

and after some resolution of family mix-ups, Horatio and Miranda, not siblings after all, marry each other.

Bound with this is THE STORY OF KAIS AND LEILA
Kais, a young poet whose father is a shiek, falls in love
with Leila at school. When their parents object and separate the couple, Kais wanders off into the desert and earns
a reputation as a love-maniac. Leila is forced to marry
someone else but retains her virginity. Kais dies saying
her name, whereupon she dies too and they are buried in the
same grave.

117: Montague, Edward   THE DEMON OF SICILY   156 pp. (Summers lists an 1807 edition in four volumes. The notes
that follow are based on an undated edition bound from
penny installments and printed by W. Dugdale, Strand.)

Ricardo, who lives with his profligate father and a sinister
priest in a purportedly haunted castle, falls in love with
a beautiful peasant, Louisa. Louisa is kidnapped by three
masked men, agents of a lecherous Count, but is rescued by
a nobleman formerly ruined by Ricardo's father and currently
leading and reforming a troop of banditti. Ricardo inherits
from his father and restores the nobleman's fortune. Having
discovered that his mother was murdered at his father's instigation, Ricardo explores the haunted wing of the castle
for her remains, wishing to bury them, but she is not to be
found.

Ricardo and Louisa marry and have two children. The
first, a boy, they give to a monastery, as he has no prospect of income. The second, Angellina, grows up to be beautiful and good. Not so a friend's daughter who is left in
Ricardo's care. She is vain, passionate, and has affairs.
It becomes necessary to send her to a convent, where she is
given the name of Agatha. When Ricardo and Louisa die, Agatha's father becomes Angellina's guardian. He desires her
and employs the usual villainous devices to make her marry
him — threatening, locking her up, etc. She loves a nice
young man named Lorenzo who helps her escape to a convent,
whence she is extricated by papal decree. She discovers
that her grandmother died of stab wounds there, which is
why Ricardo did not find her body in the castle. Lorenzo
is thrown into a dungeon but escapes in time to break up a
forced wedding between Angellina and her guardian. Lorenzo
and Angellina elope to a monastery to be married.

At the monastery we find 1) the bones of an unfortunate
trio — Ugo de Tracy; his wife, Fair Isabella, who after her
suicide was decapitated by her frustrated would-be rapist;
the villain, who does ghostly penance once a month; 2) Bernardo the monk, driven by Satan to a frenzy of lust, and

willing to sacrifice his soul for a chance at a beautiful
woman; 3) bad Agatha, who, when not distracted by sexual opportunity, spends her time trying to escape. Both she and
Bernardo kill nuns who hinder their designs. The eloped
couple unfortunately ask Bernardo to marry them; the devil
puts it into his head to kill the groom and make off with
the bride, and the monk nearly succeeds in this piece of
villainy. But Lorenzo recovers from the effects of Bernardo's dagger and sounds the alarm, thereby both saving Angellina and causing the apprehension of Agatha, whose current
attempt at escape is promising well. Agatha and Bernardo
are taken by the Inquisition and burned with generous de-
scriptive detail.

118: Moore, George   GRASVILLE ABBEY. A ROMANCE   3 vols.
      London: G. G. and J. Robinson, 1797

Clementina is put in a convent by her father for economic
reasons but runs away with a rich gentleman named Percival
Maserini. They marry and hide in caves to escape pursuit
by officials who think Clementina poisoned her sister in the
convent before she escaped (she did not). Maserini goes to
his father's home, Grasville Abbey, but finds the bellpull
rusty, his father dead, and talk of "strange doings" in the
Abbey, which his wicked Cousin D'Ollifont inherited after
killing Maserini's father with false reports about the
deaths of his children. D'Ollifont is afraid to sleep in
the abbey. Maserini is determined to explore it; the next
morning a servant finds footprints, blood, and the miniature
Maserini was wearing, with the ribbon torn as if by wrench-
ing.
     Clementina bears twins, Alfred and Matilda, and lives in
Paris. When she dies shs writes Alfred a note to tell him
who she thinks killed his father but dies before she puts
the name down. The twins go to their only receptive relative, a rich liquor merchant in London. The son of the family teaches Alfred gaming and helps D'Ollifont pursue Matilda. When Alfred hears this and discovers that the woman he
loves is being taken out of town to avoid him, he repents of
his association. Count D'Ollifont intends to seduce Matilda
and carry her off, but an anonymous warning permits Alfred
to shoot and wound him. Alfred and Matilda go to live in
Grasville Abbey and take in a stray girl, Agnes. At the
Abbey, mysteries are unraveled. Supernatural effects were
provided by a hermit who has been blackmailed into assisting
D'Ollifont's villainy. The twins' father returns to explain
his mysterious abduction. Agnes is reunited with her mother. D'Ollifont dies in guilty agonies.

119: Moore, George   THEODOSIUS DE ZULVIN, THE MONK OF
         MADRID. A SPANISH TALE, DELINEATING VARIOUS TRAITS OF
         THE HUMAN MIND.   4 vols. London: G. and J. Robinson,
         1802

Alphonso de Mellas dies in a shipwreck, leaving his twin
sons orphaned. Orlando is educated by his uncle Don Diego,
Osmund by his uncle Don John. Their educations are very
different, for Diego is a reformed rake who keeps Orlando
rather cloistered, while John, dissipated and extravagant
since the death of his family, gets Osmund a tutor and sees
that he mixes with boys of his own age. Orlando grows up
shy and awkward but certain that he can unmask all temptation, none of which he has experienced. Osmund is polished
and worldly but has been influenced for the good by his uncle's old steward Fabian. The uncles send both boys, at
seventeen, to Madrid with Osmund's tutor Zadok Bellzenipp;
they wish to see the effects of their educational systems in
practice. On their way to Madrid the boys have experiences,
one night at an inn, which will have later repercussions.
The monk Father Theodosius, who often stops at the inn and
permits nobody to sleep in the room next to his, is there
with a young girl. Orlando spies on him and perceives that
he is a sorcerer. Things not in the room appear in a mir-
ror, most notably a man with a stabbed and bloody young
woman draped over his arm. Orlando keeps his discovery a
secret, hoping to unveil the monk's wickedness and consequently to cut a fine figure in Madrid. In the same inn Osmund's servant finds and gives to his master a silver casket, apparently left behind by the girl, with a miniature
portrait, gold bracelets, a letter to "Leonora" from Theodosius, and some manuscript poetry. Osmund falls in love with
the girl in the miniature.
     In Madrid Orlando fantasizes and wishes with conspicuous
futility that people would admire him. He falls in with a
gambler named Don Esau, though warned by his more sophisti-
cated twin that the odds are against him. Despite further
warnings from the tutor, he becomes fond of gaming and loses
money. Further, he is gulled, seduced, and blackmailed by a
prostitute. His servant Otto encourages him in wickedness.
Orlando seduces an innocent girl and steals money from his
host's desk. Father Theodosius catches him at the latter
trick and in return for his protection and silence makes Orlando his slave. He encourages Orlando to rape his host's
daughter Cassandra, whom for reasons of his own he wishes
ruined or dead, but Orlando is deterred by a mysterious
groan. Meanwhile Laura, the victim of Orlando's seduction,
has confessed and run away, her mother has gone insane, and
her father has killed himself. Following Orlando when he

leaves town, Theodosius nearly browbeats him into poisoning
a gloomy stranger who turns out to be his own father, Alphonso, alive after all. Wherever he goes Orlando is followed by Theodosius, who can apparently go through locked
doors and who shows up when least expected. At one point
Orlando is persuaded to steal the life savings of a cottager
who has nursed him through a fever. With this stake he
starts life in a new spot and cultivates a reputation for
piety, even charitably establishing in a hovel the mendicant
family of the cottager whom he ruined. When he is caught by
the husband in an attempt to rape the wife, he has the man
sent to the galleys and the whole family put in jail on a
trumped-up charge of robbery. They all die. Later yet he
dices with Don Esau on the latter's deathbed and wins all
his money. When he attempts to remove Laura, who has turned
to prostitution, from the establishment where she works, he
discovers that she has taken poison. Once again Theodosius
comes just as Orlando is considering repentance and directs
him to stab a particular man. As Orlando stands with his
dagger ready, an earthquake knocks down part of the castle;
his victim, who has been drugged and veiled, is revealed to
be Alphonso. The assassination attempt having been thwarted
by the arrival of Osmund and his friend Albert, Theodosius
kills Orlando and himself.

   While all this has been going on with Orlando, Osmund
has been having a different set of adventures. It is he
whose letter of introduction has installed the twins in the
home of Don Everard de Gosmond, father of Cassandra and Albert. Theodosius is the family's confessor, a situation
that seems to cause them some unease. Albert admits that
his father has some gloomy secret in which the monk seems to
be involved. Spending a night in the forbidden east cham-
bers of the house one night after a narrow escape from an
amorous assignation, Osmund hears groans and is seized by a
cold hand. After he discovers the original of the miniature
in a cottage outside the city he becomes involved in further
mystery, for the girl disappears after her elderly female
companion dies. Ursula, the old woman, earlier told Osmund
that Leonora was languishing under her villainous father,
Theodosius, and signed an accusation that Theodosius had
murdered a girl called Lucretia de Ravillina. Meanwhile
Albert's father is trying to make him marry a girl whom he
does not know — Leonora again. In fact, Theodosius has
carried off Leonora and locked her up in Don Everard's east
wing. He is furious that Leonora and Osmund love each other
and tortures Osmund by telling him with a smile that Don
John is at that moment being stabbed on a forsaken heath,
which is true. As we discover after the timely arrival of
Osmund and Albert at the attempted assassination above, Leo-

nora is not Theodosius's daughter after all but Don Everard's. As the result of a colorful background of jealousy,
assassination, and babyswapping, Theodosius earlier murdered
his own daughter Lucretia in mistake for Don Everard's
child. He has been a villain all along — guilty of, among
other things, seduction, fraud, intimidation, murder, and a
manipulation whereby his own father died a slave rather than
profiting from a political exchange. Various mysteries
about who was groaning, and who had the miniature when, are
resolved at the end, and all the good people recover from
their illnesses and traumas.

120: Moore, John   ZELUCO. VARIOUS VIEWS OF HUMAN NATURE,
      TAKEN FROM LIFE, AND MANNERS, FOREIGN AND DOMESTIC
      2 vols. London: A. Strahan and T. Cadell, 1789

When Zeluco is ten years old, his father dies, leaving him
to the care of an overindulgent mother; hence his evil passions flourish uncurbed and he becomes a walking demonstra-
tion of the effects of bad childrearing. In his boyhood he
kills a pet sparrow whose tricks dissatisfy him. This incident is representative of the obsessive selfishness which
later leads him to abandon several pregnant girls out of
boredom, to kill with neglect a widow whom he has married
for her money, to be cruel to his subordinates in the army.
He is not at first actually sadistic, merely uninterested in
the sufferings of his victims, but he learns to enjoy punishing slaves and finally beats one to death. When Zeluco
finds Laura, a girl who is not to be had for the asking (she
prefers the military hero Carlostein), he pursues her relentlessly and at last leads her a reluctant bride to the
altar.
      Laura and Carlostein discover that they are in love but
suppress their inclinations. Laura's virtue does not save
her from her husband's jealousy, however, for his new and
wicked mistress Nerina plants in his diseased mind a notion
that Laura's new baby too closely resembles its maternal
uncle. Nerina's poisonous suggestion leads Zeluco to stran-
gle the baby in a fit of passion, and she suggests that he
might kill Laura, who is nearly dying of shock and horror,
as well; she hints that laudanum is said to be effective.
Laura's hysterical reaction to a Massacre of the Innocents
picture — one of the killers looks like Zeluco, she thinks
— makes her brother suspicious. He writes "Zeluco" over it
to test his brother-in-law, but Carlostein manages to draw
Zeluco's consequent rage onto himself to avoid familial
slaughter. On his way to duel Carlostein, Zeluco is stabbed
by a man whom he discovers in Nerina's bed. Dying, he realizes that other people seem to have a certain nobility which

he lacks and understands that he has never had a friend.
Laura marries Carlostein and charitably extricates Nerina
from prison.

121: Moore, Thomas   THE EPICUREAN. A TALE   1 vol. London:
    Longman, Rees, Orme, Brown, and Green, 1827

Alciphron is elected, at twenty-four, to be chief of the
Epicureans. Unfortunately he is constitutionally not much
inclined to pleasure. He dreams that a man tells him to go
to the source of the Nile for eternal life and he sets out,
contemplating ruins and Time. In Memphis he sees and begins
to pursue an extraordinarily beautiful girl. He rows to the
city of the dead and pursues her into pyramids and finally
down a well. Letters of fire lead him toward a secret. To
reach it he must go through a forest of burning trees with
serpents of fire, through a flood with wailing specters
floating down it, and up a set of stairs which break away
under his feet. Then he dangles from a brass ring which ultimately lets him down in a garden where a priest tells him
that he has won victory over his body. He is initiated into
the odd sect responsible for these adventures, but at the
moment of Great Illumination the beautiful girl persuades
him to run away with her. A secret Christian, she takes him
to her brethren. Alciphron pretends, and even tries, to
convert so that he will be allowed to marry her, but in his
heart he cannot believe in this new religion. However, they
are betrothed. When they go back to the city she is mar-
tyred and dies in his arms, after which he really becomes
a Christian and dies in a later persecution.

122: Palmer, John, Jr.   THE HAUNTED CAVERN. A CALEDONIAN
    TALE   1 vol. London: B. Crosby, 1796

The novel begins during the reign of Henry VI. Sir James
Wallace, who owns a ruined castle in Aberdeenshire, is a bad
man — "of a sordid disposition, deceitful, cruel, and designing, his heart...a stranger to humanity or compassion."
He sends his wife Matilda away to a corrupt convent in Rouen
but keeps his infant daughter Jane at home. Matilda, who
was given him in marriage by an ambitious father, loved Alan
Duntrone, who is said to have died of wounds in France.
Jane is raised with and falls in love with her cousin Eldred, son of Matilda's mysteriously missing brother Archibald. Her father, however, supports the suit of Donald of
the Isles, a ferocious man who is willing to take her by
coercion. A forced wedding is planned, but Jane and Eldred,
with the blessing of a veiled and mysterious female figure,
elope and are hidden by Ambrose the hermit. (Ambrose has

interesting tales to tell of the wars, of Joan of Arc, of
pirates and imprisonment and captivity by one Muley Abdallah, whose daughter effected Ambrose's release.)

Shortly after the elopement Jane takes a nap under a
tree and disappears; Eldred falls ill. He finally discovers
Jane at Donald's, looking pale and unhappy. When he tries
to carry her away he is wounded and captured. In his dungeon (the cavern of the title) he discovers a rusty dagger
and a skeleton and hears unaccountable moans. One day a
manuscript written by his missing father falls on his head;
Eldred concludes that the bones are his father's too. When
he is released from his prison he sets about avenging his
father's death, but his attempts are interrupted by a pilgrim who removes a false beard and claims Eldred as his son.
Other reunions follow: Eldred rescues Jane just as she is
being forcibly married to Donald; Jane's mother, the mysterious female who blessed the elopement, is restored to her;
and Ambrose identifies himself as Alan, the long-lost love
of the now fortuitously widowed Matilda Wallace.

123: Palmer, John, Jr.   THE MYSTERY OF THE BLACK TOWER.
     A ROMANCE   2 vols. London: William Lane, 1796

Leonard the peasant boy goes off to fight the Scots and
makes good. He becomes friends with Edgar de Courci, a
local nobleman who loves a girl named Julia. Leonard himself loves Emma but nearly loses her when his parents neglect to give her the letters he encloses in theirs. His
adventures include exposure to some apparently supernatural
phenomena in the Black Tower when he goes home on leave, and
an encounter, back in the army, with a crazy, half-naked recluse named Hildebrand. (Hildebrand unwittingly killed his
own son, whom he misunderstood to be an adulterous visitor
to his wife.) Emma is kidnapped by the vicious Lord Edmund
Fitzallan, who locks her up in the Black Tower. She is put
in a haunted room to sleep, and when one morning she is
missing the maid is certain that a ghost has taken her.
Meanwhile Leonard has been captured and imprisoned by a
lecherous Baroness; unfortunately, when she tries to kill
her husband he kills her instead, and she dies without explaining that Leonard is locked up. Leonard, notwithstanding, makes his escape, in the course of which he falls
through a floor, accidentally puts his hand on a "clammy and
putrid" corpse, and has other mishaps. He also finds and
rescues Emma, killing Fitzallan, who tries to prevent their
escape. Fitzallan, dying, produces a confession which clar-
ifies family relationships: the murdered son of the recluse
Hildebrand was Leonard's father. As children, Leonard and

his sister were imprisoned in the Black Tower with their mother, who tied a miniature on him and dropped him from a window. Leonard is restored to his title and marries Emma; his sister Julia, the same Julia loved by his friend Edgar, is a friend of hers. The Black Tower is converted into a monastery.

124: Parsons, Eliza   ANECDOTES OF TWO WELL-KNOWN FAMILIES
       3 vols. London: T. N. Longman, 1798

Elinor reads romances and lives in the castle where her father is chaplain. A little foolish as a result of inexperience, she stands in contrast to both the sophistication of the lords and ladies and the plainspoken common sense of some of the servants. She wanders about the castle trifling with keys and cabinets, suspects that she has parents who will not own her, and fantasizes about a mysterious lover who has sent her a letter signed "Edmund." The tone of the first volume is best represented by the incident in which she discovers a miniature in a drawer — in which a servant is hunting for bile pills. The curious thing about the novel is that Elinor's view of the world proves to be essentially correct. The love letters are genuine and written by the son of the castle's new owners; he has been hiding in the house and flitting around the grounds, apparently from love of her, and in the end marries her. Further, she is discovered to be the child of Baron P (who earlier planned to seduce her) and his wife. Elinor turns out well and has a happy life.

125: Parsons, Eliza   CASTLE OF WOLFENBACH. A GERMAN STORY
       2 vols. London: William Lane, 1793

En route to Zurich, Matilda Weimar and her servant are forced by a storm to shelter in the Castle of Wolfenbach, said to be haunted. Matilda is not much daunted by the supernatural; what frightens her are the advances of her guardian/uncle, whom she is fleeing as the story begins. The aunt with whom she had planned to take refuge died before her arrival, so Matilda is on her way to another relative who may protect her. At the Castle of Wolfenbach she finds, living in secret, Victoria, Countess of Wolfenbach, a woman who is popularly supposed to be dead and who gives Matilda a letter of introduction to her sister in Paris. The next night the Countess has disappeared and her attendant is found murdered. Too weak to drag the body away or to dig a grave, Matilda and an elderly servant stuff the dead attendant into a chest.

Later, Victoria's sister in Paris tells Matilda that
their father forced the marriage to Wolfenbach, who had evidently abused a former wife into her grave. The lecherous
uncle follows Matilda to Paris. First he says that he is
not really her uncle and proposes; then he says that anyway
he is her guardian and tries to get her back.

The household goes to London, where they find the Countess Victoria, who tells a bloody story of how the Count
killed the man she truly and innocently loved, slowly, in
front of her eyes, and locked her in a closet with the body.
The shock induced labor, and her husband carried off the
baby but permitted her to live under a vow of secrecy, from
which a chaplain has just absolved her. Matilda's uncle,
still following her, arrives in London. She retreats to a
convent, but her uncle Weimar gets a king's order to take
her out, and they get on a boat for Germany. When attacked
by Turks he is led to confess that he really is her uncle
and that he killed her father out of jealousy. Matilda and
her mother are reunited, while Weimar grows pious and decides to be a monk. De Bouville chases her through half
a dozen countries to clear up a misunderstanding and marry
her. Count Wolfenbach, dying, repents and receives his
wife's forgiveness. He tells her that her son is alive and
signs papers to restore everyone to his proper situation.

126: Parsons, Eliza   THE HISTORY OF MISS MEREDITH. A NOVEL
     2 vols. London: Printed for the Author, and sold by
     T. Hookshaw, 1790

Harriet Meredith does not believe in love, so is willing to
marry Authur Williams, the son of an old friend, to please
her father. Emma Montague, her correspondent, is in love
with George Oldham, a libertine, and is prepared to lose
£25,000 by marrying without the consent of her parents.
Each girl fruitlessly tried to persuade the other out of
her folly. Emma's story is simple enough: her husband takes
all the money he can get and leaves her, after which she
goes abroad to avoid the humiliation of going home; her
mother pines and dies, and Emily at last comes penitently
back. Harriet and the Earl of Bleville are greatly attracted to one another, but too late, for she has promised herself to Williams. (Both Williams and Bleville write to and
confide in their friend Sir Edward Stanley.) Harriet's marriage is not easy: Williams becomes jealous and difficult,
resenting even Stanley; a villainous Lord Richmore contrib-
utes to his suspicions. At last Williams dies of a fever.
Stanley, who has married Emily's sister Isabella, tells
Bleville to come home and marry Harriet, which he does.

127: Parsons, Eliza   THE MYSTERIOUS WARNING. A GERMAN TALE
      2 vols. London: William Lane, 1796

Count Renaud, to please his family, marries a loud woman
whom he does not love. This union produces his first son,
Rhodophil. When his wife dies he marries Caroline, her more
desirable kinswoman, and Ferdinand is born. He has, as
well, a mistress of whom he tires after she has borne him
a daughter. As the novel begins, the boys, now grown, are
very different from each other; briefly, Rhodophil is bad,
Ferdinand good. But Rhodophil is so accomplished a hypocrite that Ferdinand fails to see through his displays of
fraternal affection. When Claudina, whom they both fancy,
chooses and marries Ferdinand, Rhodophil makes a show of
soliciting his father's pardon for Ferdinand's unprofitable
match. In fact, he manages to keep the two from reconciliation and causes Ferdinand to miss a deathbed blessing. Further, he hides the latest will and magnanimously buys Ferdinand a commission in the army. This enables him to keep
and seduce his sister-in-law. When Ferdinand comes home on
leave, a mysterious voice (belonging to Ernest the discerning servant) tells him to flee Claudina as he would sin and
death. She agrees that this warning is justified and goes
to a convent without letting Ferdinand know where.

    In the course of subsequent melancholy wandering, Ferdi-
nand finds and rescues a couple who for twelve years have
been locked in separate dungeons by a sadistic recluse. The
male victim, Count M--, becomes Ferdinand's companion after
his wife decides to go into a convent. They meet two girls,
one of whom (Louisa) has been victimized by wicked Count
Wolfran, who married, discarded, denied, and imprisoned her.
The other girl (Theresa D'Allenberg) is saved from a marriage to Wolfran by hearing Louisa's story. After they go
back to the army Ferdinand and Count M-- are captured by
Turks but later escape, bringing out of Turkey with them a
cooperative jailer named Heli and his favorite wife Fatima,
a particularly unscrupulous female who embarrassingly turns
out to be Ferdinand's illegitimate half-sister. Information
she drops seems to make clear that she is also Claudina's
sister. After a final crisis in which Heli and Wolfran
shoot each other and Ferdinand is jailed for murder and robbery, things begin to improve. Wolfran and Rhodophil die.
Heli goes home. Fatima kills herself. Claudina turns out
to be the daughter not of Renaud but of Count M--'s elder
brother. Both Claudina and Count M--'s wife die, whereupon
Ferdinand and the Count marry, respectively, Theresa and
Louisa.

128: Patrick, Mrs.   MORE GHOSTS!   3 vols. London: William
     Lane, 1798

Mary Morney lives in a Yorkshire abbey with her father and
Thomas Grey, a young man whom her father has raised and intends for her husband. They are constantly in the company
of Betsey Bolton, the vicar's daughter, who has an eye to
Thomas herself. Hoping to take Thomas away from Mary, she
contrives a story about seeing the ghost of Thomas's mother,
who sends him the message "Beware of incest!" She manages
to persuade him that his guardian Mr. Morney raped his
mother and that Mary is doubtless his half-sister. When he
confronts Mr. Morney with this fantasy Mr. Morney is highly
annoyed and says that if Thomas is such a great fool he will
not save Mary for him after all. Thomas's mother is Mr.
Morney's sister, who did something so bad that he helped her
leave the country. Thomas is sent away to college, and Mary
is exposed to a season in London. These expeditions into
the world are not altogether successful. Mary does not care
for men of fashion, especially since they at first think her
Mr. Morney's mistress and are rude to her, but she does meet
a nice clergyman named Mr. Seymour, whom she finally marries. She has a light attack of Modern Philosophy but gets
over it.
     Thomas drinks and gambles and goes to a fortune-teller,
wearing feminine clothing for a prank. What is worse, Betsey announces that she is pregnant, a plausible story, for
she came weeping to Thomas's room the night before he left
for college and managed to seduce him. When he refuses to
marry her, his guardian threatens to take him out of college
and apprentice him. He is extricated from this difficulty
at last by the admission of Mary's brother Charles that he
has had Betsey too, and that he knows her to have been plot-
ting to acquire Thomas.
     The "ghost" that has been making occasional appearances
in the abbey during the course of these social entanglements
is discovered to be Thomas's living mother. She has a complicated and bigamous history of her own, which resulted
in her taking the veil in a French convent, where she was
thought to have died. In fact, the nuns were evicted during the French Revolution and she found her way to her old
home, where she has been hiding ever since.

129: Pickersgill, Joshua, Jr.   THE THREE BROTHERS.
     A ROMANCE   4 vols. London: J. Stockdale, 1803

This plot is so complicated that it will be best to un-
tangle it from the start. The sequence of events is not
represented below, for much of the information is not re-

vealed until the end of the novel. The three brothers are Arnaud (later known as Julian), Louis (usually known as Claudio), and Henri.

Arnaud/Julian. As a child Arnaud is much petted by his parents. He is the eldest. Despite a sadistic streak he is a general favorite, for he is attractive, quick-witted, and articulate. When he is eight he is wounded by banditti and taken hostage; the robbers try to nurse him, but when his parents recover him he is a cripple, hunchbacked. He goes home to find that his younger brother Louis has supplanted him as favorite. When the family moves to France he stabs Louis and tells his parents that his brother has gone on with the servants. Some time after their arrival in France, his father casts him and his mother off, for his mother is only a kept woman, previously an escaped nun, and the Marquis wishes to bring home his real wife and legitimate son Henri. Children perpetually jeer at Arnaud for his deformity, and later his misery is intensified by the discovery that the only girl who is nice to him, and whom he consequently loves, is his father's courtesan. At last Arnaud decides to pursue evil and makes an arrangement with Satan whereby he acquires a new, handsome body, having discarded the old one and left it in a cave. He is thereafter called Julian and appears in the narratives of the other two brothers.

Louis/Claudio. Claudio is found and raised by peasants, along with a nobleman's daughter named Camilla. Their foster father, a bandit, sells Claudio as a page to their neighbor Larina. Time passes. Camilla is kidnapped by pirates on her wedding day. Claudio joins the army and is captured by Henri, who makes friends with him and takes his prisoner home. (It is here that the novel begins.) Claudio and Henri spend the night in a house belonging to a frightening and apparently supernatural Cavalier, who is in fact Julian. Henri sees his own family crest on the bedhangings. In the morning Henri is missing and Claudio is offered poison for breakfast but does not take it. Julian forces him to go to Genoa on some political errand by threatening that Henri's life will be forfeited if he does not. Later Claudio finds Camilla in a Moorish harem. He gets her out and brings her home and marries her, though it is fairly obvious that she does not at all dislike her foreign husband. Henri takes the couple in, but this domestic arrangement is not good, for he tries to seduce Camilla and she finally runs away, leaving the impression that she succumbed to him.

Henri. Henri's real adventures begin when he is imprisoned by Julian on his way home from the wars. His dungeon is in the house occupied by Larina, an associate of

Julian's, and the woman for whom Claudio once worked as a
page. Larina's current page, Laurian, loves his employer
so much that he tries to poison Henri, whom he sees as com-
petition. He is correct in his assessment, for Larina goes
about seducing Henri with an efficiency that is striking
even in a Gothic villainess. There is one remarkable scene
in which she clamps him into a torture chair of some kind
and sets about stirring him up. When Laurian's worst suspicions are realized, he hangs himself, and the guilty couple rather casually toss his body into the vault. (Claudio
later has the misfortune to thrust his hand into Laurian's
wormy chest cavity while he is hunting for Henri.) Henri
discovers his father wasting away in another of the building's several dungeons. When, after various complications,
Henri returns to society, he becomes more and more wicked,
despite Claudio's hopes of reforming him. Besides being a
libertine and a glutton, he grows violent and bloody and
even cuts his dying father's head off with a sword.

Circumstances bring the three brothers together again
near the end of the story. Julian is in so much trouble
that he decides to resume his old body and identity on the
one night when this deed may be done, but he needs fresh
blood, a human sacrifice. Claudio falls into his hands and
is taken to a cave. Actually, Julian appears to like Claudio a little and is almost hoping that someone will come by
to interrupt his plan. The person who comes by is Henri,
with an evil ecclesiastical confederate. When Claudio flees
to his protection, announcing that they are brothers, Henri
drags him back to the cave and shoots at him. Julian is
glad to have Henri, whom he hates, in his hands and forces
him to trample a crucifix before he kills him, as he wishes
his legitimate brother not only to die but to go to hell.
Claudio shoots at random and hits Julian, but the latter is
not angry and joins Claudio in his flight from the cave.
He is nursed by a priest to whom he confesses and is turned
over to the Inquisition. They condemn him to the rack, but
it is clear that only an ambulatory body is left when the
morning of his execution arrives. To the disappointment of
the audience, he does not even cry out, but there is a storm
that knocks down buildings, and the scaffold and body burn
together.

Claudio rediscovers Camilla, but their meeting is not a
happy reunion. Camilla is a penniless wanderer and carries
with her a black baby, child of her previous husband the
Moor. The child was apparently a factor in her earlier
departure from Henri's house. Claudio catches up with her
just as the peasants decide to throw the black baby around
to see if it can fly. It cannot, and lies in a mangled lump
at Claudio's feet as he catches up Camilla in his arms.

Pickersgill points out that anything further would be anticlimactic and stops the novel there, but several years later
he adds a note that tries without great success to draw a
moral from the story and adds that the strain of her vicissitudes was too much for Camilla, who was imbecile for the
rest of her life. Claudio could get near her only by stain-
ing his face brown so that he looked like the Moor and he
was too scrupulous to take sexual advantage of the illusion.
Camilla lived on with him, celibate and feebleminded, and he
supported them both by laboring in the Pyrenees.

130: Polidori, John William   ERNESTUS BERCHTOLD, OR, THE
     MODERN OEDIPUS. A TALE   1 vol. London: Longman, Hurst,
     Rees, Orme, and Brown, 1819

Ernestus and his twin sister Julia have been raised by the
priest Berchtold and Berchtold's married sister ever since
their mother died in childbirth. Ernestus has learned to
love heroism and public virtues but has little control over
his private passions. One day a beautiful woman (Louisa),
whom he meets by chance, inspires him to join the army,
where he meets her brother Olivieri, has various adventures
and close escapes, and gains popular fame. After Father
Berchtold dies, Ernestus and Julia make their home with Olivieri's father, Filberto Doni. Olivieri proves to be a libertine, seducing Julia and leading Ernestus into deep gaming. His father appears a kind and virtuous old man but is
involved in traffic with the occult; as we discover later,
he can ask his supernatural affiliate for money or other
forms of aid but for each favor gained must pay the price of
some domestic loss or pain.
    What with occultism and libertinism and seduction and
gaming, the Doni household is increasingly troubled: Julia
dies in childbirth; Olivieri is arrested as head of a band
of robbers and is condemned to die; Louisa is dying of consumption, after nursing a man whom Ernestus wounded in a
misguided quarrel. Despite her illness Louisa marries Ernestus and the couple experience a brief happiness. Then
they decide to decorate their quarters with portraits of
Louisa's father and Ernestus's mother, the latter newly
painted from a miniature. They think that the portraits
will surprise Louisa's father, as indeed they do, for he
realizes that the woman is his lost wife and the Berchtold
twins his own children. The final penalty exacted for his
occult dealings is the knowledge that his children have committed double incest. He writes a confessional autobiogra-
phy for Ernestus, supplying an account of the old man who
bequeathed him the fatal secrets of occult procedure, and a
description of the consequent chicanery and misunderstanding

in which he has been involved. At the end of the novel,
Ernestus, Louisa having died, is left a solitary penitent,
nursing visions of reunion with her in paradise.

131: Polidori, John William   THE VAMPYRE. A TALE   1 vol.
      London: Sherwood, Neely, and Jones, 1819

Aubrey travels with an older and interesting nobleman named
Lord Ruthven but later disapproves of and leaves him. Ruthven seems chiefly interested in ruining young men with gaming and young girls with debauchery. Aubrey begins to think
that Ruthven may be supernatural. Later Aubrey meets and
becomes attached to Ianthe, an innocent but well-informed
Greek girl, who tries to tell him about vampires. He does
not listen until a vampire, Lord Ruthven in fact, kills
Ianthe. Aubrey falls ill from shock and Ruthven nurses him.
Ruthven is wounded by robbers and, dying, makes Aubrey promise not to reveal his death for a year and a day. During
that period Ruthven appears and courts Aubrey's sister.
At the expiration of his oath Aubrey manages to tell about
Ruthven, but it is too late; the vampire has married the
girl and taken her away.

132: Porter, Anna Maria   ROCHE-BLANCHE, OR, THE HUNTERS
      OF THE PYRENEES. A ROMANCE   3 vols. London: Longman,
      Hurst, Rees, Orme, and Brown, 1822

The year is 1557. Eustache de la Marot de Roche-Blanche,
stepfather of the heroine, Aigline, has ludicrously deluded
notions of his attractiveness and of his literary and musical ability. His wife is shallow and unfeeling and makes
Aigline, her daughter by a previous marriage, wait on her
youngest child Celine, who is horribly spoiled. Their other
two children are away from home — Lolotte with a relative
and François with his tutor at Pau. Their neighbor Mr. Willoughby has one son, Clarence, who is Aigline's friend and
companion.
    Clarence dreams of knighthood and military glory; he
especially relishes tales about his hero Adhemar de Bourbon
and desires to go in the army. His father holds him back
until Clarence meets Adhemar on a wolfhunt and is invited
to join his troops. While Clarence is away, Lolotte comes
home. She is remarkably beautiful but behaves oddly — gal-
lops through the flower beds and says things that make no
sense. Aigline realizes that Lolotte is imbecile and adds
her care to her other domestic duties. Lolotte's imbecility
notwithstanding, Adhemar, having come home with Clarence,
falls in love with her, nor can he altogether overcome his
attraction after he assesses her condition. Clarence and

Aigline by this time realize that they are in love as well,
but Aigline's mother has made her promise to stay single and
take care of Celine. For a while things go badly for everyone: Clarence is seeking from the English government ac-
knowledgment of his legitimacy and arouses Queen Elizabeth's
ire; he and Adhemar become estranged; Aigline is pining; her
stepfather has to flee his creditors; Lolotte is put in a
convent — the family is Protestant, but Lolotte's parents
think she will not know the difference — to keep her away
from unscrupulous money-hunters, but she runs away and dies;
François loses his job as page; Celine has consumption.
Adhemar and Clarence are reconciled when the former dies
saving the latter's life. A man whom Aigline dreaded as a
suitor reveals himself to be interested in her only because
he is her uncle. Queen Elizabeth decides that Clarence is
entitled to the claims his father has made for him. The
lovers marry and Celine finally dies.

133: Radcliffe, Ann   THE CASTLES OF ATHLIN AND DUNBAYNE.
     A HIGHLAND STORY   1 vol. London: T. Hookham, 1789

The castle of Athlin is inhabited by the widow Matilda and
her children Osbert and Mary. When Osbert is old enough to
participate in the traditional feud against the house of
Dunbayne, he attacks the Baron Malcolm with the aid of his
friend Alleyn and is captured. The Baron covets Mary and
says she may be exchanged for Osbert, who will otherwise be
killed. Mary heroically consents to the exchange, though
she loves Alleyn, a relationship that is discouraged because
he is a peasant, despite his refinement.
    Meanwhile, Osbert has found a secret panel and gone ex-
ploring. He discovers Laura, a young woman with whom he
falls in love. She is locked up with her mother, who was
married to the late Baron, Malcolm's elder brother, and to
whom the castle should belong. Osbert escapes and is attacked at his castle by the Baron, who dying confesses that
Laura's brother is not dead after all. The Baroness sees a
birthmark and recognizes Alleyn as her missing son, so he
is permitted to marry Osbert's sister. Since Alleyn has
twice rescued Mary from kidnapping and has all the while
borne the snobberies of Osbert, it is no less than he de-
serves.

134: Radcliffe, Ann   GASTON DE BLONDEVILLE, OR, THE COURT
     OF HENRY III. KEEPING FESTIVAL IN ARDENNE   4 vols.
     London: Henry Colburn, 1826

Two English travelers go to see Kenilworth and there pur-
chase from an old man an illuminated manuscript apparently

from the period of Henry III. The convention of "finding"
the principal story in a manuscript is nothing new, but Ann
Radcliffe's use of the device is a little unusual. The manuscript is divided into day-by-day accounts of a period when
Henry kept festival in Ardenne, and each day is prefaced by
an illumination which the author describes in some detail.
She also discusses, after the Gaston de Blondeville plot has
run its course, whether the traveler has been correct in his
dating of the manuscript. I am not aware of any other novels that maintain the notion of the manuscript with compa-
rable scrupulosity.

Gaston de Blondeville, the King's favorite, is to marry
Barbara, one of the Queen's prettiest attendants. His felicity is broken by a merchant named Hugh Woodreeve, who accuses him of being a robber and the murderer of Sir Reginald
de Folville. He says that Blondeville has Folville's sword,
which has mysterious writing on its blade. Blondeville
makes counteraccusations. Although the author permits the
reader to believe Blondeville for a while, she makes it
clear long before the denouement that the merchant's accusation is justified. Woodreeve, who has no influence at
court, is imprisoned while the accusations are investigated;
Blondeville is not. However, he has trouble at his marriage
feast, which is beset by uninvited guests and unscheduled
pageants about robbery and murder. A stranger seen at the
wedding feast makes a number of appearances, during which
he points to an unmarked stone in the priory, bleeds three
drops from his forehead onto Blondeville's clothing, and so
on. The Prior, who is in league with Blondeville, tries to
make Woodreeve run away and inadvertently reveals around his
own neck a chain belonging to the murdered Folville. Woodreeve is accused of witchcraft in connection with his identification of the chain. The accusation is false, but the
chain appears to have some magical properties: when Blondeville takes it in his hand, the three drops of blood previously shed by the stranger spread all over the side of
his garment. Finally Blondeville is challenged to combat
by a knight (the stranger again) whose eyes flame through
his visor and whose sword bears messages in fire and blood.
The guilty knight faints and dies. Still Woodreeve is to be
executed, and the mysterious stranger comes yet again, demanding the merchant's release and showing the company where
to find his own bones. It is Reginald de Folville. Woodreeve is released. Henry III feels that he has had enough
of Kenilworth and never goes back.

135: Radcliffe, Ann   THE ITALIAN, OR, THE CONFESSIONAL
OF THE BLACK PENITENTS. A ROMANCE   3 vols. London:
T. Cadell, Jr., and W. Davies, 1797

Vincentio di Vivaldi falls in love with Ellena Rosalba, whom
he has seen in church. The attraction is reciprocal and Ellena's aunt permits Vivaldi's suit. His mother, however, is
outraged because Ellena has neither title nor wealth. Consequently, the Marchesa di Vivaldi and her evil confessor
Schedoni conspire to kidnap Ellena the week before Vivaldi
plans to marry her. When Vivaldi tries to go to Ellena's
house, a mysterious monk, who seems to be supernatural,
warns him away. Pursuing, the hero finds Ellena in a convent, where the Abbess is forcing her to take the veil. He
helps her escape, with the assistance of her friend Sister
Olivia. But their wedding is interrupted by men who claim
to be officers of the Inquisition and summon Vivaldi for abducting a nun. He is wounded and Ellena carried off again.
We know from a previous conversation that Schedoni has
agreed to kill her.

   Ellena is locked up in a derelict marble house near the
sea and guarded by an old man. When Schedoni comes to stab
her, he discovers that she is wearing a miniature of him as
a younger man and concludes that she is his daughter. That
being the case, he wants her to marry Vivaldi after all and
sets about freeing the prospective bridegroom from the cells
of the Inquisition. In the meantime, Vivaldi has been secretly told to ask certain questions at his trial; they result in Schedoni's being accused of fratricide and of the
violation and death of his brother's widow. Olivia turns
out to be the widow in question, not dead after all, and in
fact Ellena's mother. She assures Ellena that Schedoni is
not her father but her cruel uncle. Vivaldi's mother has
the decency to repent and die. Vivaldi and Ellena marry.

136: Radcliffe, Ann   THE MYSTERIES OF UDOLPHO. A ROMANCE
4 vols. London: G. G. and J. Robinson, 1794

Emily St. Aubert is so full of sensibility that her father
worries about it. When he dies during a family trip, he
cautions her on his deathbed about this weakness. She needs
the warning, for she is obliged to move in with a vain,
arrogant, and stupid aunt, who makes her life extremely un-
comfortable. The aunt quite unjustly suspects Emily of indiscretions and forbids her to see Valancourt, whom she met
during the trip with her father. She and Valancourt are in
love; their sensibilities are similar. At one point the
aunt has decided to permit their marriage, but then she her-

self makes a most indiscreet marriage to the villain Montoni and Emily's real troubles begin.

First the household moves to Venice, where her new uncle tries to force her into marriage with a man she dislikes. From there they move to the castle of Udolpho, which is full of passages, rumors, and unexplained ancestral scandals. Emily's difficulties at Udolpho include the discovery of corpses both real and waxwork, the misapprehensions that her aunt has been murdered and that Montoni is the captain of a bandit troop, the aunt's actual death from misery and neglect, and Montoni's determination to imprison Emily until she signs over her inheritance. Once she thinks that Valancourt is imprisoned in the room beneath hers, but when she falls into the arms of the captive he proves to be a stranger called Du Pont, also in love with her. (It was he who used to leave mysterious sonnets in the fishing house at her old home.) Du Pont rescues Emily from the castle and takes her to stay with friends of his. (The young lady of that family, Blanche, provides an interesting instance of a girl who comes to live in a decaying building accompanied by her entire family and consequently finds it pleasantly exciting.) Because an old servant sees in Emily a strong family resemblance to a former employer we are vouchsafed several stories about St. Aubert and his wife and sister, some of which put to rest unspoken anxieties of Emily's that her father had a guilty secret in his past. Valancourt reappears, but as he has acquired a taste for vicious pleasure Emily is prepared to renounce him. After he has cleared himself of some charges, repented of youthful follies, and been caught in acts of secret charity, Emily is reconciled to him and finds fulfillment in love.

137: Radcliffe, Ann   THE ROMANCE OF THE FOREST   3 vols.
    London: T. Hookham and J. Carpenter, 1791

Pierre de la Motte is in debt and obliged to leave Paris quickly if he wishes to avoid arrest. During their flight from Paris the La Mottes acquire a companion, the girl Adeline, who is thrust upon them at gunpoint by her cottager father. (Adeline is an involuntary participant; she was taken from the convent where she went to school by this father who seems not to want her.) They find a ruined abbey and decide to stay there, as their carriage is incapacitated by a broken wheel. The La Mottes are reunited with their soldier son Louis, who fortuitously discovers their hiding place.

The abbey seems a good refuge until the owner arrives; he is the Marquis de Montalt, with whom La Motte has evidently had previous dealings. He is accompanied by the

young chevalier Theodore, whom Adeline clearly likes. Louis
loves Adeline but his passion is not reciprocated. Montalt
wants Adeline too and employs La Motte to encourage her ac-
quiescence to his alternating propositions and proposals.
All this while there are other adventures and misunderstandings: Adeline finds a room with a bloodstained dagger and
the manuscript notes of a captive; Madame de la Motte thinks
Adeline is having an affair with her husband and is cold to
her. Finally Montalt kidnaps Adeline and takes her to a
plush establishment from which she is rescued by Theodore,
who has turned deserter for her sake. (The Marquis de Montalt is unfortunately his colonel.) The pair are full of
rectitude and try not even to talk about love during the
delicate circumstances of their escape. At an inn Theodore
is attacked and taken away by military police, and Adeline
is carried back by the servants of the Marquis.

The Marquis, when he sees the mark of a seal in Adeline's possession, loses his sexual ambitions and wants La
Motte to kill her instead. La Motte, however, is not altogether a bad man; he helps her to escape. At an inn at Sav-
oy she falls ill and is nursed by the La Luc family, with
whom she afterward lives. As it turns out, Theodore is La
Luc's son, and Louis arrives to explain that the young man
is in a military prison under sentence of death. There are
affecting scenes in the prison between Theodore and his ailing old father, but at the last moment a respite is granted
because Madame La Motte has written a letter bearing on Montalt's character. (At this time we discover that the Marquis was blackmailing La Motte for having once robbed him in
the forest.) Other answers are supplied. Adeline is really
the daughter of Montalt's elder brother, whose journal of
imprisonment she had read in the abbey; this conclusion is
not easily reached, for we briefly suppose her to be the
bastard child of Montalt and an Ursaline nun. His villainy
having been revealed, the Marquis de Montalt poisons himself
and Adeline inherits. Theodore is pardoned; he marries Adeline after a period of mourning for her real father. La
Motte is banished. La Luc's health improves. The La Luc
daughter marries a pleasant minor character, and Louis later
finds a suitable wife.

138: Radcliffe, Ann   A SICILIAN ROMANCE   2 vols. London:
     T. Hookham, 1790

Upon the death of his wife, Ferdinand (the Marquis of Mazzini) marries again and goes away with the bride and his
young son. His two daughters, Emilia and Julia, are left
at the castle to be educated and overseen by Madame de Menon, an old friend of their mother's. They are attractive

and talented young ladies with little chance at society; Julia especially — she is livelier — is delighted when Ferdinand comes home with his entourage to give a coming-of-age party for his boy. Julia and Count Vereza fall in love right away. This does nothing to endear Julia to the new Marchioness, who is an adulterous sort and has long had her own eye on Vereza. (She has been doing typical stepmother tricks as well — moving the girls to a shabbier set of rooms so that she can have theirs, ignoring their complaints of spectral noises in their new quarters, etc.) The Marquis wants Julia to marry the Duke de Luovo, who is cold and tyrannical; her brother urges her to escape by eloping with his friend Vereza. The execution of the latter scheme is interrupted by the Marquis, who stabs Vereza and puts Ferdinand Jr. in a dungeon. Julia runs away.

The pursuit of Julia by her father and would-be husband is fraught with complications, including the temporary capture of the Duke by a bandit chief revealed to be his own runaway son. At one point the Marquis and Duke capture the wrong girl and are obliged to let her go, while Julia is captured and let go by the pursuing father of the other young lady. She and Madame de Menon, who has left the Marquis's employ upon discovering the Marchioness's infidelity, take refuge in a convent. There they find Vereza's sister; she has been crossed in love and dies. The Abate of the convent succumbs to the Marquis's threats and gives Julia a choice between the Duke and taking the veil without a novitiate, so young Ferdinand is obliged to find and rescue her. Vereza is still alive. Back in the castle, after further complications of escape and capture, Julia discovers that her mother is alive, having been imprisoned, and has been responsible for the ghostly moans in the dungeons. Faced with the embarrassment of two living wives, the Marquis resolves to poison the first one. At the same time he discovers the infidelity of the second and is consequently poisoned by her. She afterward stabs herself. The first wife, having escaped the homicidal machinations of her husband, is discovered by her son Ferdinand to be safe and alive and staying with Julia and Vereza in a lighthouse.

139: Radcliffe, Mary Ann   MANFRONÉ, OR, THE ONE-HANDED
      MONK. A ROMANCE   4 vols. London: J. F. Hughes, 1809

This is a complicated and not very skillful tale of intrigue, with lots of dungeons, passages, rescues, and assassinations. The heroine Rosalina is subjected to four kidnappings, two imprisonments, two attempted rapes, and four miscellaneous attacks. Small wonder that she sits in church reflecting on the "instability of human grandeur." Most of these attacks come from the Prince di Manfroné, alias Grimaldi, alias Romellino, whom her father wishes her to marry in discharge of a debt; a few of the attacks (but none of the rapes) are by her father himself, who has had a long career of treachery and bloodshed. Rosalina's lover is Montalto, whose father we discover to be not, as suspected, dead, but imprisoned by Rosalina's father, the Duca di Rudolpho. Rosalina has a bad time with weddings, too. A forced marriage to Manfrone is thwarted by a specter in monk's garb who refuses to perform the ceremony. A private marriage to Montalto is thwarted by an attack on the monk and the kidnapping of Rosalina. (No matter; we know later that the monk was no clergyman at all, but Manfroné. The marriage would not have been valid.) When Rudolpho finally decides to encourage the marriage, both he and Montalto are stabbed on the eve of it, the former fatally. The principal villain of the story — both fathers of the couple are fairly villainous as well — is Manfroné, later disguised as the monk of the subtitle; he lost his hand during an early rape attempt on Rosalina, when her father, not recognizing him, cut it off. The skeletal hand is later found wrapped about the dagger in Rudolpho's breast. Manfroné almost wins, for he locks Rosalina up at the end of the novel — if she does not consent to marriage at the end of a week, he will rape her — but on the climactic night Montalto rescues her just in time, and they end happily.

140: Reeve, Clara   THE EXILES, OR, MEMOIRS OF THE COUNT
     DE CRONSTADT   3 vols. London: T. Hookham, 1788

As the subtitle suggests, the Count de Cronstadt's adventures are principal to this epistolary novel, though Reeve devotes some space as well to his two friends and correspondents, J. S. Berkeley and Monsieur de Courville. De Cronstadt's father, turned out by his family for marrying a social inferior, died prematurely, as did his wife and all his children except the hero. After the death of his parents, de Cronstadt was taken in by his paternal uncle, a not unkindly miser and alchemist, who immediately forbade clandestine marriage on pain of disinheritance. But one day de Cronstadt rescued a beautiful cottage girl, Jacqueline Volker, from sexual assault. He and Jacqueline fell in love, despite her mother's anxieties about class difference, and somehow passion, misunderstandings, and good intentions combined to lead him into the very circumstances he was supposed to avoid. His clandestine marriage has been happy, and De Cronstadt has managed to escape his uncle's attempts to matchmake. But when the correspondence of the novel takes place, matters have been intolerably complicated by

De Cronstadt's marrying his general's daughter Melusina; he
has succumbed to social and professional pressures despite
his love for Jacqueline and their little boy Frederic. The
difficulties of maintaining two good marriages are aggravated by Peter-Paul Schneider, a vengeful and blackmailing
servant (earlier dismissed by De Cronstadt) who wants Jacqueline for himself. Schneider finally destroys her, first
sending her into a decline by telling her about De Cronstadt's bigamy and then sending her into shock by brandish-
ing a pistol. De Cronstadt pursues and kills him but in
the process is fatally wounded. His will amply provides for
both of his families, his uncle having previously died in an
alchemical mishap and left De Cronstadt his fortune.

141: Reeve, Clara   THE OLD ENGLISH BARON   1 vol. First
     published as THE CHAMPION OF VIRTUE. Colchester:
     W. Keyner, 1777

Sir Philip Harclay discovers when he comes home from the
wars that his friend Lord Lovel is dead and that Lovel's estate is in the hands of the Lord Baron Fitz-Owen. Edmund
Twyford, a cottager whom Fitz-Owen has taken into his family
and educated, reminds Harclay of his lost friend and so wins
his heart that, after making an unaccepted offer to adopt
him, he promises Edmund his protection at any time. Later
Edmund comes to need it, both because the Baron's jealous
nephews try to bring his name to dishonor and because he begins to have odd suspicions about his parentage. As a trial
of courage, Edmund is sent by his foster father to sleep for
three nights in an apartment said to be haunted, it having
been the scene of some shocking murders connected to the
late Lord Lovel's family. He is visited by the ghosts of
his real parents, Lord and Lady Lovel, an experience that
is reinforced by the conversation of a faithful old servant
and a priest who wish to see Edmund come into his own, and
by further if less spectacular supernatural encouragement.
He discovers that he was born out of doors as his mother
was fleeing from the scene of his father's murder and was
brought to his foster mother by the man who found his mother's corpse. Although Edmund is distressed that his benefactor the Baron should feel some part of the disgrace
attendant upon the fall of the murderous kinsman who sold
him Lovel's estate, he goes to Sir Philip Harclay for aid in
establishing his rights. Harclay challenges the usurper and
wounds him, causing him at last to confess to the murder of
Edmund's father. When Edmund returns home the doors of the
castle spontaneously fly open to receive him. After he has
given proper Christian burial to the bones of his parents,
he is married to Emma, the Fitz-Owen daughter, with whom he

has for some time been in love. He settles down on the family estate and lives a long and happy life with his family and friends.

142: Reeve, Clara   THE SCHOOL FOR WIDOWS. A NOVEL   3 vols.
     London: T. Hookham, 1791

Mrs. Strictland hears that her old friend Mrs. Darnford, whom she is trying to find, is living in a haunted house and taking care of a madwoman. The two widows correspond; their letters, describing the difficulties of their marriages, supply the greater part of the narrative. Mrs. Darnford's husband was affectionate but dissolute. In debt as a result of profligate living, he tried to sell Mrs. Darnford (or rent her, perhaps) to his friend Lord A, and in retaliation she left him. After his death she worked for a while as a governess and then started a little school; everywhere she went she left people influenced for the better, girls set up in honest trade, and so on.

Captain Maurice, the father of one of Mrs. Darnford's pupils, asked her to take care of mad Isabella during his absence. Isabella and her late husband Don Antonio escaped together from monastic life and were close friends with Captain Maurice. Don Antonio after a time became strange and withdrawn and at last died of a beating administered by Maurice in self-defense; Isabella has been mad since his death. She buttons his clothes over a chair and talks to them. Maurice loves her but has not taken sexual advantage of her dependence.

Mrs. Strictland's husband was the opposite of Mrs. Darnford's — he had no vices except avarice but was exceedingly disagreeable. After their wedding he took her home to Woodlands, a purportedly haunted old house where she felt imprisoned. The Strictlands finally achieved a kind of marital truce, despite Mrs. Strictland's patronage of the child Reginald Henry Marney, said to be the rightful heir to Woodlands, whom her husband beat for begging at the door. Mr. Strictland's will is fairly equitable but raises obstacles to her remarrying.

At the end of the novel an uncle arrives to provide for Reginald, Isabella gets a new keeper, and the principal characters still living retire happily to Woodlands, which no longer feels gloomy.

143: Reeve, Clara   THE TWO MENTORS. A MODERN STORY
     2 vols. London: Charles Dilly, 1783

Edward Saville's guardian, Richard Munden, wishes to make him a man of the world, i.e., something of a rake. To this

purpose he sends Edward to visit the racy Lady Belmour, who
guarantees to loosen his principles. Edward's virtue is
preserved by his own sound judgment, though he does not perhaps walk quite so straight a line as his old tutor, the
Reverend Mr. Jarvis Jones, would like. Jones writes him
affectionate and morally improving letters that provide a
nice counterpoise to Lady Belmour's influence. Edward makes
friends with Sukey Jones, Lady Belmour's goddaughter, formerly ruined by Lord C but now reformed and penitent. At
one point Lady Belmour waggishly locks the pair in a bedroom
overnight; they spend the night in conversation but pretend
to have made love, thus satisfying their hostess's expectations.

       After Edward goes to stay with another acquaintance,
Sukey keeps him informed of the machinations of the Belmour
set, a kindness especially useful after one Belmour disci-
ple, a Lord S, kidnaps Sophia Melcombe, to whom Edward has
just proposed. Sophia is locked up with Miss Freewill, who
has been kidnapped by Lord S's friend Clayton, until the
girls are rescued by Edward and his friend Mr. Elliot, who
covets Miss Freewill. The whole kidnapping episode is unusually cheerful; for instance, the notes that the rescuers
lift to the girls' window rhyme ("Be of good cheer/ Relief
is near"), as do the girls' replies. In the end Edward marries Sophia and Mr. Elliot marries Miss Freewill, who is a
little fast but has money.

144: Reeve, Sophia   THE MYSTERIOUS WANDERER   3 vols.
     London: Printed for the author by C. Spilsbury, 1807

As much of the story depends upon events already past, an
early explanation of histories will be useful.
       Frederick Howard's father and uncle are on bad terms,
having quarreled over their father's will and other matters.
Frederick has been given by his father to Captain Howard,
the uncle, not out of generosity but because the father
feels that the pair are disgustingly similar — upright,
good-tempered, etc.
       Captain Howard as a young man flirted with an ugly spin-
ster named Deborah Tangress, who subsequently proposed to
him. His father and brother pressed him into an intolerable
marriage with her. Later he left her and met, loved, and
bigamously married Ellenor. When Deborah pursued him to his
new home, Ellenor, pregnant, ran away, telling the Captain
to look her up after Deborah's death but not before.
       Tilton is an old friend of the Captain's. He has been
struggling to retain an inheritance in the Barbados. He
supplies useful pieces of information, including the tale of
       Holly Howard, who was married under duress to Sir Horace

Corbet. Sir Horace became a domestic tyrant, while the man
Holly really loved died of a broken heart. Since her husband's death her son has been behaving unkindly toward her
and has at last run away.

The mysterious wanderer of the title is a desperate
seventeen-year-old who asks protection from Captain Howard
and begs to come on board his ship, the *Argo*. He says that
he is Henry St. Ledger and sticks to this story, though the
Captain questions him closely, secretly hoping — the boy
looks like Ellenor — that Henry is his son. Later the Captain discovers that his fugitive is young Sir Henry Corbet
and tells him that he will have to go home. Sir Henry
leaves and apparently drowns, a circumstance the more pain-
ful for the Captain since a letter left behind by the boy
demonstrates that he has seen Ellenor and might have effected a reunion. At last Ellenor is recovered and Deborah
conveniently dies. The shocker of the story is that Sir
Henry (he is still alive and Ellenor is his aunt) had good
reason for abandoning his sorrowing mother — she destroyed
the will by which he would have inherited, locked him up,
planned to have him declared insane, and once threatened his
life with a knife. Her confederate is the steward, by whom
she was pregnant when she married Sir Horace. The fruit of
that union was a girl, Louisa, with whom Sir Henry has been
falling in love. Even at the end of the novel the steward
tries to kill Sir Henry with a chisel (a nice touch; his
name is Mallett) but is prevented. The wicked mother runs
away and later dies of fever. The virtuous find suitable
mates.

145: Robinson, Mary   VANCENZA, OR, THE DANGERS OF CREDULITY
     2 vols. London: Printed for the Authoress, 1792

Elvira, raised by Count Vancenza and his sister the Marchioness as a companion to his daughter Carline, is known as
"The Rose of Vancenza." One day Prince Almanza, son of the
Count's old friend, is wounded in a boar hunt and brought
to the castle by his companion, the Duke Del Vero. Elvira
binds up his wound with a magic veil and heals him; she also
falls in love with him. Hence, when she hears a passionate
voice under her window asking for a tryst, she hopes it is
the Prince and agrees. Upon discovering that she has made
an assignation with the Duke by mistake, she falls ill from
embarrassment; the Duke wishes to forget the incident too,
for she is after all lower class. When the household goes
to Madrid, Carline is pursued by the Marquis Petrozi, a
flattering snake who presently tries to kidnap her. Her father prevents the abduction but is wounded by the Marquis's
poisoned dagger and dies, leaving Elvira a mysterious key.

At home again, Elvira keeps fruitlessly trying her key in all the locks. She also spends time in contemplation of a melancholy poem scratched on a castle window by some anonymous mother and begins to worry about living on the charity of the Marchioness. Her plans to work are interrupted by a misunderstanding (the Marchioness thinks that Elvira fancies the Duke) which when resolved ends in a proposal from the Prince. Decorating for the wedding, Elvira finds behind a picture in the gallery a little panel with a lock that her mysterious key fits. Inside is a golden casket containing a red velvet case containing in turn a manuscript by Elvira's mother, who also wrote the poem on the window. The details of her mother's confession make it clear that the Prince is Elvira's half-brother. The mere sight of the wedding decorations makes her shudder now, and she lies down and dies in a matter of hours. Carline, some years later, goes into a nunnery. The Prince, who never has any notion why all this is happening, goes into the army. And the Marchioness, having erased all the family names from the manuscript, gives it to the University of Naples library.

146: Roche, John Hamilton   A SUFFOLK TALE, OR, THE PER-
    FIDIOUS GUARDIAN   2 vols. London: Printed for the
    Author, 1810

Marshall Duroc leaves France for political reasons and goes to live in Ireland as De Claridge. His son Alfred, at a military academy, makes an exceedingly bad friend — William O'Connor, who plans to be a doctor. Alfred becomes a soldier and is stationed near William, to whom he confides his love for Louisa, a beautiful cottage girl. William advises seduction rather than marriage, but Alfred proposes and goes to tell his family. When his father refuses consent, Alfred and Louisa run off to Gretna Green. William, who wrote a misleading letter to Alfred's father and thus helped dissuade him from giving his consent, continues to make epistolary trouble in hopes of becoming Alfred's guardian, in charge of paying out his allowance. He gets his chance when Alfred goes into foreign service at his father's request, having been promised a later family reconciliation. William is now in a position to defraud Alfred of both affection and property.
    Alfred and Louisa go to Fredericton, New Brunswick, where Louisa dies of what sounds like pneumonia. During their absence De Claridge dies of a broken heart. When Alfred, who has been pining and writing poetry about Louisa's death, goes home on leave, he finds that William's house is remarkably elegant for a village apothecary's and begins to suspect some financial fraud; when he asks for an account,

William has him arrested for debt. His imprisonment causes
his mother to die of shock, and William will not even let
him out to bury her. After several months of imprisonment
Alfred becomes mildly insane, finally killing himself.
Nothing happens to William except that he is not happy, for
nobody likes him.

147: Roche, Regina Maria   BRIDAL OF DUNAMORE, AND, LOST
    AND WON   3 vols. London: A. K. Newman, 1823

Bridal of Dunamore: In this exceedingly complicated novel
Roche traces the Glenmorlie family through six generations
and an unlikely number of pages to focus at last upon Rosalind, who does nothing spectacular. Dunamore, in Ireland,
is part of the Glenmorlie inheritance and the cause of a
long-lasting rift in the family. The first Earl of Dunamore
was twice married and had a son by each marriage. His second wife persuaded him to pass over his elder boy Rodolphus
in favor of her own son George. In the succeeding generations, right-thinking descendants of George adopt or otherwise nurture descendants of Rodolphus, whose side of the
family is prone to hard luck. The family tree becomes more
and more complex and at last a Colonel Glenmorlie sires the
heroine.
    Rosalind and her friend Anna Woodburne have a busy so-
cial life which occupies the later part of the novel. Rosalind visits people (e.g., the shipwrecked Countess of Mont-
eagle), explores an abbey, and receives a number of suitors,
many of whom briefly appear to be the one she will marry,
and one of whom commits suicide upon losing her. At last
she marries a Lord Dunamore, presumably from the other side
of the family, a man formerly engaged to her friend Anna.
Both Rosalind and her husband die not long after their marriage, leaving her father Colonel Glenmorlie the only remaining heir to Dunamore.
    Lost and Won: When Emily St. Orme's stepfather Mr. El-
more goes to America in hopes of making money, Emily decides
to stay with her mother's cousins, the O'Brady family. Emily is a snob (a fault that will be rectified in the course
of the novel) and finds the O'Brady household rather second
rate. She is attracted to the Duke of Holmsdale, whom she
meets on a walk, and sees him several times but is disillusioned about his intentions after one nocturnal tryst. Subsequently she goes to stay with the Tibbs family, relatives
of Mrs. O'Brady's who have the advantage of living in London. They introduce her to Mr. Villers, who is smitten,
but he is a tradesman and Emily despises trade. After a
social season during which Emily snubs old and new acquain-
tances and is in turn snubbed by others, as opportunity af-

fords, she is faced with accumulating bills and is obliged to take a job as governess with the Somers family. In that position she once again meets Mr. Villers, whom she had encountered intermittently throughout the story, and, despite the efforts of Miss Somers to secure him for herself and the pursuit of Emily by Sir Marmaduke, they finally marry. Mr. Elmore returns from America and lives with them.

148: Roche, Regina Maria   THE CASTLE CHAPEL. A ROMANTIC
    TALE   3 vols. London: A. K. Newman, 1825

After the death of his wife, O'Shaughnessy O'Neill discovers that he can buy back a decayed castle formerly owned by his family. He moves into it with his two children, Eugene and Grace, and his sister, Miss Agnes Flora Judith, who is put in charge of their education. The children are likeable and high-spirited, their aunt well meaning but highly eccentric. She is a great believer in phrenology and decides that if she can shave the children's growing heads and fit them with metal caps their cranial bumps will be certain to turn out on the most desirable pattern. When she suggests this, Eugene is convulsed with laughter, Grace furious. But Miss Agnes Flora Judith is a determined woman and persuades the local barber/apothecary to drug and shave Grace, who faints from rage and horror when she sees herself in the morning. Family relationships are strained for some time. Eugene, who goes as a midshipman, is also affected by his aunt's teaching; he is at one point court-martialed but let off because his examiners find his phrenological justifications so lunatic.

While Eugene is away, Grace acquires as a companion the miller's daughter, Rose. Eugene, home again, falls in love with Rose and persuades her to make private vows of their own devising, though the pair delay both marriage and consummation. At about this time in the story the villain enters; he is Mr. Mordaunt, former owner of the castle, who has stored things in some unused rooms. Rose and Grace, influenced by romance-reading, peep into his storerooms and imagine, when one night they see three men bury a chest in an excavated grave, that the chest contains bones and that Mr. Mordaunt is involved in the business. The author's tone suggests to the reader (certainly to this reader) that the girls are having Radcliffean fantasies. Nevertheless the chest does contain bones, the bones of Mordaunt's wife; not liking her, he impulsively put laudanum among her medicines as she recovered from childbirth, and she died of it as he had half intended. The child (Rose, we discover later) was taken away by a nurse. Mordaunt is shocked and confused to discover his daughter still alive — he had been told that

she was dead — and kidnaps her with the apparent and para-
doxical intent of restoring her rights. At any rate he proposes to provide for her by marrying her to Eugene, whom he
has earlier persecuted to the extent of having him falsely
accused of murder. Rose, however, has all along felt so
guilty about her indiscreet vows to Eugene that she has once
tried to kill herself, and these feelings of shame are now
aggravated by the acquisition of a homicidal father. Mordaunt takes her at her request to a furnished cottage in
North Wales, whence she wanders off to be brought back in a
hearse, dead of a broken heart. Eugene goes away to fight
for Greece.

Grace, in the meantime, has been having difficulties of
a lighter sort. While little more than a child she promised
herself to the orphan William Delamore, her friend, who was
leaving for the East Indies. She was not in love with him
but found the exchange of letters and locks of hair divert-
ing. The William who returns some years later is an impressive figure, and Grace is obliged to fight for him against a
scheming and unscrupulous rival. She is never in much danger of losing him, but there are misunderstandings which delay for a while their happy ending.

149: Roche, Regina Maria   THE CHILDREN OF THE ABBEY.
     A TALE   4 vols. London: William Lane, 1796

Fitzalan, scion of a once illustrious and lately impoverished Irish family, fell in love with and secretly married
Malvina, the Earl of Dunreath's daughter. The machinations
of Malvina's stepmother and stepsister Augusta caused the
Earl to disown Malvina and precipitated her early death.
The adventures of Fitzalan and Malvina's two children, Oscar
and Amanda, especially the latter, provide the substance of
the story.

As the story begins, Amanda leaves home to escape the
advances of Colonel Belgrave, a libertine who is both her
brother's commanding officer and her father's creditor. She
goes to stay with her old nurse in North Wales, where she
soon meets Lord Mortimer, the son of her father's old friend
the Earl of Cherbury. The rest of the plot is concerned
principally with the vicissitudes of Amanda and Mortimer's
relationship (which quickly identifies itself as love) and
the survival of Amanda's reputation under the assaults of
jealousy, malice, scandalmongering, and so on. The principal antagonists (besides Belgrave, who continues to be a
villain) are Amanda's aunt Augusta and cousin Euphrasia;
the latter is an unpleasant and ill-favored girl whose fortune the Earl of Cherbury wishes to annex by marrying her
to Mortimer. Toward the end of the novel, just when all the

malicious rumors have been cleared away and Amanda has real
hope of marrying Mortimer, Cherbury secretly tells her that
he will kill himself if she does not give up his son, for
he needs a rich daughter-in-law to extricate him from gaming
debts. Amanda concurs and further misunderstandings result,
but Euphrasia elopes with someone else at the last moment
and dies when her carriage falls over a precipice, and Cherbury confesses his interference with Amanda, so Amanda and
Mortimer are able to marry.

Oscar, Amanda's brother, has fallen in love with Adela
Honeywood, his general's daughter, and has watched her
endure an unhappy marriage to Belgrave. Oscar is court-
martialed for dueling Belgrave over a matter of excessively
severe military discipline, but at last he too has a happy
ending. Belgrave takes to drink and dies in mental agony,
leaving Adela free to remarry. Further, Oscar ceases to be
penniless, for during some of her own difficulties Amanda
goes, with a family to whom she is governess, to stay at
Dunreath Abbey, her mother's family home. (It is during the
abbey visit that identifiably "Gothic" scenes take place.)
There she encounters and briefly mistakes for a specter her
stepgrandmother, who has been locked away by her own thank-
less daughter Augusta. The old woman produces her husband's
real will, previously concealed, by which Amanda and Oscar
inherit through their mother.

150: Roche, Regina Maria   CLERMONT. A TALE   4 vols. Lon-
     don: William Lane, 1798

Madeline Clermont is brought up in a cottage by her father,
who is clearly of good blood but has withdrawn from society.
He later gives her into the protection of the Countess de
Merville, an old friend. Madeline falls in love with De
Sevigne, who is full of sensibility; unfortunately he behaves oddly and seems, like the Countess, to have a private
grief. One problem with De Sevigne is his poverty. The
Countess promises to give Madeline a good dowry if the young
man can produce a respectable reason for his being poor —
he must not, for instance, be a peasant or an ex-gamester
— but he fails to cooperate.

The Countess is fatally wounded by an assassin sent by
her son-in-law D'Alembert, but her daughter Viola, who is
not responsible for the wickedness of her husband, becomes
friends with Madeline. The lives of the characters at this
period are further stimulated by disturbing noises and tales
of ghosts. Suddenly D'Alembert arrives with three carriages
full of roisterers and pursues Madeline despite Viola's efforts to keep her out of sight. Someone poisons the old

servant Agatha. After a terrifying experience of fleeing
and being caught on a hook in the dark, Madeline is told to
escape to her father. Young Clermont appears and recites a
complicated story of disinheritance and frustrated love, the
gist of which is that he has been done out of his rights on
a charge of illegitimacy and must clear his mother's name.
Madeline begins to entertain some suspicion that her father
has murdered his half-brother Lord Philippe (whose picture
looks like De Sevigne).

After Viola dies, D'Alembert proposes to Madeline; she
is blackmailed into accepting. Her father admits that he
did kill his brother, having been deluded into thinking that
the brother had wronged him, and that while he was hiding,
Madeline's mother gave birth and died. When Madeline hears
a rumor that Viola is still alive, she refuses D'Alembert,
and her father goes to secrete himself in the wilds. Her
servant Lafroy, under pretense of helping her escape, decoys
her to Paris and into D'Alembert's clutches. Just when
things are worst, De Sevigne comes to the rescue and proves
to be the son of Clermont's murdered brother, who did not,
after all, die of his wounds. Lord Philippe is restored to
his elderly father. Lafroy confesses his considerable involvement in all the villainy. D'Alembert commits suicide,
while his father, who helped with the villainy, goes to
a monastery. Viola is not dead after all and remarries.
Madeline and De Sevigne marry too and live happily.

151: Roche, Regina Maria   CONTRAST   3 vols. London:
      A. K. Newman, 1828

There are two pairings in this novel, one of which ends happily, one unhappily. Horatio de Montville and Adelaide have
a happy ending, after some tensions and complications, for
Adelaide is both the girl Horatio's godfather wishes him
to marry and the nameless girl whom he discovered confined
to a crumbling villa and instantly loved. For Helena and
Mountflorence, whose father and mother, respectively, have
just married each other and are now matchmaking for their
children, a promising beginning comes to no good. Helena
marries Mountflorence reluctantly, though she appears to
love him; the wedding is full of ill omens — the bride
faints, the bridegroom loses the ring and discovers it outside on a tombstone. The problem is that Helena was previously married to an unpleasant man whom she believed to
be drowned in a shipwreck, along with all witnesses to their
marriage. Having unexpectedly seen him alive, she runs
away, forgetting to leave the explanatory note that she has
written to Mountflorence. Although her first husband really

does die subsequently, Helena is ignorant of this and dies too. Mountflorence is grief stricken and has nothing to look forward to except the Resurrection.

152: Roche, Regina Maria   THE DISCARDED SON, OR, HAUNT
     OF THE BANDITTI. A TALE   5 vols. London: Lane,
     Newman, 1807

Captain Robert Munro is gifted but has not made a success of his life. He has been cast off by his father (owner of Castle Glengary) for marrying a Spanish girl; her parents have disowned her as well. Munro resorts to farming in an attempt to support his wife and children — they have two, Osmond and Elizabeth — and to pay his son's Oxford fees. Their lives go on in ordinary ways (except that there are rumors of local ghosts) until Lord O'Sinister arrives in the neighborhood. He restores the Captain to military life with a post in the militia and assumes Osmond's university expenses, in exchange for which the Captain signs a bond. Elizabeth is proposed to by an older man, Mr. Eaton, and meets a handsome young stranger, Captain Delacour, in some ruins. Delacour rescues her when someone throws a lighted brand through her window. When an anonymous note warns her against an unnamed villain, her mother thinks that the villain may be Delacour, but Elizabeth hopes that it is Mr. Eaton. Soon Elizabeth is kidnapped by a ruffian claiming to have been hired by Delacour and is rescued by Eaton, who persuades her to marry him in gratitude. The wedding (in a ruined chapel) is interrupted by a figure in gray who announces that Eaton is Lord O'Sinister. Later Elizabeth finds herself subject to the advances of a second villain, Mr. Ruthven; they are guests together at a place called Black Crag, and although Ruthven keeps grabbing her, Elizabeth is afraid to go home, for her father is away and Lord O'Sinister is not.

O'Sinister is making trouble for Osmond too. Rather than giving him the living he promised he wishes to send the young man to Jamaica. Osmond avoids Jamaica by accepting a post as chaplain on Delacour's ship and has assorted adventures — banditti, kidnapping, imprisonment. He and a Miss Cordelia Raymond fall in love, but Osmond's discovery that her father is Lord O'Sinister, whom he has just wounded in a duel, conjures up an apparently unconquerable hindrance to their marriage. Meanwhile Captain Munro has been imprisoned for his debt to O'Sinister and the only way to free him seems to be in Elizabeth's hands: she reluctantly agrees to marry a man who offers in return to get her father out of jail. Just in time Signor Barbarino, Mrs. Munro's father, arrives and releases his son-in-law. So Elizabeth marries

Delacour after all, and Lord O'Sinister dies penitent (from
another duel), telling Cordelia to marry Osmond.

153: Roche, Regina Maria   THE MAID OF THE HAMLET. A TALE
        2 vols. London: Long, 1793

After Matilda's parents die in America, where her father
was sent on military duty, she is adopted by their dearest
friend, Mr. Belmore. Mr. Belmore has lost his patrimony to
a distant relative who discovered some long-lost and pertinent papers, but he and Matilda are not destitute. They
move to a smaller house and in the new neighborhood find two
particularly interesting men. The first is Bromley — young,
elegant, and sexually unscrupulous. He has designs on Matilda and pursues her unremittingly despite her lack of
response and, later, her change in marital status. Roche
presents from time to time evidence of Bromley's earlier
escapades, e.g., a discarded woman with three children, a
spaniel once given him by a woman he ruined.
    More interesting than Bromley is the recluse Charles
Howard, said to be mad, proved to be philanthropical, and
clearly attracted to Matilda despite his disillusionment
with women. He has some reason to be jaundiced, for he is
married to, though apparently not living with, an especially
perfidious woman, formerly the wife of his friend Pelham.
(She told him that she was a widow, when in fact she was
divorced.) Matilda likes Howard very much, but while he
is away with the army she marries Hartland, a friend of her
guardian's, more from amiability than from love. In the
end, however, Hartland dies and Howard's wife is drowned
in a shipwreck, so Matilda and Howard marry each other.

154: Roche, Regina Maria   NOCTURNAL VISIT. A TALE
        4 vols. London: William Lane, 1800

In the hamlet of Wyefield, between Chester and Holywell,
lives the virtuous curate Mr. Greville. He has brought up
with his own family a young female named Jacintha; there is
some mystery about the girl which Mr. Greville will not reveal, even to his wife. Mrs. Greville would be a bad depos-
itory for delicate secrets in any case, for she dislikes
Jacintha, partly because the child outshines her own daughter Gertrude, and is cruel to her as often as possible. One
Christmas when Jacintha and Gertrude make their annual visit
to their friends the Franklands, Jacintha, then seventeen,
attracts the honorable intentions of Egbert Oswald, second
son of the Marquis of Methwold. Greville, although he approves of the match, insists that the marriage wait until
Egbert comes of age. Jacintha worries about the London

charms of a visiting Miss Woodville, Egbert about the approaching stay of the local nobleman Lord Gwytherin, an
attractive libertine. Mr. Greville tries to keep all his
family away from the dangerous pleasures of the castle, but
Gwytherin's attempts on Jacintha are so pressing that Egbert
in desperation undertakes to carry her off to Scotland for a
fast wedding, an indiscretion finally prevented by a broken
wheel. When Mr. Greville perceives their desperation he admits that he has delayed the marriage because Egbert's fortune has been lost and that he has been trying to save dowry
money for Jacintha. Egbert leaves for Jamaica to cope with
the embezzlers of his fortune.

After Egbert's departure, Mrs. Decourcy, Mr. Greville's
sister, comes with her husband for a visit and befriends Jacintha, whom she takes back to town with her. While Jacintha is away from home her foster father dies. Given the
opportunity, Mrs. Greville casts her off, but Mrs. Decourcy
promises to take care of her. Soon, however, Mr. and Mrs.
Decourcy begin to treat her with coolness, perhaps because
they suspect her of being involved with Lord Gwytherin. He
has indeed been lurking around the grounds in order to speak
to her, but his message is that he is her real father. Her
mother, he says, is a sister to Mr. Decourcy; she is the
Countess of Dunsane. He himself has complicated the affairs
of that family considerably, having seduced and impregnated
Mr. Decourcy's sister and having attempted to carry off the
present Mrs. Decourcy, who was afterward hired as a companion to the pregnant Miss Decourcy. Some troublemaker spread
the rumor that the child subsequently born belonged not to
Miss Decourcy but to her companion. Uncertainty and suspicion about the story have poisoned the Decourcy marriage.
Jacintha relieves domestic tension by going to stay with the
former Miss Frankland, who is now, confusingly, Mrs. Falkland. Troubled there by the attentions of another libertine, she returns to the Decourcy house and finds its owners
gone out of town. At that point Lord Gwytherin offers to
take her secretly to France to see her real mother, and she
goes. The mother is a widow now and Gwytherin hopes to win
her back. The Countess is upset to see her long-kept secret
made flesh in the person of her daughter; how upset becomes
evident when she sends Jacintha to a castle in the Pyrenees,
ostensibly so that they may become better acquainted, but in
fact so that Jacintha may be locked away for the rest of her
life.

In the castle Jacintha discovers a secret panel to a
second room. One night when she finds it open she tries to
close it and is seized by a cold hand. The hand belongs to
Henri, a local shepherd and accomplished flautist. Henri
loves her and helps her escape to a convent, but the abbess

is not a good woman. Jacintha discovers the Earl of Endermay's wife locked in a tower at the convent; her vow to tell
the captive's relatives where she is gives way, for ethical
reasons mysterious to this reader, to a later vow of secrecy
forced upon her by a sinister nun. When Henri once again
helps her escape, she comes back to town to find all her
connections dead or out of town indefinitely, except Mrs.
Greville, who is not helpful even when Jacintha loses her
purse in a coaching accident and is set altogether adrift.
Further misadventures include an interlude with a kept woman, and another abduction, this time by a Mr. Loveit whose
brother is Lord Endermay. Ultimately an old servant of Endermay's reveals secrets pertinent to Jacintha's mysterious
parentage. She is really the child of Endermay and his
wife Eglantine, the lady imprisoned in the convent tower.
Eglantine and Jacintha have both suffered from the malevo-
lence of Endermay's brother and sister, and from an episode
of babyswapping among nurses. Jacintha is identified by a
cherry birthmark, Lady Endermay is released from her tower,
Henri is shown to be the heir to Dunsane, and Jacintha's
foster sister Gertrude, who has been seduced and deserted,
dies of grief and infamy. Egbert and Jacintha marry.

155: THE ROMANCE OF THE APPENINES   2 vols. London: Henry
     Colburn, 1808

A young outcast arrives in Naples and is mistakenly identified as a bravo. He is taken to Roberto, who is shocked to
see in the boy's face a resemblance to his murdered brother
Henrico. The boy is no boy at all, but Roberto's niece Viola in masculine clothing. Roberto had supposed her to be
dead, having arranged for her murder himself when he had her
father killed. (Roberto was jealous of both Henrico's inheritance and his wife.) During the little time Viola
spends in her uncle's house — he soon sends her into the
keeping of some banditti — his guest Lorenzo, Duke d'Urbino,
falls in love with her. The bandits are not a bad lot.
Both Rinaldo, the leader, and Beatrice, a female member of
the troop, are kind to Viola, and the melancholy bandit Vincentio is particularly interesting. Actually Vincentio is
not a proper bandit; he was released from the bandits' dungeons and has saved Rinaldo's life. Viola soon discovers
that he is her father Henrico, who did not after all die
under Roberto's attack. Lorenzo, accompanied by Viola's
servant Rondello, comes to release her, though she dislikes
escaping without her father, and takes her to his own parents. Then Lorenzo disappears and Rondello, through Roberto's machinations, is accused of his murder and brought to
the Inquisition, where he in turn accuses Roberto. The mat-

ter is resolved by the sudden arrival of Lorenzo. Roberto
bursts a blood vessel and dies, Vincentio/Henrico is released, and Lorenzo marries Viola.

156: Ross, Mrs.   THE BALANCE OF COMFORT, OR, THE OLD MAID
     AND MARRIED WOMAN. A NOVEL   3 vols. London: A. K.
     Newman, 1816

Mrs. Vernon, who married imprudently, is living a meager
life with three daughters still at home. The eldest,
strong-willed and socially ambitious, marries a rich man who
proves to be parsimonious. They quarrel and are unhappy.
The second daughter is a romantic and marries a poor clergyman; they anticipate an idyllic love-and-a-crust rural life.
But the clergyman is extravagant beyond their means and
proves to be jealous of the baby. As people of excessive
sensibility, they suffer even more than the other couple.
The youngest and brightest daughter, Althea, visits her sisters and is appalled. She begins to consider being a spinster like her mother's friend Mrs. C., a wise and charming
woman whose independence, contentment, and gracious domestic
arrangements look a lot better than the available specimens
of matrimony. Mrs. C. rather hopes to convert her to spin-
sterhood; Althea is her favorite. However, Althea finally
makes a really good marriage and concludes that she is hap-
pier than she would have been alone, but that in general a
single life is best. The moral, explicitly stated, is that
the old maid loses occasional happiness and avoids much
trouble; the balance will not change until more reason is
brought to bear upon marriage.

157: Ross, Mrs.   THE MARCHIONESS!!! OR, "THE MATURED
     ENCHANTRESS"   3 vols. London: A. K. Newman, 1813

Lionel Southampton means well and is an affectionate husband
and father, but when he goes off to Parliament his wife worries more about his morals than about those of her son at
Eton. She needs to worry about her husband, for he falls
into the clutches of a fascinating woman, the Marchioness,
who teaches him to gamble. His wife stops writing, his son
frets himself into the grave, and his daughter declines.
The Marchioness tells him that it is all his own fault: how
could he have supposed that anyone who loved him would start
him gaming? He finally dies. The Marchioness neither reforms nor dies in agony; at the novel's end she is as un-
abashedly worldly and loose-living as ever.

158: Sarratt, J. H.   KOENIGSMARK, THE ROBBER, OR, THE TER-
ROR OF BOHEMIA   1 vol. London: William Cole, 1801

Herman and Theodore are sitting in a German inn, talking
about Adolphus Rosenburg, who was assassinated in the forest
after one year of marriage. He was lured to his death by
a woman's cries and a white form. Another man in the inn
tells a related story about an ancestor of his who was asked
by a lady in the forest to destroy a spider. The spider had
yellow eyes and grew larger and then disappeared; the man
was unable to kill it; his sword bounced off the spider as
it would off a rock. The next day he saw a wolf turn into
a man. On both days he heard mysterious voices speak of his
"punishment."

   Herman and Theodore hear a plot against Rosenburg's
father-in-law; Koenigsmark evidently wishes to capture Adelaide, Rosenburg's widow. The two heroes, with friends, attack the robber and his men, but Koenigsmark's body is apparently impervious to knife-blades. Theodore is imprisoned
by Koenigsmark but later helped to escape by a kindly robber
who is of noble origins. Rosenburg's ghost has offered encouragement from time to time and now asserts that Theodore
should not kill himself, for Adelaide's child needs him.
Certainly it needs someone, for its mother, who has become
mildly deranged, loses it in the forest. It is recovered,
however. (Adelaide is not the only lunatic in the story;
another woman sits under the gibbeted bones of her hanged
lover and raves.) After Koenigsmark's capture, Rosenburg's
shade makes a final appearance, and Adelaide, electing to
follow it, dies. A man with a mask passes by and stabs
Koenigsmark as he is put on the rack. Since the robber dies
this time, albeit with a loud laugh, everyone assumes that
the masked man was an evil spirit.

159: Shelley, Mary   FALKNER. A NOVEL   3 vols. London:
Saunders and Otley, 1837

John Falkner is raised after his mother's death by a female
relative who has a daughter named Alithea. Although the two
young people have an idyllic juvenile romance, the girl later marries while Falkner is in India. When he comes home
he plans an elopement to which she consents, but her child
is accidentally left behind and she has convulsions and
drowns before Falkner can take her home to it. He buries
her secretly and for the rest of his life feels like a murderer. The novel takes place during the years of his guilt-
stricken wanderings. He adopts Elizabeth, an orphaned child
who keeps him from committing suicide on her mother's grave,
taking her partly out of gratitude and partly because her

mother is discovered to have been a friend of Alithea's.
Their paths cross several times with those of the Nevilles,
the husband and son of Alithea who are hunting for her ab-
ductor and planning revenge. Elizabeth falls in love with
the Neville boy, Gerard, and vice versa, which is awkward.
Finally Falkner confesses his identity to the Nevilles and
is prosecuted after the body has been exhumed, but the pos-
tilion who helped with the elopement is persuaded to testify
to the accidental nature of Alithea's death, and Falkner
goes free. He is never free from guilt, however, and never
forgives himself. Despite some doubts about the propriety
of their union, Elizabeth and Gerard marry and are happy
with the decision.

160: Shelley, Mary   THE FORTUNES OF PERKIN WARBECK. A
     ROMANCE   3 vols. London: Henry Colburn and Richard
     Bentley, 1830

Mary Shelley believes that Perkin Warbeck was indeed the
Duke of York who was thought to have been killed in the
Tower by Richard III. The novel follows his adventures from
his late childhood to his execution. The particulars of his
attempts and ultimate failure to regain the throne of England, which constitute the principal part of the plot, may
be omitted here, since there cannot be much suspense about
events that have become history. Much of the novel's interest lies in the delineation of characters — the boy Richard;
his betrayer Robin Clifford, who destroys himself by his own
dishonor; Richard's sister Elizabeth, who suffers as the
wife of Henry VII; Monina de Faro, who loves Richard and
promotes his claim; the elderly Jane Shore, and others.

161: Shelley, Mary   FRANKENSTEIN, OR, THE MODERN PROMETHEUS
     3 vols. London: Lackington, Hughes, Harding, Mavor, and
     Jones, 1818

The frame story concerns a Captain Walton, whose ravenous
curiosity has driven him to organize a dangerous expedition
to the polar regions. Walton's ship rescues Victor Frankenstein from a drifting fragment of ice and Walton hears his
tale.
     Victor Frankenstein has a propitious upbringing in the
midst of a loving family and is especially blessed in his
foster sister Elizabeth and his best friend Henry Clerval.
He is consumed, however, with a quasi-scientific lust for
knowledge and is drawn to the outmoded alchemical books in
his father's library. Later at the University of Ingolstadt
he takes up modern science, especially chemistry, and discovers how to create life. The "monster" which crowns his

labors, and which he never names, horrifies him with its
ugliness, though he had expected to find it beautiful. He
goes trembling to bed, leaving his creation unsupervised;
later he awakens to see it standing over him and flees the
house. When he forces himself to come home the next day,
the monster has disappeared. Six months later a letter from
his father arrives with the news that his youngest brother
William has been murdered. When he arrives at his father's
house he sees his monster lurking behind some trees and
knows at once what has happened, though the murder is offi-
cially blamed on Justine, a devoted member of the household,
upon whose person has been found a miniature which the child
was wearing before he was killed. Justine is hanged (having
falsely confessed in order to be shriven), and Frankenstein
feels that he has two deaths on his own conscience.

When the monster arranges a confrontation with his creator, he demands that Frankenstein do his duty and make him a
female of his own kind. The story of his tribulations wins
some degree of pity from the reader but seems not to impress
Frankenstein. After wandering away from the house where he
was given life, the monster has various educational experiences pertinent to food, warmth, and human animosity, after
which he takes refuge in a little shed attached to a cottage. Watching the cottagers (people of good blood and
background) every day, he learns to love them and does them
anonymous favors around the grounds. He learns also to
speak and to read, after which he educates himself by ab-
sorbing three books which he finds by chance — *Paradise
Lost,* Plutarch's *Lives,* and *The Sorrows of Werther*. Thus,
he explains, he learns to love virtue and to abhor vice.
At length his longing for companionship leads him to speak
to the blind father of the family when he is alone; the conversation goes well enough until the son comes home and
beats the monster with a stick. The family quickly packs
up and goes away, after which the monster burns their cottage and sets out again into the world. His intentions,
when he sees William Frankenstein, are to capture him and
bring him up without prejudice against deformity; when William, who is already past training in that respect, threatens the monster with his father's name, the possibilities
of revenge against an unloving creator become clear. The
monster incriminates Justine largely because she represents
joys from which he knows himself to be hopelessly excluded.

Frankenstein agrees to make his monster a female companion, but at the last moment he changes his mind and destroys
her. The monster retaliates by killing Clerval and Elizabeth, the latter on the night of her wedding to Frankenstein. Frankenstein's father dies of shock and grief.
After that Frankenstein dedicates himself to the monster's

destruction, following him to the arctic, where Walton meets
him. He is determined to kill the creature with his own
hands, and apparently the monster has something of the same
sort in mind, for he leaves behind him on his trail occasional notes and food so that his pursuer can keep up. When
the exhausted Frankenstein dies on Walton's ship, as he soon
does, the monster comes through a window and grieves over
him. Feeling guilty and lonely, the monster announces that
he will go farther north and immolate himself on a funeral
pyre. Having been persuaded by Frankenstein's tale to give
up his analogous folly, Walton turns his ship back toward
home.

162: Shelley, Mary   THE LAST MAN   3 vols. London: Henry
       Colburn, 1826

The Last Man takes place in the twenty-first century, though
it is not (barring the dates, the abolition of the British
monarchy, and a reference to air-balloon transport) a dis-
cernibly futuristic novel. Lionel Verney and his sister
Perdita, early orphaned, bring themselves up in Cumberland.
Lionel, according to his own description, is changed from
beast to human by the sudden friendship of Adrian, the son
of England's last king, who abdicated in 2073. Adrian is
in love with a Greek princess, Evadne, a young friend of his
mother's, but he is passed over in favor of Lord Raymond, a
rather Byronic gentleman who is a hero of the Greek wars and
something of a public figure. Raymond, however, appears
to be planning a marriage to Adrian's sister Idris, through
whom he hopes to restore the monarchy. (Adrian is a firm
republican.) At the last moment he abandons his political
aspirations to marry Perdita instead, which leaves Idris
and Lionel free to marry each other. The two couples and
Adrian, friends all around, settle down in the neighborhood
of Windsor Castle.
      Later Raymond is chosen Lord Protector, and he and Per-
dita move to London. There he accidentally finds Evadne,
destitute, and resumes a relationship with her. Perdita,
who has been feeling a growing estrangement, shuts off her
love for Raymond and returns to Windsor. Raymond and Adrian, after a bit, go to Greece to fight the Turks. Having
heard a rumor that Raymond is dead, though she does not believe it, Perdita goes to Greece to find him. He is in fact
a prisoner, but the Turks free him lest he cause political
trouble by dying in their dungeons; he is a great hero in
Greece. Despite his weakened condition he leads an assault
against Constantinople, a city that proves to have been emptied by the severity of the plague, and that his men are
afraid to enter. He rides in alone and is blown up by some

cleverly contrived powder charges. Although Perdita insists
upon staying by his tomb in Greece, Lionel unwisely drugs
her and puts her on a boat for England. She jumps overboard, wearing a tag that will direct her corpse to Athens,
and drowns.

Soon, and here we come to the central business of the
novel, the plague that emptied Constantinople spreads over
Europe. Further, the weather is taking unaccountable turns
and a report comes in from the East that a black sun had appeared along with the regular one. England avoids contagion
for a little longer and is filled with refugees, but at last
the plague begins in London. Adrian consents for humanitar-
ian reasons to be Lord Protector. Shelley describes changes
of attitude and behavior brought about by the progress of
the malady, especially the leveling of social distinctions.
In 2096 the survivors, fewer than two thousand, decide to
leave England for a more moderate climate. Before they go,
Lionel's elder boy dies of the disease, while he himself has
it and recovers. Idris appears to be dying of grief and expires in a snowstorm as they go to the rescue of a deserving
cottager and her rheumatic mother, who have been abandoned
in the general emigration. Lionel's family now consists
of a younger son, Perdita and Raymond's adolescent daughter
Clara, and Adrian. Arrived in Paris, the refugees fall into
three contending factions, including an especially vicious
and fanatic religious one. Adrian reconciles the other two,
and the refugees arrange to spend the summer in Switzerland.
The journey is nightmarish, with decayed bodies and spectral
figures all along the way, and nearly everyone dies. Finally, in Switzerland, only Lionel and Adrian and the two chil
dren are left alive. The plague seems to be over, but that
winter the younger child dies of typhus. Soon after that
Adrian and Clara drown and Lionel is left alone. He lingers
in Rome for a while, writing his memoirs, and then sets off
with a few books (Homer and Shakespeare, mostly) to hunt for
another survivor.

Lionel's story, according to the Author's Introduction,
was found written on leaves and bark, in a variety of lan-
guages, in the Cumaean Sibyl's cave in 1818. This eccen-
tricity of chronology is acknowledged but not explained.

163: Shelley, Mary   LODORE   3 vols. London: Richard
     Bentley, 1835

Lodore is the surname of a virtuous, obscure, and vaguely
unlucky family. The son Henry (who had at Eton a friend
remarkably like the juvenile Shelley) marries Cornelia Santarre on her sixteenth birthday. She is so dominated by her
mother that he takes the baby Ethel and goes to the States

after offering her a chance to come along. Twelve years
later, on the way home, he is killed in a duel. Ethel lives
with her paternal Aunt Bessie, her fashionable mother having
rashly promised not to see her. Affection develops between
Ethel and Edward Villiers, who was her father's second in
his duel. Though poor, he is a gentleman; he somehow sacri-
fices his prospects to marry her. Ethel and Edward survive
in London on love and little else, ducking bailiffs until
he is finally arrested. The couple is "living within the
rules" in a horrid house when Ethel's mother finds them and
resolves to give them everything and retire to Wales. En
route to Wales she comes down with scarlet fever, and the
couple later finds her in the same town as Aunt Bessie,
grown thoroughly lovable.

164: Shelley, Mary   MATHILDA   1 vol. Chapel Hill: Uni-
     versity of North Carolina Press, 1959 (Written 1819)

Mathilda, whose mother died giving her birth, is brought up
by an unloving aunt and dreams constantly of her father's
return. When he comes back their relationship is briefly
idyllic, but soon he becomes negative and withdrawn and repulses her caresses. Bent on getting at the source of his
trouble so that she can comfort him, she pushes him into
confessing that he desires her. She is terrified and appalled and dreams of trying to catch him as he leaps over
a precipice. Her dream is precognitive, except that she arrives too late even to try. After her father's suicide she
breaks down and, when she recovers a bit, goes off to be a
hermitress. Her only companion in sorrow is Woodville the
poet, and even he refuses to make a suicide pact with her.
At last she gets lost, sleeps out in the rain, and develops
consumption. She is happy in the contemplation of death,
for she expects to be reunited with her father.

165: Shelley, Mary   VALPERGA, OR, THE LIFE AND ADVENTURES
     OF CASTRUCCIO, PRINCE OF LUCCA   3 vols. London:
     G. and W. B. Whittaker, 1823

A novel more full of wars and politics than my summary may
suggest, *Valperga* deals with the life of a real Italian
nobleman who was an ally of Emperor Louis of Bavaria. Valperga is the name of a castle to which Castruccio and his
mother were to escape in case of emergency. It is also the
home of his childhood friend Euthanasia, with whom he is
later in love. At fourteen Castruccio goes to Florence
to see dramatic representations of hell from Dante's then
unfinished manuscript. At seventeen he goes out into the
world and begins his career. He spends some time in En-

gland, where he becomes friends with Piers Gavaston, but he is obliged to leave after he kills a nobleman.

Besides Euthanasia there is another woman in Castruccio's life — Bertha, the daughter of Wilhelmina of Bohemia, who claimed to be the Holy Ghost incarnate, come to earth for the salvation of her sex. Bertha, too, is given to public prophecy and is taken by the Inquisition, who force her to walk on burning plowshares, a task that she accomplishes unscathed. Bertha is beautiful and makes sexual overtures to Castruccio from a conviction that God wishes her to surrender to him. No promises are made but she seems to presume that he is hers permanently; she is in consequence much distressed when he leaves her to go back to Euthanasia. Later she appears at Valperga as a pilgrim on her way to Rome. Euthanasia, in the meantime, has refused Castruccio and has further declined to surrender Valperga. (He and she are on différent sides of the Italian wars.) He carries her away to Lucca with no animosity and she forgives him in a detached way, demanding a return to Florence. A flood delays her going back. Bertha, who has once again been captured by the Inquisition, successfully solicits Euthanasia's intercession with Castruccio. Bertha is by now preaching a malevolent God ("Time opens the shell, the seed is poison") and has abandoned all notion of divine guidance. During her wanderings she fell for three years into the power of an evil man, and emerged from the experience feeling more than three years older. She goes to a witch, Fior de Mandragola, who is on nobody's side and is interested only in power, in hopes of achieving control over Castruccio. She is told that she can see Castruccio by magic. At the confrontation, which is not after all magical but real, she collapses; she is too changed for him to recognize and she dies insane.

Meanwhile, politics march on. There is a conspiracy against Castruccio which is eager to enroll Euthanasia. She is told that by joining she can save his life, so she agrees. But the conspiracy is betrayed by a villain and Euthanasia is put into prison. Castruccio releases her and sends her to Sicily, but on the way the ship is lost in a storm. Except for a postscript on the death of Castruccio at forty-seven, the story ends with Euthanasia's demise.

166: Shelley, Percy   ST. IRVYNE, OR, THE ROSICRUCIAN.
    A ROMANCE   1 vol. London: J. J. Stockdale, 1811

The novel opens with outcast Wolfstein, in the middle of a storm, considering throwing himself off a mountain. Instead he joins a troop of bandits. He becomes good at banditry but competes with the chief for Megalena, a captive. After the chief threatens to rape her, Wolfstein poisons him and

escapes with Ginotti, the chief's right-hand man, who saw
him put the poison in the cup. Ginotti exacts a promise
that Wolfstein will, on demand, listen to his story and will
bury him when he dies.

Megalena has escaped too; she and Wolfstein go to Genoa
and have a love nest, but he begins to find gaming a more
alluring mistress. On several occasions he is disturbed to
find Ginotti among the company or in some disguise. Ginotti
hints that he is not what he seems. Megalena persuades
Wolfstein to kill her rival Olympia, but at the last minute
he is unable to do it. Olympia, however, stabs herself at
his refusing her, and though Wolfstein now hates Megalena
they flee Genoa together. Wolfstein inherits a castle in
Bohemia, and when Ginotti appears there, too, he is dread-
fully shaken. Ginotti, who was as a youth atheistic, over-
curious, and self-loving, seems to have sold himself to
the devil for the secret of immortality. He now wishes to
be rid of this information by passing it on to Wolfstein.
Wolfstein wants it but refuses the stipulation that he deny
his Creator. Suddenly the devil carries Ginotti away; although Wolfstein consequently dies of shock, we assume that
he is not damned.

In the subplot, Wolfstein's sister Eloise is also an
outcast, and innocent as well. When her mother dies she is
attracted to a stranger, Frederic de Nempere (really Ginotti, we discover at the end), who seduces her. Nempere's
kinder associate Mountfort wins her from him at the gaming
table and sends her to live in a cottage with his poetic
bachelor friend Fitzeustace. The two fall in love and Fitzeustace accepts Nempere's bastard child. They marry to
placate Fitzeustace's father.

167: Shelley, Percy   ZASTROZZI. A ROMANCE   1 vol. London:
     G. Wilkie and J. Robinson, 1810

The villain Zastrozzi and the passionate and unscrupulous
Matilda are in league against the lovers Verezzi and Julia,
Matilda because she wants Verezzi herself, and Zastrozzi to
avenge the seduction and abandonment of his mother by Verezzi's father. Verezzi is imprisoned, starved, and then
told that it was all a fever dream. After he recovers, he
saves Matilda from jumping off a bridge. She takes him home
and works on him — counterfeits sensibility, declares her
love. Finally she tells him that Julia is dead (a lie) and
nurses him through his consequent collapse. (Her nursing
is counter to the doctor's recommendation, for Verezzi
tends to faint whenever he finds himself in Matilda's arms.)
After setting up a scene in which she rescues him from stabbing, Matilda finally persuades Verezzi to marry her. Be-

cause the Inquisition has begun to pursue her, she takes
Verezzi to Venice, where he chances to see Julia, alive.
After some fluctuation he commits suicide, for Julia arrives
just as Matilda has won him back. Matilda snatches the dagger from his bosom and kills Julia as well. She and Zastrozzi are both taken by the Inquisition. She has a pretty
vision and repents, but Zastrozzi stays imperturbable and
mean to his last gasp on the rack.

168: Sickelmore, Richard   MARY JANE. A NOVEL   2 vols.
     London: Printed for the Author by William Lane, 1800

Radmill, a businessman, takes his family to Brighton. He
has a son, Henry, and an adopted orphan, Mary Jane. Radmill's old friend Northcote goes into fits of rage every
time Mary Jane talks to a man; in the case of Barville this
is a sound reaction. He is a dissolute young man with a
reputation as a seducer, and he kidnaps Mary Jane during a
theater fire, after which he shuts her in a castle in Wales
and tries to take "indecent freedoms," which are somehow
deterred by a miniature of her parents. In the castle Mary
Jane drops her candle while exploring and inadvertently
picks up, instead, a human jawbone with scraps of putrefying
flesh, a mistake that she fails to notice until a servant
discovers it on her table. Later she comes upon the corpse
from which she had removed it — Sickelmore provides loathsome detail — and pockets a diamond ring lying nearby. Barville is just prevented from killing her by someone whom we
later discover to be her foster brother Henry, who has been
having adventures of his own while in pursuit of her.
    Mary Jane escapes and goes home by public transporta-
tion, only to find the house locked up and to discover that
she has lost the fare for the hackney coach. She gives the
coachman the diamond ring. A pawnbroker recognizes the ring
and reports it, but Henry arrives just in time to save Mary
Jane from the officers of justice. We discover that Mary
Jane is the child of Barville's elder brother by Northcote's
daughter. Barville kills himself. Henry and Mary Jane
marry.

169: Siddons, Henry   THE SON OF THE STORM. A TALE
     4 vols. London: Longman, 1809

Lord John Oceanus O'Carroll, who was born aboard ship and
consequently has a passion for the sea, finds a pair of orphans and adopts them. They are Henry and Laura, to whom
O'Carroll has added the surname Tempest. Henry becomes a
clergyman and Laura proposes to keep house for him, having
refused an offer from Dalton, whose social rank exceeds

hers. O'Carroll is subject to what his friends think are
fits of lunacy: once a year at midnight he sees his father's
ghost. The ghost turns out to be a manifestation of his
guilty conscience; he broke a promise to his father and contracted a secret marriage. He discovers at last that the
twins are his own children from that marriage, sent back to
England by their mother. Laura accepts Dalton's proposal.
The author makes much of filial piety and the misery that
results from disobedience or secrecy.

O'Carroll is instrumental in solving the problems of
some other people in the novel. Charles Woodville is engaged to marry Susan, daughter of the Duke of Montcastle.
Though only fifteen, Susan has a serious vice, learned from
an older school friend — she is addicted to gaming. Despite
the sympathy of her cousin Arthur (a playful young man who
is given to surreptitious charity, e.g., he adopts a baby
and supports an old lady), Susan falls into bad company and
accumulates heavy debts. It is Lord John O'Carroll who pays
them when Susan reforms. At first she feels too corrupt to
marry Woodville, but he persuades her in the end.

170: Sleath, Eleanor   THE NOCTURNAL MINSTREL, OR, THE
        SPIRIT OF THE WOOD   2 vols. London: A. K. Newman,
        1810

The Baroness Fitzwalter sits with her attendant Winifred
in her castle near the Scottish border and listens to the
lovely and mysterious music that issues from the forest at
twilight. She likes to think that it may be the benevolent
spirit of her husband, to whose memory she is faithful despite the importunate courtship of Sir Reginald Harcland.
In fact, she would very much like to send Sir Reginald home
and finds an excuse to do so upon learning the otherwise
disheartening news that the Earl of Ormond is coming to see
her and can by royal authority marry her if he wants. (She
is a ward of state, her husband having complicated their
lives by espousing the cause of Perkin Warbeck.) Winifred,
however, admires Sir Reginald and supports his courtship;
her support is of some moment, for Winifred is a wily domestic tyrant who bullies the other servants and especially
persecutes Ethelind and her boyfriend Edgar, who are, respectively, a peasant girl under the Baroness's protection
and the promising son of a vassal. Sir Reginald behaves
badly upon being asked to leave and claims to have had a
dream in which the late Baron's ghost said that he did not
want his wife to marry Ormond.

People begin to hear clattering, as of falling armor,
in the late Baron's chamber. Cruel Winifred shuts Ethelind
up in the chamber for claiming to have seen an armed figure

there, but she is consoled by Edgar, who creeps in disguised
as Mr. Motley the jester. The Baroness takes all the uproar
as additional evidence of her late husband's disapproval and
tells Ormond that she will not marry him, the king notwithstanding. Ormond is kind and humble, really a thoroughly
nice man, and offers to sit up in the haunted room. On the
third night he follows a beckoning ghost, but this is a mistake, for the "ghost" is Sir Reginald, who locks him in a
subterranean vault. People think Ormond has disappeared
in some uncanny way and hold a special mass, which is disrupted, even demoralized, by knockings from under the floor
(they are Ormond's). At this point a kind of wizard arrives
and offers to lay the castle ghost. During the subsequent
ritual he reveals himself to be the still-living Baron; Sir
Reginald had lied to the Baroness about his death, and had
told him in turn that the Baroness was dead. Edgar finds
and releases Ormond and is made steward in the place of the
corrupt incumbent, who like Winifred is demoted to ordinary
vassal. Ethelind and Edgar marry. Ormond procures a pardon
for the Baron, marries someone else, and becomes a family
friend. Sir Reginald repents and makes a pilgrimage to
Rome. The Baron and the Baroness, who are still young, produce a son who grows up and marries Ormond's daughter.

171: Sleath, Eleanor   THE ORPHAN OF THE RHINE. A ROMANCE
     4 vols. London: William Lane, 1798

Julie has a son, Enrico, by the Marchese de Montferrat, who
pretended to marry her. Later the Marchese gives her an
additional infant (someone else's) to raise. The child is
Laurette; she and Enrico like each other very much. When
the children are grown, Julie moves to new quarters and
makes friends with an abbess who tells her about a Sister
Cecilia, whom Julie suspects to be Laurette's mother. But
Cecilia dies, denying that she ever had a daughter, and Julie is beginning to fear that Enrico and Laurette, who are
falling in love, are half-brother and sister.
     A man named LaRoque, whom Julie frees from a tower where
he is imprisoned and guarded by Montferrat's servant Paoli,
tells a story of stabbing his wife accidentally when he intended to stab his mistress. Discovering that Julie had a
hand in LaRoque's escape, Montferrat has her kidnapped.
Meanwhile a white-robed monk gives Laurette a miniature supposed to be of her real mother and promises to reveal the
secret of her birth. The monk also says "Beware the Marchese de Montferrat" — good advice, for Montferrat later
proposes to Laurette, is turned down, and kidnaps her.
Enrico, home on leave, has gone to hunt for his mother and
comes back to find Laurette missing as well. Fortunately

LaRoque helps him to recover her and tells him that his
mother is safe too. LaRoque also informs him that he is
the lawful child of the Marchese, for the marriage was valid
after all. When Laurette's origins are clarified, it appears that she is not Enrico's sister, so the couple are
free to marry.

172: Sleath, Eleanor   PYRENEAN BANDITTI. A ROMANCE
        3 vols. London: A. K. Newman, 1811

Count St. Angouléme hates his handsomer and more prudent
brother. Also, he is jealous of his wife's nephew Theodore
St. Leon, for whom she has reserved a portion of her fortune, and shuts her in the castle so she cannot see him.
It is into this villain's hands that his niece Adelaide
falls upon the death of her father. After inventing and
claiming not to believe a rumor that Adelaide was substituted in infancy for his brother's real child, he produces,
with signs of regret, a confession to that effect from the
nurse whose child Adelaide is said to be. The DeLaunés, a
singularly unappealing couple, claim Adelaide and say that
she can either come home with them or go into service; the
Count with apparent generosity offers to let her stay on at
the castle, but not as an heiress. Her main worry, however,
is that she cannot seem to love her new father, DeLauné.
Soon she is kidnapped by banditti and taken to a purportedly
haunted castle; although she has never believed the stories
about it, she sees a bloody ghost with a taper and faints.
Adelaide is told various lies about who has arranged the
kidnapping and why. Perouse, the other "prisoner" who helps
her to escape, is really DeLauné's son and one of the villains. The "aunt" to whom he takes her for refuge was hired
from a Paris brothel for the occasion. Adelaide is under a
good deal of pressure to marry Perouse, but even when she
supposes him to be good she finds him unpolished and unat-
tractive. The faithful servant Jacques is her only support
until she becomes acquainted with a young man for whom, it
later turns out, Jacques's grandmother keeps house.
    Adelaide nearly loses the young man, Montroi, when he
hears a mistaken report that she is ruined, but truth prevails in the end and the pair marry. Before that Adelaide
is arrested for possession of a diamond-studded ring which
DeLauné has given her. She refuses to tell where she got
it, for she thinks that it proves her father a murderer and
feels that she will be a parricide if she tells. Jacques
saves her from torture and solitary confinement by arriving
at the trial and supplying necessary information about the
ring. The Count, who was behind all the trouble and wished
DeLauné to kill her, is poisoned by his mistress. (Marrying

Adelaide to his son was DeLauné's own idea.) Specters at the castle are explained as special effects supplied by the banditti.

173: Sleath, Eleanor   WHO'S THE MURDERER? OR, THE MYSTERY
      OF THE FOREST   4 vols. London: Lane and Newman, 1802

Sleath's title is a little misleading, for the plot is principally concerned with the identification of Cecilia, the heroine, as sufficiently upper-class to marry the Marchese de Varano's son. As a small child Cecilia passed through a number of hands before coming to Madame Villeneuve and her brother De Sevignac, who raised her, so her origins are difficult to trace. However, she fortuitously encounters her half-brother, who recognizes a parental miniature in her possession in time to establish her identity for Varano. The Varano family seems not to be put off by the particulars of her background: her father married an escaped nun and was burned by the Inquisition; Cecilia's mother sent her away in her infancy because her old convent wanted the baby as a penitential offering. Horrid touches include a body in a sack, nightmares of blood and death, and the tortures of the Inquisition.

174: Smith, Catharine   BAROZZI, OR, THE VENETIAN SORCERESS.
      A ROMANCE OF THE SIXTEENTH CENTURY   2 vols. London:
      A. K. Newman, 1815

Rosalva Barozzi is handsome and spoiled but essentially good. One day he rescues from kidnappers a girl named Rosalina, who unbeknown to him was being carried away by agents of his wicked father, Augustino. Her father has been murdered by the kidnappers. Rosalva puts her under the protection of his aunt, who thinks it best to change her name to Rosa Falieri in case someone is still after her. Some time later at a masquerade a woman dressed as Medea identifies herself as a sorceress and indisputably acts like one. She knows Rosa's real name and that she is in danger from the Marquis de Barozzi. As Rosa is leaving town with her protectress she is kidnapped from the carriage by a woman who gives her a sleeping potion, which she kindly says is for Rosa's own good. At about this time Rosalva finds a ruined castle in which he discovers his father's dagger, a secret panel, and a room containing occult paraphernalia and a woman laid out in a white robe. He also discovers his father in conversation with the sorceress, who is demanding Rosa for a human sacrifice and pointing out that after all he has not scrupled to kill both her parents. A female rises through the floor with a scroll containing the warning, written in blood, that if the Marquis does not get on with the killing, Rosa will inherit the Barozzi fortune. Barozzi tries to stab his son, who has leaped out to say that he does not want to inherit under those circumstances.

At Barozzi's subsequent trial a great deal of information is supplied. In brief, Rosa/Rosalina's father was twin brother to Rosalva's. Her father, Fernando, married her mother secretly and thus exposed himself to the machinations of his sinister twin, who wanted all the inheritance. Augustino, the bad brother, told his sister-in-law that her marriage was invalid, had his brother assassinated, and burned the house over the heads of his sister-in-law and infant niece. He supposed the latter two pieces of villainy to have been successful, but such was not the case. Fernando was rescued by fishermen and later acquired by Algerine corsairs and sold into slavery. The Marchioness was carried off at the time of the fire by a courteous bandit whose booty she later inherited. At the trial Rosalva produces Fernando, and the sorceress appears and reveals herself to be Rosalina's mother. They are all glad of the reunion. Rosalva and Rosalina marry and have a child. The assassins die on the rack.

175: Smith, Charlotte   MARCHMONT. A NOVEL   4 vols. London: Sampson Low, 1796

After her mother's death, Althea Dacres was raised by her aunt Mrs. Trevyllian; her father married a second wife who bought him a baronet's title and bore him several children. When Mrs. Trevyllian is obliged to nurse a friend with a contagious fever, Althea is sent to stay with her father and his family. Though her father rather likes her, her stepmother does not, nor do her sisters, and she is pursued by "odious Mr. Mohun," a rude and conceited lawyer whom her father wishes her to marry. Mrs. Trevyllian herself falls ill and dies, leaving Althea an unwelcome and incompatible guest in her father's shallow and vicious household. Intractable on the question of marriage to Mohun, she is sent as punishment to a remote and decaying manor house that formerly belonged to the Marchmont family. Althea has already met young Mr. Marchmont at the home of the Eversleys, friends of her aunt, and has found him attractive. Stories of his virtue and of his hardships abound at her new residence and she is increasingly prepossessed in his favor. He has been trying hard but without much success to meet the debts left by a profligate father and to support his mother and sisters.

As winter closes in on the manor house, Althea and the servants begin to hear disquieting noises and to see inex-

plicable sights (e.g., an unidentified animal running down
the corridors). These are explained by the discovery of
Marchmont, hiding in his old home from an unscrupulous crew
who would clap him into prison for debt. The principal villain is an unusually loathsome attorney named Vampyre. Althea helps Marchmont flee into exile; in the course of his
escape they discover their mutual attraction and achieve a
vague understanding about future affiliation. After the
sudden death of her father Althea feels stripped of refuges
and arranges to board with the Marchmont family, who after
some hesitation are going into trade. Althea adds her fan-
cywork to the productions of the Marchmont sisters and despite unkind gossip, difficulty about collecting the interest due from her small inheritance, and some doubts about
the propriety of staying after Marchmont returns, she finds
the arrangement a happy one. When Marchmont comes home
they marry. After three weeks, however, Vampyre and company
catch up and send the bridegroom to prison. Disasters and
betrayals multiply, but just when spirits are at an all-time
low and Marchmont is about to try writing as a trade, Althea
inherits money from a cousin, an unexpected and elderly relative befriends Marchmont, and old friends generally rally
round, so they have a happy issue out of all their afflic-
tions.

176: Smith, Charlotte   THE WANDERINGS OF WARWICK. A NOVEL
      1 vol. London: J. Bell, 1794

Captain Warwick is a friend and brother-in-law to Orlando,
the hero of *The Old Manor House* (published in the year previous). He has inherited General Tracy's estate and returned to England with his wife Isabella. This volume is
his account to Orlando of their wanderings from the time of
their marriage until their coming home. They have been to
North America and to Jamaica and have spent some time in
Spain and Portugal. Several of the anecdotes seem to have
other people at the crux of the adventure; the narrative
is studded with military exploits, privateers, flagellation,
suspicions of infidelity, bullfighting, imprisonment, and so
on. Warwick at one point reduces his family to beggary by
gaming but asserts that poverty was good for him, because it
made him consider himself the steward of his two boys rather
than a man of the world.

177: Smollett, Tobias   THE ADVENTURES OF FERDINAND COUNT
      FATHOM   2 vols. London: W. Johnston, 1753

Sometimes cited as a precursor of the Gothic, Smollett's
novel concerns the adventures of Ferdinand, who was born in

a wagon between Holland and Flanders, his mother a camp
follower and his father unknown. His stepfather, Fadom by
name, teaches him to suck brandy and gunpowder through the
touch hole of a pistol, but he moves on to higher-class
tutelage when he is taken in by Count Melvil, a wounded officer whom his mother forebears to kill and loot on the bat-
tlefield. Ferdinand is brought up as a page to Melvil's son
Renaldo and given the same education. Because he is canny,
and graceful in his bearing, he is able to insinuate himself
into the family affections and to make the much more virtuous Renaldo look boorish by comparison.

As he grows up, Ferdinand tries to marry the Melvil's
daughter, seduces the daughter's maid, cheats Rinaldo, deserts from two armies, and generally engages in theft, wom-
anizing, and double-dealing. He leaves behind him a rather
spectacular train of lunacy and grief, but his most treacherous deed is his coming between Renaldo (who has just forgiven him previous abuses and retrieved him from debtor's
prison at great sacrifice) and a lovely and virtuous girl
named Monimia. Ferdinand tries both seduction and rape on
Monimia but is doubly thwarted. Just as Renaldo is beginning to hear reports about Ferdinand's true character he
receives a letter from Monimia which, she says, will arrive
after her death. When he recovers from his consequent illness, Renaldo goes to spend a few melancholy nights sobbing
on her grave. The scene is solemn and is perhaps after all
somewhat Gothic — midnight, the church deserted, owls hoot-
ing. The second night Renaldo hears organ music and sees
Monimia's spirit, or what he supposes to be her spirit.
In fact she is alive, having recovered from her illness, and
her friends have conspired to make a test of Renaldo's devo-
tion. Having passed the test, he marries her. Before the
wedding, however, she is discovered to be Selina, the long-
lost daughter of a secondary character named Don Diego. As
for Ferdinand, the virtuous couple find him dying in "ex-
tremity of indigence, squalor, and distress," clutching a
confession of his sins and watched over by his wife, a woman
whom he earlier ruined. Selina and Renaldo procure medical
aid that saves Ferdinand's life, and pension him off to England.

178: Stanhope, Louisa Sidney   THE CONFESSIONAL OF VALOMBRE.
     A ROMANCE   4 vols. London: A. K. Newman, 1812

Theodore is left in infancy at the monastery of Valombre by
a man who murders the abbot. He is raised by Father Betsolin and is good, though a little passionate. He wants to
become a monk, but Betsolin tells him to see the world
first. At about that time a mysterious stranger offers to

help Theodore discover his origins, binding him with a terrible oath of secrecy. Theodore goes on a mission for the monastery and discovers Montaubon, the mysterious stranger, operating as the leader of banditti. Montaubon identifies himself as Theodore's father; the boy is horrified but develops an interest in saving his father's soul. Montaubon seems to imagine that he sees the ghost of the murdered abbot. Later a ghost tells him to repent, and he falls downstairs and fractures his head. But Father Betsolin reveals that Theodore's father was really the murdered Duke of Vermandois. In fact, Montaubon is Theodore's uncle and the murderer in question. Theodore finds a sister, as well as identifying his parents, and manages to dig up and move his mother's bones to the family vault. He marries Juliette, a convent boarder with whom he has been in love, and attributes his good fortune to Father Betsolin's correct principles.

179: Stanhope, Louisa Sidney   THE CORSAIR'S BRIDE. A
     LEGEND OF THE SIXTEENTH CENTURY   3 vols. London:
     A. K. Newman, 1830

The Della Monti family go to Sicily, where mother and baby die, leaving Rosalita alone with her father. She and Arthur de la Pole are in love, but Arthur has to go back to England, where he has political connections; he is Clarence Plantagenet's grandson. When he gets home, everyone is gone. They have been arrested, and he sees one of his brothers beheaded. Meanwhile a shipwrecked stranger has been talking passionate love to Rosalita and saying that she cannot escape him. And indeed she cannot, for pirates later carry her off to Hayradin Barbarossa, who turns out to be the importunate stranger. He is now gentle but firm in his insistence and marries her in a Christian ceremony, so she is obliged to recognize the validity of the union. Rosalita's father and Arthur weep over her supposed dishonor. However, she escapes, disguised, with the help of one of Barbarossa's other wives, and there is a joyful scene of reunion. They wash the dye from her face and persuade the Pope to annul her marriage. The novel ends happily except for the political executions of some secondary characters in England.

180: Stanhope, Louisa Sidney   DI MONTRANZO, OR, THE
     NOVICE OF CORPUS DOMINI. A ROMANCE   4 vols. London:
     A. K. Newman, 1810

As the novel begins, Adelheida is dying an agonizing death. She has been poisoned, presumably by someone in the household, but all the occupants — her secret husband Huberto, who was brought up with her as a foundling; her father, the Conte Alverani; her servant Vannina — are clearly appalled. Not even the Conte's confessor and confederate, the evil monk Father Brazilio, seems in control of events. Dying, Adelheida tells her husband some terrible secret and swears him to slience. That night her father leaves the castle for a life of eternal solitude; his explanatory note vaguely alludes to guilt. The rest of the novel is devoted to explaining the events of this calamitous night and to discovering Huberto's family origins and uncovering various usurpations and villainies.

A few other principal characters are introduced: the Duca di Monte Melissario, whom Huberto nurses after he is attacked by banditti; the pilgrim Isidore, who claims to have an identical twin sister in a convent; a virtuous old canon, who takes an unusual interest in the vicissitudes of the other characters. Major explanations occur on the occasion of Huberto's trial by the Inquisition for the murder of his wife and the concealment of a nun. Isidore is female — hence the "twin sister" fantasy; she has been indulging in transsexual dressing and is in love with Huberto, while Vannina is misguidedly in love with her. The Duca discovers her to be his missing child. The Conte Alverani rushes in and stops Huberto's examination on the rack to announce that he killed Huberto's father (his own brother) and usurped Huberto's inheritance. He is wrong, however; his brother survived his attack. The benevolent canon reveals himself as Di Montranzo, Huberto's living father. Adelheida was accidentally poisoned when Huberto brought her a restorative which had been doctored by the Conte and Father Brazilio on the assumption that he wanted it for himself. Father Brazilio has been responsible for a lot of trouble; he loved Huberto's mother and pursued her so unremittingly that she killed herself rather than be raped by him. Huberto (now Flodoardo) and Hemelfride (formerly Isidore) decide to marry.

181: Stanhope, Louisa Sidney   MADELINA. A TALE FOUNDED
    ON FACTS   4 vols. London: A. K. Newman, 1814

Madelina and Rosamond are dissimilar sisters. Rosamond is playful and lighthearted; she marries Sir Essex St. Aubin after a pleasant and uneventful girlhood and has no particular troubles. Her sister Madelina is more serious and suffers from complications of the affections. She and Captain Glenmorris are in love, but her father wishes her to marry Lord Ormington. Madelina and Glenmorris part, promising to live for each other, but Madelina later hears a story that

Glenmorris has married a rich heiress. After she recovers
from the decline into which this news precipitates her, she
marries Lord Ormington to please her father. Ormington dies
in the end, and Glenmorris is single after all, so Madelina
is free to marry the man she loves.

Many of the incidents in the novel seem designed principally to show the characters of the two sisters, though
there is also a Gothic sighting of a white monk at some
ruins and an account of a mysterious voice which says, "My
hour is not yet come." There are, as well, some minor characters more lurid than the heroines and their heroes. Two
girls suffer acutely as a result of relationships with men.
Janetta, the "pity of all Rhydol," is insane during the two
years she survives her drowned lover and runs wild in all
weathers gathering flowers for his grave. Ellen, an orphan
raised by Margaret Annendale, is betrayed and seduced by a
friend of the family with whom she is left while her guardian travels to India. At the time of the novel she is pregnant and mildly deranged, and at last she goes into a decline and dies.

182: Stanhope, Louisa Sidney   MONTBRASIL ABBEY, OR,
      MATERNAL TRIALS. A TALE   2 vols. London: Lane,
      Newman, 1806

The Elvington sisters, Elenor, Agnes, and Constance, have
separate histories which occur simultaneously and are woven
together through the family correspondence.

Elenor, who is romantic and convinced that love amidst
poverty has some innate attraction, is courted by Richmond.
When her mother rejects him as a suitor for her, feeling
that he has no prospects, he and Elenor elope. Although,
or perhaps because, she feels guilty, she does not write to
her mother afterward. She and Richmond are wretchedly poor.
Two of their three little girls die; Richmond himself has
died before the birth of the third child. At last her sister Agnes finds her and takes her home to Mrs. Elvington.

Agnes, who is determined to marry wealth, visits Mel-
bourne Castle, where she hears ghost stories which she passes on to her romantic sister Elenor, and where she meets two
young men. She and the Honourable Major Arbuthnot fall in
love; he is a rather freespoken young man, but not quite a
rake. She foolishly marries the Marquis of Montbrasil instead, apparently not for his greater worthiness, though he
is the better man, but for his social position. She has a
child and attempts to distract herself with gaming, but neither these diversions nor her good intentions stifle her
continuing love for Arbuthnot. Arbuthnot consciously decides to throw away virtue, but he is not a ready villain,

for he has scruples and suffers. Nevertheless, he and Agnes run away, taking along the baby and pursued by the Marquis, who in the end kills Arbuthnot. The Marquis at first flees the country but later decides to come back and stand trial. He is acquitted. His return permits him to be at hand so that Agnes, who is dying of grief, remorse, and shame, may expire in his arms. He returns to live in France, leaving his child with the Elvingtons.

Constance, who has always argued for a "thankful middle station," has been with her mother through the escapades of her sisters. She loves Edward Beverly, whose father wishes him to marry an orphaned cousin and withholds his sanction from Constance. At last he comes to admire Constance's honorable resistance to Beverly's suit and permits them to marry. It is clear that Constance's middle way is best.

183: Stanhope, Louisa Sidney   THE NUN OF SANTA MARIA DI
        TINDARO. A TALE   3 vols. London: A. K. Newman, 1818

The narrator shelters overnight at a convent and is given for her moral instruction the memoirs which make up the body of this tale. They tell the story of Helena, a nun who has recently died and whose bad experiences in the outside world caused her to take the veil.

Helena's father has withdrawn from the world and done his best to make her suspicious of everything; he is cynical because Helena's mother ran off with De Beaufort. He tells Helena that if she has anything to do with any De Beauforts he will put her in a nunnery. Unfortunately she meets the son of the man her father so dislikes and they fall in love. Under constant threat of nunneries, Helena runs off with her lover and they undergo a marriage ceremony which later proves to have been invalid. Her father takes her defection badly. Eugenius, her husband, goes to fight for the aristocracy in the French Revolution, and Helena stays with the mother of his friend Angerville. She has a baby.

Angerville covets Helena and begins to scheme. He leaves in plain sight a letter that mentions that Eugenius is already married to someone else. Eugenius, who does love her, returns to nurse her through the shock of the disclosure but admits its truth; the other marriage was undertaken as some kind of duty and is loveless. He trusts his friend Angerville to take care of Helena when he has to leave again. Angerville wins her sympathies by weeping on her shoulder about an unidentified woman whom he loves; not knowing that it is herself, she prays for his happiness. He is such a villain that he betrays Eugenius into an ambush and imprisons him, then acts solicitous. Helena still believes in him, even though she has a dream about his being evil. After she is given a chance to save her husband by giving herself to some other unspecified man, she overhears Angerville's voice and realizes that he is a villain. The shock is acute. Eugenius dies attempting to escape. Helena finds that her mother has given herself to the Prefect to save her father, who is in prison too. She removes herself to a convent and writes her memoirs, which the narrator says have been most uplifting.

184: Stanhope, Louisa Sidney   THE SIEGE OF KENILWORTH. AN HISTORICAL ROMANCE   4 vols. London: A. K. Newman, 1824

Baron Hanslape, doing penance at a cross one rainy night, was presented with a male child by a stranger who then disappeared. A voice said — as it does at intervals throughout the story — "Vows to Heaven savour not of the vows of this world." Hanslape is greatly relieved at the end of the novel to discover that the voice belongs to a live Knight Templar, not to a spirit. (The Knight Templar is obsessed with that line because his wife, a runaway nun, said it as she died at the altar on their wedding day.) Hanslape is inclined to be superstitious; he fears that his wife and one of his children died because he had failed to go on a promised pilgrimage and suspects that his other two children were spared so that God could punish him some more later. Stanhope makes it clear that this is nonsense.

As the story begins, Hanslape is starting on his long-delayed pilgrimage and the children are growing up. Adopted Hubert is nicer than the Baron's son William, but William is not really bad. Isabel, the Baron's daughter, is devoted to Hubert, and it is a sad day when she leaves for convent school. Sixteen years later she is quite ready to come home again, though the country is in such chaos with the rebellion against Henry III that the Baron would rather like her to become a nun for her own safety. William has become a rebel, for he has fallen under the spell of the sinister Ingelrica Fitzparnel. His father tearfully and reluctantly disowns him, but William and Hubert (a royalist like the Baron) manage some secret meetings across enemy lines. At one point Hubert receives a summons, purportedly from William, which is really a trap devised by Ingelrica. She is simultaneously cold and seductive, a thoroughly frightening woman; there is one chilling scene in which she springs between Hubert and the door and throws her gold chain over his head. Hubert is locked up, later to be freed by William, but not before he has been given a harrowing glimpse of the mad Duchess of Kent, whose husband's wrongs are the rebels' rallying cry. After other imprisonings and releases, including Isabel's, family troubles reach a climax: William, who has been feeling increasingly penitent, more or less deliberately dies in battle. Hubert fears that William's intentions were suicidal, but as he dies making a confession of faith we are probably to conclude that he is not damned. At the siege of Kenilworth Hubert finds the Knight Templar, who explains to him his parentage — he is the son of the Duke and Duchess of Kent. Hubert and Isabel marry.

185: Stanhope, Louisa Sidney   TREACHERY, OR, THE GRAVE
     OF ANTOINETTE   4 vols. London: A. K. Newman, 1815

Corisande de Roussillon's somewhat despotic father promises her in marriage to the Duke de Briançon, though neither her mother nor her brother Mortaigne approves of the engagement. Despite this involuntary engagement Corisande is having a romantic life, for she is finding anonymous poems in a purportedly haunted boathouse from which music emanates at odd hours. Further, she sees and afterward dreams about a youthful hunter, who will turn out to be Louis D'Avignon, boathouse poet and ultimately husband. He also saves Mortaigne's life in battle and becomes his friend, subsequently sharing adventures like going through trapdoors in ruins and being locked in.

Both Corisande, gone into a convent to escape the threatened marriage to the Duke, and Mortaigne, in his gentlemanly wanderings, meet some people who will be unexpectedly important to the denouement — two cottage girls, a hermit, a nun, etc. The gist of the revelations is that Louis is the brother of Gabrielle, a cottage girl who asked Mortaigne to take her to a religious sanctuary, and that both Louis and Gabrielle are the offspring of the hermit, formerly Everard St. Sauverne, who is brother to the nun Mathilde, a new convent friend of Corisande's and an old friend of her mother's. Louis and Gabrielle's mother (Antoinette) died in childbirth through the cruelty of her brother (Corisande's father), the Marquis de Roussillon. Everard was in love with Corisande's mother Hortense and once arranged to elope with her, but De Roussillon somehow substituted himself for Everard and married her instead. Everard was driven to the religious life by his cozening brother Eugene but seems to have embraced it sincerely, for we find him trying to induce the Marquis de Roussillon to repent, which the Marquis does at last on his deathbed. Corisande marries Louis; and Mortaigne marries Louis's sister Gabrielle, to whom he has proposed earlier in the novel.

186: Sykes, Mrs. S.   MARGIANA, OR, WIDDRINGTON TOWER.
A TALE OF THE FIFTEENTH CENTURY   5 vols. London:
Lane, Newman, 1808

Margiana Widdrington's father is a supporter of Richard II
but tells his daughters to attend Henry IV's court. Margiana finds Ethelred Winburne Lord Delancey engaging but does
not return his love. The excitement begins when the girls
stay with their uncle Bertram. Margiana reads manuscript
romances and hears shrieks in the night; the next day her
uncle unconvincingly explains that he was unwell and cannot
bear pain. They meet Ethelred's younger sister Arlette, who
is fond of dressing up in armor and playing imaginative
games.
      Later in the novel Margiana disappears and is thought to
have been murdered. She is discovered half-starved and imprisoned with her faithful dog. Since Ethelred has believed
her dead he has married her sister Genevieve. Genevieve
dies of shock at a false rumor that Ethelred is dead, but
even though Margiana now loves him he cannot marry her, for
he is her brother-in-law. This problem is resolved when
papers reveal Genevieve to be the child, not of Margiana's
father and his mistress, as he thought, but of the mistress
and a page. Ethelred and Margiana marry. Ethelred's father
is shown to have committed fratricide; he has killed himself
as well. There are many other complications — an aunt tortured by thumbscrews, Arlette's flight to the North Pole
which leads to her reunion with her mother, and so on, but
everything comes right in the end.

187: TALES OF THE DEAD   1 vol. London: White, Cochrane,
1813

The collection, edited and translated ("principally...from
the French") by Sarah Utterson, contains six tales, as follows:
      1) "The Family Portraits": This is a horribly complex
tale involving two portraits of people whose ghosts walk.
There is a woman's portrait which frightens a young girl and
later falls on her and kills her. The other portrait, of a
man named Ditmar, is even more frightening; it is said that
while it was being painted a child-specter kept making it
look deathlike. Ditmar, who has killed an enemy's son by
giving him a poison kiss, is condemned to ghosthood and the
repetition of his guilty deed — he must kiss the sons of the
family and mark them out for death. The narrator and hero
of the story has visited the family in question and seen the
curse fulfilled. It looks for a while as though the hero, a
descendant of the female in the portrait, will be obliged to

marry a girl named Clotilde, thereby somehow tranquillizing his ancestress. It turns out that he can accomplish the same thing by marrying Emily, sister of the ghost-kissed boys, whom he loves. We are informed that Ditmar raised the female in the portrait, though she was the daughter of his enemy, and we learn of his frustrated and bloody deeds. At the end his portrait fades away.

2) "The Fated Hour": Florentina is nervous about her approaching marriage, as a paper left to her by her father predicts that she will die at the ninth hour on the eve of her marriage. Her father died at the ninth hour and so did her sister Seraphina. Seraphina had a doppelganger, or did astral projection, or both. She prophesied her own death, and her father's, and it is perhaps her prophecy that Florentina read. The household also has guilty secrets and flitting lights. At the fatal hour the shade of Seraphina appears and the girls embrace. One of them — friends cannot tell which — says, "I am thine forever." Florentina drops down dead.

3) "The Death's Head": Calzolaro comes back to the town where his schoolmaster father had lived, to dispute his father's will. He is with a carnival troupe and does things with magnetism, electricity, and ventriloquism. Colonel Keilholm asks for a performance of ventriloquism with a death's head, so Calzolaro sends the local sexton to dig up a skull. The sexton craftily digs up the schoolmaster's skull, having heard that a child can bring his parent's head to life. It is evidently so, for Calzolaro faints away during the performance and says, when he comes to, that the skull assumed his father's features and accused him for a parricide, as he more or less broke his father's heart. Calzolaro repents, dismisses the troupe, drops the lawsuit, and comes out of the whole thing well by marrying his father's heiress.

4) "The Death Bride": The frame story is about Ida, a girl whose twin, Hildegarde, has died. Hildegarde had a strawberry birthmark that distinguished her from Ida. A Duke comes and wants to marry Ida, though he seems to have seen the ghost of Hildegarde in a gallery in Paris and to have the two girls confused. The family opens Hildegarde's coffin in case she should be missing, but everything is in order. In order to marry Ida, the Duke has broken an engagement to another woman and he becomes very nervous when the narrator, who knows something about him, tells the following tale.

Felippo and Clara pledge to each other eternal faithfulness and drink their blood mixed with champagne, saying that if one of them proves unfaithful, he or she will be forced to come among the dead to join the other. Felippo later runs off with Camilla and hears mysterious shrieks. A strange and uninvited lady appears at the wedding dinner; she is masked and wearing Camilla's ring. Felippo's white wine looks red to him. The lady will not unmask. There is shrieking. Clara's ghost blows out the candles at the wedding. Felippo dies.

The Duke's wedding proceeds, and the Duke goes away, he thinks, with Ida; the real Ida, however, has not seen him. He is found dead. But the ghost with whom he went away is evidently not Hildegarde; she is a local ghost who can assume various appearances and whose curse is the obligation to seduce away an engaged man.

5) "The Storm": Isabella de Nunez is in perpetual mourning and says she has done something so bad that she is beyond the help of religion. She tells her friend Emily, swearing her to secrecy, that on a certain night something terrible will happen. On that night a carriage is heard to arrive (the arrival impossible, one would think, in such a dreadful storm), a locked door opens, and Isabella dies under "circumstances of unexampled horror." Emily faints and dies of brain fever.

6) "The Spectre Barber": Francis goes to make his fortune and win his love. Once he stays with a man who flagellates guests, but his honesty (i.e., rudeness) so charms the host that the ritual is omitted. Some time later he sleeps in an empty castle and has his hair and even his eyebrows shaved off by a whiskery ghost. As the ghost apparently wishes to be shaved too, Francis cooperates. The ghost is thus freed from a curse and thanks his benefactor by giving him clues to hidden treasure.

188: THE THREE GHOSTS OF THE FOREST. A TALE OF HORROR.
AN ORIGINAL ROMANCE   36 pp. London: J. Ker, 1803

The place is Orleans, the year 1640. The Baron Arnhalt has three daughters; if any one of them should die unmarried, her share of the estate will go to her cousin Orlando, Count Brissac, who Arnhalt hopes will marry one of the girls. Isabella, who is noble and amiable, is eighteen when her father dies. Octavia, the next eldest, is handsome and witty but wicked and designing. Adela, the youngest daughter, who is boarding in a convent, resembles Isabella in character. Orlando and Octavia are friends, which means in effect that Orlando knows her character too well to marry her; he prefers Isabella. Octavia marries Honorio, whom she has stolen from Isabella, and later (we discover at the end) persuades Orlando to have him murdered. Widowed, she moves back in with Isabella, whom she shortly persuades Orlando to abduct. After Orlando's death-or-dishonor threats, even the one he makes while wearing a Tartar disguise, fail to move Isabella, who prefers death, Orlando is rather sorry about the abduction but feels that he must keep her incarcerated. At that point Adela complicates matters by coming home from the convent and winning Orlando's affections. Terrified that Octavia may tell Adela that he is a villain (and, as he later says, hearing that she plans to poison him), Orlando arranges to carry Octavia to a convent; one of the hired ruffians stabs her, on his own initiative, and is informed by Honorio's ghost that he died by the same sword. On that same night, Isabella escapes from imprisonment only to be killed by a robber before she has gone very far. People claim to see three ghosts in the forest, Isabella's and Honorio's together, and Octavia's skulking along separately. Isabella's ghost leads Adela aside one evening and makes what is for spectral tradition an unusually long speech, warning her to shun Orlando. Orlando dies soon, making a deathbed confession to Adela, who afterward becomes a nun.

189: Tomlins, Elizabeth Sophia   ROSALIND DE TRACY   3 vols.
     London: Dilly, 1798

As the novel begins, the heroine, Rosalind de Tracy, is riding alone through a gathering storm and blunders into a stone quarry frequented by drunken smugglers, where she is forced to spend the night. The next day she informs a kind lady named Mrs. Smith, who puts her to bed and gives her tea, that she has no friends and at eighteen has lived quite long enough. She has been raised by Sir Raymond Cecil and his wife since her mother (no relation to the Cecils) died in childbirth. As Rosalind explains to Mrs. D'Acre, a cousin of Mrs. Smith's who takes the girl to live with her, Lady Cecil has died — she was chased, while pregnant, by a pet buffalo and subsequently died as a result of the terror — and Rosalind has been driven from the house by Sir Raymond's insistence that she marry a friend of his. She has escaped with three hundred guineas of her own and a pistol in her pocket; though she afterward admits that she was imprudent, Sir Raymond is irreconcilable.

The man he intends for her, and whom she properly fears, is Signor Mondovini; he may have been the owner of a hand that seized her arm in her room one night. She is also pursued by Mr. Johnson, son of the family's late housekeeper, who lurks unpleasantly in the park and gives her an unsolicited miniature of himself. As the novel proceeds, Mondovini's villainy and Rosalind's identity are made plain, for Mrs. D'Acre was once engaged to Mondovini, who then bore a different name. Before the projected wedding Mondovini

went to bed with his fiancée's sister Charlotte, who later
died at the Cecil's estate after giving birth to Rosalind, a
coach accident having induced labor as she was running away.
A monument is belatedly erected to Rosalind's mother ("Char-
lotta infelix") and Mondovini is obliged to marry one of his
surviving victims, a German lunatic who has wandered into
the plot from time to time.

190: Walker, George   DON RAPHAEL. A ROMANCE   3 vols.
       London: G. Walker and T. Hurst, 1803

At the beginning of the story Don Lorenzo de Ferrara, in Madrid, is accosted by a strange girl, Agnes, who mistakes him
for his friend Count Aranda, to whose protection she is running. Consequently Lorenzo is attacked by her father, whom
he stabs in self-defense. Count Aranda is studying the Doctrine of Celestial Influences, as taught by a man he calls
"little Mahmut." Lorenzo's history is given in some detail,
but the adventure pertinent to subsequent developments has
to do with the Castle of St. Helma, into which he and a
friend once found their way. The castle was rich with mysterious figures, vapors, and so on, and possessed an especially striking room done all in black, with black candles.
He and the friend found themselves clamped into chairs there
and the friend's chair sank through the floor, while letters
of fire spelled "Lorenzo" on the wall. The principal inhab-
itant of the castle was Don Raphael, an old man in a wizard
suit, with a long white beard to his knees. He admitted
that the supernatural effects were a ruse to ensure privacy.
He had been living in isolation since he stabbed a cuckold-
ing friend. Lorenzo discovered Don Raphael's best-kept
secret, his daughter Cornelia, a girl so innocent as to be
entirely ignorant of men. ("Can it speak?" she asked about
Lorenzo.) At last Lorenzo accidentally stabbed Don Raphael,
having thrust out for balance a hand with a dagger in it,
and left the castle.
    Later Cornelia appears in Lorenzo's life again and
says that she has cured Don Raphael, who now wishes to marry
her. Lorenzo is shocked, but innocent Cornelia assures him,
"I have told him I would not have him, even if he was my
father." She has discovered from some papers partially
glimpsed that he is not. Don Raphael arrives and shoots
her, apparently fatally. Lorenzo discovers that Christiana,
a girl who looks like Cornelia and to whom he has earlier
been attracted, is Cornelia's sister. When Cornelia suddenly turns up again, alive after all (though she and Agnes
dress as specters; it is a scheme of the latter's to wean
Count Aranda from the occult), Christiana is so discouraged
that she decides to take the veil. But Cornelia, having

been apprised of her own earlier, though innocent, indiscretions, takes a drug and dies. Lorenzo interrupts Christiana's veil-taking just in time and marries her.

191: Walker, George   THE HAUNTED CASTLE. A NORMAN ROMANCE
     2 vols. London: William Lane, 1794

Ignatius, fighting for King Philip, is resting in the woods
one day when he sees a girl and her elderly male companion
being attacked. He rescues them and later meets the man,
Reginald Lacé, again; Lacé offers Ignatius a chance to marry
the girl, his niece Adelais. Ignatius likes this suggestion
but wants first to solve the mystery of a particular haunted
castle that a hermit has told him was formerly owned by Manfredi, inherited by Manfredi's brother, and subsequently
sold. As Adelais is said to be Manfredi's orphaned daughter, the haunting is of some interest to the hero's prospective in-laws. Ignatius's own background is mysterious
(found as an infant on the bosom of a dead woman, he was
adopted by the bachelor Du Pin and later ejected by Du Pin's
heir Du Dorf), and he begins to fear, during the course of
his discoveries, that Manfredi was his father too and that
Adelais is consequently his sister. The exploration of the
castle involves sliding doors, subterranean passages, a
bloody ghost, a murder weapon, and at last a tablet identifying Manfredi's murderer as his brother Hendred. Although
Ignatius is now in line to inherit Du Pin's estate, Du Dorf
having been killed in a duel, he is upset about his relationship with (and perhaps to) Adelais and decides to go
into a monastery as Du Pin had originally wanted him to do.
At the monastery he finds the murderer Hendred, now the penitent Friar Francis, and learns that there was some babyswapping at the time of Manfredi's death: Adelais is not his
sister, but the daughter of Reginald Lacé and Lacé's murdered wife Antoinette.

192: Walker, George   THEODORE CYPHON, OR, THE BENEVOLENT
     JEW   3 vols. London: B. Crosby, 1796

Theodore, a secretive and despondent young man who refuses
to reveal his last name, saves the life of Shechem Bensadi,
the Jew, who in gratitude takes him in and treats him like
a son. The wife of the family is missing, having been
"snatched by violence" earlier; the daughter, Eve, fancies
Theodore, who once rescued her from a rapist, but he is devoted to a picture of one Eliza Hanson. When Theodore is
wounded in a street fight, trying to save an adulteress from
her husband, he confesses his whole story.
     Squire Cyphon, Theodore's father, was power hungry and

opposed his son's attachment to Eliza, the daughter of a poor but exceedingly virtuous clergyman. The Squire kept locking Theodore up and finally put him in a madhouse, where he attempted to kill himself by knocking out his brains against a wall. Followed by threats from his father, who kept track of where he was, he escaped and found the Hansons. Hanson was arrested for marrying Theodore and Eliza, and the marriage was annulled. Theodore's wicked, unscrupulous, and libertine uncle had spies and managed to trick away and ruin Eliza. The rape aborted Theodore's baby. Theodore murdered his uncle and fled. His flight was attended by rumors that he was supernatural, rumors of which he sometimes took advantage to evade capture; once, for instance, he hung on a gibbet and creaked and howled.

Shechem Bensadi's investigations reveal that Theodore's father is so nervous that he is employing guards and tasters. Eliza's brother Jason, who in the course of foreign adventures has crossed paths with Bensadi's kidnapped wife, wants to marry Eve and goes to hunt for Eliza. Eliza, who has been raped and infected by a madhouse keeper, dies of venereal ailments in a workhouse. Theodore goes to jail, confesses, and insists upon the death penalty. At his hanging he makes a speech about obeying the law, and forgives his father. He is buried beside Eliza. Eliza's brother-in-law kills the madhouse keeper and bribes the witnesses. Squire Cyphon commits suicide. Eve and Jason will marry after a year of mourning for Theodore.

193: Walpole, Horace   THE CASTLE OF OTRANTO   1 vol.
    London: Tho. Lowndo, 1765

An ancient prophecy asserts that the castle and lordship of Otranto will pass from the present family "whenever the real owner should be grown too large to inhabit it." Thus the usurper Manfred has extra cause for discomfort when a giant helmet falls out of the sky and crushes his only son, who, though unprepossessing, was on the eve of marriage to the beautiful Isabella. Manfred, never very much in control of his passions, takes out his rage and frustration on the peasant Theodore, who has chanced to observe that the helmet is like that on the statue of Alphonso the Good, an earlier Prince of Otranto. Further excited by the news that the statue's helmet is missing, Manfred imprisons Theodore under the giant helmet without any food. Other supernatural portents follow the helmet — a portrait, for instance, sighs and leaves its panel to walk about the castle — but they are perhaps no more alarming than Manfred's increasingly frantic behavior. Spurred by a combination of lust and family ambition, he decides to divorce his almost unbearably virtuous

wife Hippolita and marry Isabella himself. Since Manfred
has acted for some time as her foster father and has nearly
become her father-in-law, the suggestion borders upon incest; Isabella is so shocked and frightened that she flees
down a subterranean passage to sanctuary in the church of
St. Nicholas. She is aided in her escape by Theodore, who
has himself escaped through a gap in the courtyard's paving.

Manfred's troubles increase along with the supernatural
phenomena. Father Jerome refuses to render up Isabella or
to sanction a divorce; servants report seeing a giant leg
and foot in the great chamber. When Theodore, having been
recaptured, is brought out for execution, Manfred's daughter
Matilda (who has spoken to him from her window) discovers
that Theodore looks like the portrait of Alphonso the Good,
to which she has always been inordinately attracted, and
Father Jerome discovers from the prisoner's bloody-arrow
birthmark that Theodore is his own son. Amid the negotia-
tions and pleadings that ensue a hundred gentlemen led by
Isabella's father Frederic arrive carrying a gigantic saber.
Theodore thereby gains a kind of reprieve that permits him
to escape with Matilda's help and to fall in love with her.
Later, mistaking the particulars of a situation in which
he finds himself, he wounds Isabella's father; he has in another sense wounded Isabella herself, for she has fallen in
love with him and is jealous of his affection for Matilda.
At last Manfred, who has been trying to obtain Isabella by
offering Matilda to Isabella's father, is defeated by a
specter which appears to Frederic and reminds him of his
duty. He gives in to passion once again and stabs his own
daughter in mistake for Isabella, whom he supposes to have
spurned him for Theodore. Just as she dies the castle is
thrown down by a giant specter of Alphonso the Good. Subsequent revelations make clear that Theodore is the true
heir to Otranto; he is finally persuaded to marry Isabella
in order to "indulge [his] melancholy" for Matilda in her
company. Manfred and Hippolita go into religious houses
for the rest of their lives.

194: Warner, Richard   NETLEY ABBEY. A GOTHIC STORY
      2 vols. Southampton: Printed for the Author, 1795

Edward de Villars goes to the crusades with Prince Edward.
On the way he finds Bertram, a beautiful Sicilian orphan
whom he takes under his protection. Wounded by a poisoned
Saracen blade, De Villars is close to death until Bertram
sucks out the poison and seems likely to die in his protector's stead. At this point Bertram confesses himself to be
a woman, Isabel, who so admired De Villars at a tournament
that she has followed him in disguise. After she is rather

miraculously cured by some Saracen medicine, De Villars marries her.

Some years later De Villars, become a widower, retires with his grown offspring Edward and Eleanor to an estate near Netley Abbey. Hildebrand, Lord of Netley Castle, is the nephew of De Villars's old friend Sir Raymond Warren, who is said to have died with his daughter Agnes two years earlier. Young Edward, out for a walk, hears a feminine scream from the Abbey and tries to investigate but is sent away by the abbot. Later he goes back disguised as a minstrel, intoxicates the monks, and rescues the girl; she turns out to be Agnes Warren. Meanwhile, Sir Hildebrand has proved an unpleasant neighbor. His proposal to Eleanor having been turned down, he has become hostile to the De Villars family and even more so to a mysterious black knight whom Eleanor seems to love. The knight subsequently rescues her when she is kidnapped by Hildebrand and reveals himself to be young Raymond, the son of Sir Raymond Warren; he was away at war when his cousin Hildebrand locked up his sister Agnes, starved Sir Raymond to death, and usurped the title to Netley Castle. Agnes reports that Hildebrand was once frightened away from her by the ghost of her father. Hildebrand and the abbot from whom Agnes escaped kill one another. Raymond and Eleanor marry, as do Edward and Agnes.

195: West, Jane   THE ADVANTAGES OF EDUCATION, OR, THE
     HISTORY OF MARIA WILLIAMS. A TALE FOR MISSES AND THEIR
     MAMMAS   2 vols. London: William Lane, 1793

West says that the purpose of her novel is "to counteract evils incident to romantic conclusions which youth are apt to form" and suggests that any reader over sixteen may be bored.

When Maria Williams is taken out of school after her father's death, her mother allows her to choose their place of residence. She chooses the village where her friend Charlotte Raby lives. Charlotte is wealthy and generous but flighty. She is allowed more entertainments than Maria, e.g., a regimental ball. Maria, on the other hand, acquires a taste for philanthropy, some of it assisted by Charlotte's contributions, and establishes a little school. After marrying a Major Pierpoint (a match that does not turn out well) Charlotte tries to play go-between for a man who fancies Maria. He is really Henry Neville, a baronet, who will marry Maria if marrying is the only way to get her, but he is using the name of Stanley. Maria is pulled into the conspiracy so far as to keep Stanley's interest a secret from her mother, but she is saved from further involvement by Neville's remorseful suicide upon seeing the corpse of a girl he has seduced. Maria marries a much nicer man and at last loses touch with Charlotte, for the two women have become hopelessly unlike.

196: West, Jane   THE REFUSAL. A NOVEL   3 vols. London:
    Longman, Hurst, Rees, Orme, and Brown, 1810

West embellishes her novel with elaborate chapter titles and a witty introduction lamenting the death of Prudentia Homespun (herself). The heroine is Emily Mandaville. Her crochety uncle calls her away from the aunt with whom she has been living, to come and live with him. West refers to this move as "CHAPTER II. The heroine liberated from a convent to be confined in a castle, where, having enchanted her keeper, she prepared for herself imaginary fetters." Emily's uncle likes her and finds her a husband, Sydney Avondel, whom she marries at the end of the first volume. ("CHAPTER VIII. An instance of Mrs. Prudentia's bad management. Hymen pops into the first volume with very little prearrangement, and thus the narrative ceases to be interesting.")

Avondel struggles to be faithful to Emily despite his attraction to Selina Delamore. He and Emily have a little boy whom they call Sydney after his father. Soon Paulina, an Italian friend of Avondel's whom he describes as "original," moves into the neighborhood. Emily dreads her advent but is fascinated by her for some time. Paulina wears wild and revealing costumes and has a little boy who is also named Sydney, in honor of Avondel's having saved them from a tiger. She claims to love Avondel with holy platonic affection. Paulina works on Avondel's susceptibility and starts a rumor that Emily is her aunt's illegitimate daughter and consequently ineligible to inherit any money. At last Avondel comes to despise Paulina, who is at one point arrested as a felon. But he is killed in a duel and Emily leads a sad life as a widow. Paulina preserves her reputation by marrying a respectable man who wants her money, but she is not happy either. "CHAPTER XXXIV. Instead of distributing rewards and punishments, Mrs. Prudentia concludes with an essay on the advantages of affliction."

197: West, Jane   RINGROVE, OR, OLD FASHIONED NOTIONS
    2 vols. London: Longman, Rees, Orme, Brown, and
    Green, 1827

Emma Herbert is not wanted at home. She has been spoiled since her mother died and has acquired a stepmother who dislikes her. Her debut was not a great success, nor is she appreciably domestic. So her family sends her to Ringrove,

her grandmother's house, to get her out of the way. Mrs.
Loveday, the grandmother, is pro-feminist and against hus-
band-hunting, forced charity, misanthropy, and joyless
lives. She is fond of giving moral lectures. Emma reluctantly makes friends with Ellen, a wholesome and right-
thinking girl who lives with Mrs. Loveday. When Emma finds
herself infatuated with Frederick, the midshipman whom Ellen
loves, Ellen tries to step aside. Realizing this, Emma begins to appreciate Ellen and better evaluate her own emotions. Proposed to by a solid citizen named Dick Smith,
Emma has a happy and rational marriage. Ellen and her midshipman marry, and both survive a rumor that he is lost at
sea.

198: Wilkinson, Sarah   THE KNIGHTS OF CALATRAVA, OR,
     DAYS OF CHIVALRY   35 pp. London: B. Mace, 1804

The story takes place in the twelfth century. The knights
Theodore and Alphonso are brothers; Alphonso is the good
one, Theodore the bad. They both love Felicia, who prefers
Alphonso. Theodore has her sent to a convent, but Alphonso
follows her, and there he discovers Clara, another of Theodore's victims. Political changes free Felicia from the
convent and make it possible for her to marry whom she
likes. Theodore dies in battle, having left a confession
that he was really married to Clara but had persuaded her
that the marriage was bogus. Alphonso and Felicia marry;
Clara becomes the new Abbess.

199: Wilkinson, Sarah   THE SPECTRE OF LANMERE ABBEY,
     OR, THE MYSTERY OF THE BLUE AND SILVER BAG
     2 vols. London: W. Mason, 1820

Agnes Bennet, husbandless, is begging in order to support
herself and her three-year-old daughter Charlotte. Lady
Cecelia Martimel impulsively offers to educate the child
but, having second thoughts, decides to give her back to
Agnes, whom she is expecting to consult the next morning;
Agnes, however, discovers from Lady Cecelia's card that she
is the wife of her seducer, and never comes to the interview. Lady Cecelia is consequently less than delighted with
Charlotte and sends her with a housekeeper to Martimel Castle in Wales. There she is educated by a Mrs. Stockley, a
recent arrival in the neighborhood, who wears a black shade
over her face to hide a cancer. Nearby is Lanmere Abbey,
property of the Godolphins, whose son and daughter both died
young, the latter apparently by throwing herself in the
river to avoid a forced marriage. In fact, the Godolphins'
daughter Mary did not die — she is Agnes, currently masquer-

ading as Mrs. Stockley, and is responsible for the "spectral" visitations that punctuate the story. She only pretended to drown herself. She was married to Sir Everard
Martimel, who later, tiring of the marriage, suggested that
it probably was not legal. He has for years felt that he
killed her and has kept all the papers pertaining to the
marriage in a blue and silver bag, about which there is some
suspense in the course of the novel (e.g., it is stolen and
sent back empty).

Other complications are initiated by Alderton, the Godolphins' nephew, who was once rejected by Mary/Agnes, who
poisoned the Godolphins' son Albert, and who is now jealous
of their relationship with Charlotte. The first time he
kidnaps Charlotte, she is rescued by her mother, who has
herself escaped from confinement arranged by Alderton. The
second time he kidnaps Charlotte, he is prevented from stabbing her by the ghost of Albert. Charlotte, who has her
sewing materials, cuts letters from a book and stitches them
to a blank page and throws them out the window; they are
found by a young man named Hubert, who later marries her.
By the time Agnes dies, she and Charlotte have been reunited
with the Godolphins and everything has worked out satisfac-
torily.

200: Wilkinson, Sarah   THE SPECTRES, OR, LORD OSWALD AND
     LADY ROSA, INCLUDING AN ACCOUNT OF THE MARCHIONESS
     OF CEVETTI WHO WAS BASELY CONSIGNED TO A DUNGEON
     BENEATH HER CASTLE BY HER ELDEST SON, WHOSE CRUEL
     AVARICE PLUNGED HIM INTO THE COMMISSION OF THE WORST
     OF CRIMES, THAT STAIN THE ANNALS OF THE HUMAN RACE.
     AN ORIGINAL ROMANTIC TALE   31 pp. London: Langley,
     n.d.

The handsome stranger Rudolpho, who looks like their dead
Lord, is sheltered from a storm by two servants. That night
the castle resounds with spectral sighs, falling armor, and
so on. (Background: Oswald, who had the bulk of his mother's estate and a mean, jealous, profligate brother named
Francisco, was married to Lady Rosa. Shortly before the
birth of his second child, Oswald died of a bowel complaint
during a visit from his brother. The corpse showed signs
of poison. A false will said that Rosa was not his wife and
left everything to Francisco. Francisco locked Rosa in a
turret and carried off the infant Malvina.) Specters of
Oswald and Rosa appear to Rudolpho, telling him to "save
a sister's honour and forgive a father's murder." Just in
time he prevents Francisco from raping Malvina and learns
that he is the true heir of the castle. Francisco even
counterfeited his own mother's death; she is released from

her dungeon at the age of seventy-one. Rudolpho marries
Francisco's wealthy daughter.

201: Wilkinson, Sarah   THE WATER SPECTRE, OR, AN BRATACH
      36 pp. London: Ann Lemoine and J. Roe, 1805

Murchardus is godfather to Donald, infant son of his friend
Roderic, Thane of Dungivan. Wishing to inherit Roderic's
title and estate, he arranges for Donald's kidnapping and
drowning. Allan, to whom these tasks are assigned, discovers between the kidnapping and the murder that his own baby
has just died; his wife Jannette persuades him to keep Donald and throw the body of their dead child into the river
in Donald's place. Murchardus plans to murder Roderic next.
Some years pass while the Thane goes off to the crusades,
but the murder takes place immediately upon his return.
     The Weird Sisters, who feel a protective interest in
Donald, tell him of Murchardus's usurpation and give him a
magic white flag which will help him in one moment of danger
and one only. The Sisters also inform Murchardus, in response to questions he asks, that he will be harmed by no
human power, that he will die at the third appearance of
Roderic's specter, and that the next owner of Dungivan will
be the rightful heir with his bride Lady Catherine. Their
prophecy is doubly displeasing to Murchardus, for he is himself courting Lady Catherine and he has already seen Roderic's specter once. It appears for a second time at the
close of his interview with the Weird Sisters. Donald and
Lady Catherine do fall in love, despite apparent differ-
ences in class, and are persecuted and more than once captured by Murchardus. Donald has been taken out in a boat
and is about to be strangled when he remembers to wave the
white flag; his father's specter appears, and a second boat,
from which Murchardus is watching, sinks straightaway with
its villainous occupant. Donald's title is restored and he
marries Lady Catherine.

202: Wilkinson, Sarah   ZITTAW THE CRUEL, OR, THE WOODMAN'S
      DAUGHTER. A POLISH ROMANCE   36 pp. London: B. Mace,
      n.d.

The woodman's daughter Ingonda is engaged to marry Count
Timoska but is kidnapped before the wedding by wicked Prince
Zittaw. He also drugs and imprisons her father and the
Count. All three victims hold fast to virtue. Zittaw rapes
and kills the wife of Ingonda's servant; the servant frees
the Count in retribution. When Zittaw tries to kill the
servant, he finds the ghost of his rape victim. Ingonda
stabs him as he is in the process of murdering her father.

The Count rescues them. A dying officer (there is a battle
outside) directs them to Zittaw's imprisoned wife, who also
dies. Ingonda and the Count are married.

203: Williams, Helen Maria   JULIA. A NOVEL, INTERSPERSED
    WITH SOME POETICAL PIECES   2 vols. London: T. Cadell,
    1790

The purpose of this novel, says the preface, is "to trace
the danger arising from the uncontrouled [sic] indulgence
of strong affections," calamitous even to the virtuous, for
"though we do not become the slaves of vice, we must yield
ourselves the victims of sorrow." The plot is complicated
by the presence of three Mr. Seymours and two Miss Clif-
fords. The youngest and best of the three Seymour brothers
is Frederick, who is upright, strong, and intelligent.
Though engaged to marry Charlotte Clifford, he falls in love
with her cousin Julia Clifford. Julia loves him too, but
they try to stifle their attraction and the contracted marriage takes place. Frederick suppresses his passion less
successfully than Julia does hers. We see him treasuring
her lost glove, for instance, and telling her at intervals
how he feels, which always offends her sense of propriety.
Gossip about Frederick and Julia at last reaches even Charlotte's ears, after which Frederick becomes increasingly
lovelorn, Charlotte increasingly cold to her rival, and
Julia increasingly wretched. After a bit the two women are
reconciled, and Frederick seems to like Charlotte the better
for her tolerance. Charlotte and Frederick produce a son.
Frederick at last contracts a fever and dies, pleading to
be buried in the same grave as Julia; Julia never marries,
devoting herself to Charlotte and Frederick's child. The
author observes that, but for Julia's unconquered weakness
for Frederick, she would have been "above the common lot,
fortunate and happy."

204: Williams, William Frederick   FITZMAURICE   2 vols.
    London: Murray and Highley, 1800

Edward Fitzmaurice, whose father is ruined in fortune but
honest, is put to work in his maternal uncle Rigby's count-
inghouse. He leaves behind him two sisters; Helen, the
elder, is afflicted with too much sensibility, and Anastasia, the younger, is a bit too cold and prudent. Edward
does well in his uncle's business. He has occasional news
from home and is told that his father and Helen are dead,
and that Anastasia has married Pobjoy, a pompous neighborhood doctor. On his way to visit the Pobjoys, Edward gives
money to a needy prostitute and learns her story, in the

course of which he discovers her to be his own sister Helen.
Helen was seduced by the rector, who is Aubrey Delvalley,
Edward's friend. After having been cursed by her father and
rejected by an aunt, she fell into bad company and has been
whoring for two years. Business has been falling off lately
as she is past her prime. This information makes it impossible for Edward to accede to his uncle's desire that he
marry Delvalley's sister Augusta, who wants him very much;
consequently, the uncle disinherits him. Anastasia and
Pobjoy are not sympathetic to Helen's problems, though they
admit that the father retracted his curse before he died.
They think that Edward should work his way back into the
uncle's favor. Anastasia is sluttish, her children mon-
strous. Edward leaves saying, "Damn the world!"

An apparently demented old man named Withers is so attracted to "Damn the world" as a philosophical statement
that he follows Edward back to London, where various problems await. Delvalley avoids a duel with Edward by pretending repentance. Augusta proposes to him and threatens to
kill herself when he refuses. The uncle dies and leaves
everything to his wife, who takes on Edward as a kind of
steward. Helen, who says she cannot quite stop swearing or
drinking, joins the Society of Magdalens. Augusta, becoming
gradually more unbalanced, offers to be Edward's mistress
and threatens him with her hatred when he refuses. Augusta's friend Selina claims that Edward seduced her, which he
has not; this particular problem ends surprisingly — they
fall in love and marry. The aunt remarries, once again
stripping Edward of his prospects, and his house is taken
over by her loud fundamentalist in-laws. Just when things
are at their lowest — Edward sick, dying, imprisoned for
debt, Selina considering suicide — Mr. Withers reveals himself as Edward's paternal uncle. He pays the debts and restores Helen to society. Edward rescues the former Mrs.
Rigby from her tyrannical new husband, who has locked her
up while he sits around drunk with his drunken mother and
drunken grandmother. The aunt admits that she suppressed
her husband's final will, so Edward inherits at last. Aubrey Delvalley, his sins revealed to the bishop, takes laudanum. His death is made more garish by the appearance of
Augusta, now totally insane, who pounds on his corpse with
her fist; she is put in an asylum. The good end happily.

205: Williams, William Frederick   THE WORLD WE LIVE IN.
      A NOVEL   3 vols. London: Lane, Newman, 1804

Sigismund Archdale, though illegitimate, was raised by the
Earl, his father. His legitimate and unprincipled half-
brother Lord Portcennis has inherited. Late in the novel

Archdale, having been wounded, is nursed by Mrs. Mordent, an attractive widow whom he once met at a masquerade, and a clergyman named Hervey, who is able to inform Archdale that his father and mother really were married and that his half-brother is the illegitimate one. Archdale becomes Earl and marries Mrs. Mordent. His half-brother, now disinherited, leads an unhappy life with his shrewish wife and mother-in-law, who resent his poverty. Between Archdale's initial entrance and the establishment of his legitimacy the author employs a number of colorful devices which have little apparent bearing on the main plot: suspicions of parricide, duels, dead servants, exploration of ruined abbeys, and a madman who moans about his suicide son.

206: Yorke, Mrs. R. M. P.   THE HAUNTED PALACE, OR, THE
     HORRORS OF VENTOLIENE. A ROMANCE   3 vols. London:
     Earle and Hemet, 1801

As Edward Fitzallan, intent on vengeance, is pursuing his brother-in-law Mr. Owen through a volcanic explosion, he encounters an organization that is interested in punishing the same villain. Owen is guilty of crimes against the Society as well as domestic indiscretions like accidentally shooting his wife in the neck while trying to shoot his mistress. Before the Society can execute Owen he kills himself. Frederick, a gentleman and captain of the Society, makes friends with Edward and relates his own history: Frederick, his brother Charles, and their father all loved the same woman, Mrs. Brisac; both sons left home on the assumption that, whomever she married, relationships would be awkward around the house. After some adventures Frederick was made to join a secret society, taking oaths and drinking animal blood.

    The Society appears to have two branches, one dedicated to good and one to evil, which are constantly at war with one another. All members, whether living or dead, are obliged to come to a big annual meeting. Edward is sworn in. Ventoliene, where the friends are staying, fairly bristles with supernatural phenomena, including music, several ordinary ghosts, and a company of phantoms who come out of the lake during a storm and dance around the humans, singing about how they will rip out their insides and drink their blood. On the appointed day Edward and Frederick go off to the annual meeting, which does indeed include dead members, some visibly pursued by demons. The two friends are instructed to go back to Ventoliene and bury some bones. Ghosts direct them to the well-preserved body of a young woman, which has been sunk in a lead-weighted box, and to a one-handed female skeleton in a wall. When they give proper burial to the former, the whole chapel lights up and seraphic voices sing "I know that my Redeemer liveth." The skeleton seems to have been walled up alive for sedition; she also at one point killed a woman — the one in the lake, apparently — with a poisoned orange. The ghosts having been laid, the heroes go on to resolve their romantic difficulties. Frederick finds that Mrs. Brisac married none of the family, preferring to stay single; but, when he contracts a fever from disappointed love, some interested friends persuade her to have him. His brother Charles marries another woman who looks like Mrs. Brisac, and Edward falls in love with the niece of someone he met in the Society.

207: Yorke, Mrs. R. M. P.   THE ROMANCE OF SMYRNA, OR,
        THE PREDICTION FULFILLED!!!   4 vols. London: Earle
        and Hemet, 1801

Alphonsus has had a difficult life. He is the second son of the Duke of Aranjuez, who had a murder on his conscience and disappeared after seeing a spirit with a prophetic scroll which said, among other things, that the house will become extinct when a fair maiden is murdered by her adoring mother. Alphonsus had a sister who died in a convent. His mother was somehow suspicious of his infant son, thinking that it looked too old for its apparent age. His wife disappeared in the Lisbon earthquake and he himself, believed dead, is unable to prove he is not an imposter.
    As the story opens, a lay brother gives Alphonsus a purse, with instructions to go abroad at once. He meets a number of people in his travels and the reader is subjected to all their histories, some of which are unusually bizarre. Alphonsus's three most important acquaintances are an elderly male wanderer who passes through and will be heard of later, a book-loving child named Dick Berry whom Alphonsus volunteers to educate, and old Muley, who is retained as Dick's tutor. It is Muley who contrives to read the mysterious writing on the purse, thus causing Alphonsus to arrive at Joppa in time to discover that the old wanderer (known as Doctor Pilgrim) is his father, and to be present at his death.
    Both before and after this event the household receives a most alarming series of letters from home, revealing all sorts of bad news and shocking information. The most striking information Alphonsus receives is a deathbed history from his wife Alizra. Her parents were an escaped nun and a younger son of good family. Educated in a convent, she was removed by her uncle Don Joseph, ostensibly to be a companion to his other niece, an invalid. In fact, she was meant to replace the other niece, who was dying, as her uncle's mistress. He drugged and raped her, buying her sub-

sequent cooperation with threats of the Inquisition. Later
she was forced to marry Alphonsus. The baby is of course
her uncle's. During the earthquake Don Joseph caught her
again, but this time she informed on him. He poisoned her
in revenge.

Alphonsus's brother Xavier, too, has difficulties of the
heart. The girl he loves is in love with someone else, who
is too poor to marry her. He nobly offers to get the other
man a position as aide-de-camp to the Prince of Brazil, but
her parents stubbornly refuse; they want Xavier for her.
In a domestic altercation on this topic the mother strikes
the girl with a knife, accidentally hitting her bosom and
knocking her downstairs. This appears pertinent to the
spirit's prophecy at the beginning. And indeed both Alphonsus and Xavier die before the end of the novel, thus ending
the family line. Only Dick, who is overseen by Muley and
the ship's captain until he grows up, lives happily.

208: Young, Mary Julia   THE EAST INDIAN, OR, CLIFFORD
     PRIORY   4 vols. London: Earle and Hemet, 1799

Elinor Clifford lives with her father and widowed aunt and
has a moderately active social life. She likes Sir Clement
Darnley, who is restricted by parental will from marrying
before his twenty-fifth birthday; in the meantime (two
years) she is instructed to be nice to her father's friend
Lord Felgrove, who has proposed. Ultimately Felgrove proves
to be a villain, ruining her father and causing his death.
It is after this, when Elinor moves in with her great-uncle
Sir Gervas, that her adventures begin. Her room in Clifford
Priory has dark purple hangings on the bed and reminds her
of *The Mysteries of Udolpho*. Gervas is a nice old man, despite some parsimony and pettishness, and treats his niece
kindly. But disturbing things happen. For instance, the
coffin of Elinor's father disappears and is discovered to
have fallen through a rotten trapdoor into a vault. Elinor
reads the manuscript tale of a dead uncle's troubles and
imagines that she sees his ghost. Her worst experience oc-
curs when she blunders into the wrong room and seems to see
two unburied bodies in "her" bed. Gervas explains that they
are his wife and child, whom he is saving out of sentiment
so that all three of them can be buried together when he
dies. The figures turn out to be waxwork — the real bodies
are in crimson velvet coffins underneath them — but Elinor
has a bad moment when Sir Gervas tells her to pull down the
coverlid. At last the old man dies, and after some alarms
Sir Clement Darnley comes back and marries her.

Index to Motifs

The index that follows should not be regarded as exhaustive. First,
some major elements have been omitted by design. Castles, for instance, are so pervasive a device that no purpose can be served by the
recitation of two hundred novels that have them; similarly, the abun-
dance of murders in the novels argued the retention for the index of
specialized murders only — matricide, ax murder, suicide, and so on.
Second, the reader should understand that some novels have been more
thoroughly indexed than others. Those read or reread under clement
circumstances were indexed page by page, but others were read under
pressure of time or indexed from plot notes taken in other years for
other purposes. And while plot notes are likely to include incest
and banditti, they may well overlook such subtler elements as presen-
timents or unfinished deathbed speeches.

The index should have a number of uses. Most conspicuously, it
can lead scholars with particular interests — cavern imagery, Romantic
fascination with incest — to pertinent though obscure novels. I suppose, too, that it might have its uses for people interested in precursors and influences: how many novelists were using such-and-such
a motif before Coleridge or Scott or Keats ushered it into more high-
brow company? But beyond its original intention as a guide to titles,
it is an index that should be read through. Who would have expected
so few cabinets with secret compartments, so few ghosts wearing chains,
so many swooning males and burning buildings? Critical and historical
works on the Gothic novel overlook the richly various obsession with
falling (from heights, in holes, off horses, into rivers) which unexpectedly emerges from the tabulation. Someone, surely, must want to
know that despite plentiful seductions, weddings, and attempted rapes,
prophetic dreams outnumber erotic dreams more than twenty to one.

One heading requires explanation. *Mariticide* has from the first
been mistaken by typists and readers for a misspelling of *matricide*.
Mariticide is the killing of one's husband. Recourse to dictionaries,
district attorneys, police detectives, and academic departments of
criminal justice produced no name for this apparently unspeakable
crime, though the name of the reciprocal action — uxorcide — is
readily available. I was at last obliged to derive *mariticide* from
the rare adjective *mariticidal,* which was the closest term the *Oxford English Dictionary* could offer.

Finally, the numbers that stand in place of titles refer not to
pages but to the sequential number of the novel as it appears in the
plot summaries.

abbess: bad, 24, 29, 33, 74,
75, 78, 97, 105, 108, 112,
119, 122, 135, 137, 149, 154;
good, 29, 42, 54, 62, 65, 70,
78, 97, 119, 128, 135, 136,
171
abduction: of female, 1, 5, 17,
24, 27, 28, 29, 30, 31, 33,
34, 42, 43, 52, 53, 60, 61,
62, 63, 64, 68, 69, 70, 71,
73, 75, 78, 82, 86, 87, 88,
91, 95, 97, 101, 104, 107,
112, 116, 117, 119, 122, 123,
125, 127, 129, 133, 135, 136,
137, 138, 139, 143, 144, 147,
150, 151, 152, 154, 155, 159,
162, 166, 168, 171, 172, 178,
179, 188, 190, 192, 194, 199,
200, 202; of large group, 42;
of male, 1, 12, 20, 22, 24,
25, 26, 30, 41, 47, 50, 58,
59, 61, 63, 68, 70, 71, 76,
82, 83, 85, 86, 90, 91, 93,
112, 113, 123, 129, 137, 138,
147, 150, 152, 160, 172, 184,
187, 190, 194, 201, 207; of
wrong party, 70, 100, 138
adultery, 10, 18, 20, 32, 34,
35, 38, 49, 58, 59, 64, 65,
83, 104, 114, 119, 120, 122,
127, 128, 136, 138, 162, 171,
177, 182, 190, 192, 199, 206
animal, wild: assorted, 3; bear,
129; dragon, 67; lion, 19, 49;
tiger, 48, 196; vulture, 82,
109; wolf, 18, 69, 100, 101,
107, 132, 136, 172
apostasy, 1, 29, 99, 108, 109,
129, 177, 207
assassination, interrupted, 29,
36, 38, 42, 48, 49, 81, 88,
96, 199
atheism, 1, 57, 70, 75, 99, 104,
109, 167, 207
ax murder, 93, 107, 130

baby swapping, 22, 33, 34, 45,
56, 113, 119, 154, 191
banditti, 1, 20, 22, 28, 29, 30,
31, 38, 43, 45, 46, 47, 51,
53, 54, 59, 65, 69, 70, 74,
77, 78, 79, 87, 90, 91, 96,
97, 99, 107, 108, 109, 118,
119, 127, 129, 130, 134, 136,
138, 150, 152, 155, 158, 166,
172, 174, 177, 178, 180, 204.

See also condottieri;
highwayman; piracy
banishment, exile, and emigration, 4, 9, 35, 41, 58, 62,
66, 67, 73, 78, 87, 91, 96,
99, 107, 111, 113, 119, 128,
137, 140, 145, 159, 163, 165,
174, 175, 182, 207
banshee, 149, 151
bastard. *See* illegitimacy
battleground horrors, 24, 29,
92, 97, 130, 155, 162, 184
begging. *See* mendication
Bible-reading, dangers of, 99,
128
bigamy, 1, 33, 73, 80, 90, 97,
108, 114, 115, 119, 127, 128,
140, 144, 151, 152, 153, 177,
183
birthmark, 6, 28, 102, 107, 112,
113, 129, 133, 154, 185, 187,
193, 201. *See also* scar,
identifying
blood: alleged pool of, 53; bap-
tism of infant in, 107; boiling, 158; bowl of, dipping
daggers in, 116; as commodity,
109; cup of, in demon's hand,
10; drinking, 59, 75, 102,
129, 187, 206; on face, from
invisible hands, 108; issuing
from crucifix, 75; of lover,
on cudgel, 98; as noble orna-
ment on scarf, 100; overflow-
ing room, dream about, 137;
as payment to witch, 10; spit-
ting, 142, 155, 203; spreading
magically, 134; stains, 33,
42, 45, 70, 79, 99, 107, 108,
116, 118, 125, 134, 135, 136,
173. *See also* bosom; corpse;
message; pulp, bloody; statue,
peculiar
body. *See* corpse
body snatching, 16, 86
bones. *See* skeleton; skull
bosom: bloodstained, 9, 90, 116,
119, 166, 167; as distraction,
74, 99, 166; hag's naked, 75,
100; lover's severed heart
placed on, 33; pawed by lecherous jailer, 75; viper in
(figurative), 30, 35, 36, 46,
61, 71, 83, 108, 113, 168,
178, 183, 188, 194
brothel, 6, 119, 172, 177, 207

brothers, dissimilar, 1, 16, 29,
41, 45, 48, 49, 51, 65, 70,
75, 77, 78, 80, 83, 86, 90,
94, 109, 119, 127, 133, 134,
135, 137, 140, 142, 144, 154,
155, 172, 174, 185, 186, 198,
200, 204, 205
burial: alive, 3, 19, 47, 70,
80, 100, 187, 206; refused,
129; secret, 75, 112. *See also*
funeral, sham

cabinet with secret compartment,
7, 29
cannibalism, 1, 9, 109, 129
cave, 1, 18, 19, 24, 29, 33, 38,
43, 44, 54, 56, 62, 65, 70,
75, 76, 77, 78, 83, 95, 97,
98, 100, 102, 107, 108, 118,
122, 129, 133, 136, 138, 150,
151, 152, 155, 165, 167, 178,
187, 193, 201
cemetery as trysting place, 75,
159, 178, 186
chains, rattling of, 191
child or infant, dead, 3, 10,
24, 29, 40, 44, 47, 50, 60,
61, 64, 71, 72, 74, 80, 81,
83, 88, 95, 99, 105, 109, 113,
120, 127, 129, 130, 140, 161,
162, 170, 174, 175, 180, 182,
184, 187, 197, 199, 201
clergyman: evil, 1, 4, 24, 29,
31, 34, 45, 52, 53, 66, 70,
76, 78, 95, 96, 97, 99, 107,
108, 109, 110, 119, 129, 134,
135, 138, 179, 180, 185, 204;
good, 9, 10, 11, 52, 53, 60,
73, 92, 94, 95, 97, 109, 111,
127, 128, 130, 137, 149, 180,
205. *See also* monastery
coffin: body sitting up in, 16;
broken, 70; carried by skeleton, 88; crumbling, 29; doppelganger in, 59; erect, 70;
fallen through trapdoor, 208;
marked with name of protagonist, 190; open, 9, 29, 64,
65, 80, 100, 187; red velvet,
208; stones in, 70; voice in,
6
condottieri, 136
confinement: extralegal, 1, 5,
20, 23, 24, 26, 28, 29, 31,
33, 38, 42, 43, 45, 48, 49,
51, 52, 55, 61, 62, 65, 66,

67, 68, 69, 70, 71, 74, 75,
76, 77, 79, 81, 83, 85, 86,
87, 88, 90, 93, 95, 97, 98,
99, 106, 107, 108, 109, 112,
118, 119, 120, 121, 122, 123,
125, 127, 130, 133, 135, 136,
137, 138, 139, 144, 149, 150,
151, 154, 155, 160, 162, 167,
170, 171, 172, 174, 178, 180,
183, 185, 186, 188, 190, 191,
192, 194, 199, 200, 202, 204;
legal, 4, 16, 19, 24, 30, 35,
42, 50, 51, 55, 56, 64, 68,
71, 80, 84, 92, 99, 111, 114,
127, 129, 130, 132, 136, 137,
144, 146, 149, 152, 159, 160,
162, 163, 165, 168, 170, 172,
177, 183, 187, 192, 204, 207,
208
convent: corrupt, 75, 97, 122;
escape from, 6, 36, 60, 100,
118, 132, 135, 145, 173, 184,
200, 207; eviction from, 17,
74; as haven, 5, 33, 35, 42,
59, 62, 74, 87, 97, 99, 112,
117, 120, 125, 138, 149, 154,
171, 183, 185, 207; as prison,
4, 6, 24, 29, 33, 34, 36, 60,
61, 74, 75, 76, 92, 97, 99,
117, 118, 119, 128, 129, 135,
176, 178, 180, 183, 198, 206.
See also abbess; monastery;
novice or nun; veil-taking
conversion, religious, 24, 39,
54, 64, 69, 82, 105, 111, 121,
128
corpse: in bed, 205; behind cur-
tain, 136; bleeding, 38, 56,
66; blue, 108; burnt, 33, 191;
changing places with, 177;
disguised, 1, 123; dragged
past heroine's dungeon, 5; as
entertainment for villainess,
46; equestrian, 67; under
floorboards, 72; hanging, 16,
42, 43, 93; mangled, 1, 43,
73; naked, 24; physical contact with fresh, 1, 24, 33,
47, 74, 75, 100, 111, 119,
130, 136, 149, 154, 162, 193;
physical contact with moldering, 9, 23, 29, 99, 107, 110,
123, 129, 130, 133, 168, 191,
204; plural, in piles, 28, 33,
97; preserved, 60, 66, 129,
130, 134, 187, 206; produced

corpse (*continued*):
  as evidence in trial, 167; in
  sack, 119, 135, 173; of seduced woman, provoking hysteria in seducer, 195; shut in
  with, 75, 99, 125, 177; stumbling over, 177; talking, 30,
  127, 129; thrown over precipice, 33, 123; in trunk, 91,
  125, 148; walking, 43, 129;
  waxen representation of, 136,
  208. *See also* body snatching;
  child or infant, dead; pulp,
  bloody; putrefaction
cross, adverse reaction to, 67,
  75, 99, 129
cross-gender dressing, non-
  erotic, 1, 5, 6, 29, 33, 36,
  41, 47, 58, 62, 65, 67, 71,
  72, 75, 83, 86, 88, 89, 90,
  92, 95, 100, 103, 106, 108,
  120, 142, 155, 162, 165, 180,
  183, 186, 194; confusion of
  affections resulting from, 36,
  47, 86, 92, 110, 180
curse, 19, 71, 83, 107, 109,
  119, 127, 129, 183, 187, 204;
  release from, 6, 43, 75, 99,
  101, 109, 187, 206

death: emotionally induced, 1,
  6, 9, 11, 13, 15, 16, 20, 24,
  31, 49, 50, 55, 57, 61, 64,
  69, 71, 74, 75, 78, 81, 83,
  85, 90, 100, 106, 109, 114,
  116, 119, 120, 122, 123, 126,
  130, 144, 145, 146, 148, 149,
  150, 151, 155, 157, 161, 162,
  165, 174, 175, 182, 183, 186,
  189, 191, 193, 199, 207; pre-
  nuptial, 45, 65, 69, 145,
  161, 181, 184, 193, 199, 203,
  204, 207; sad and/or pious,
  11, 29, 33, 36, 37, 38, 40,
  48, 64, 71, 74, 80, 114, 120,
  130, 136, 139, 140, 146, 149,
  154, 174, 180, 193, 203, 204,
  207
deathbed: agonies, 4, 7, 11, 25,
  26, 29, 30, 33, 42, 43, 53,
  71, 76, 109, 114, 118, 119,
  126, 130, 135, 136, 146, 149,
  195, 203, 204, 206; blessing,
  missed, 24, 40, 127; speech,
  unfinished, 16, 29, 62, 71,
  83, 86, 94, 105, 108, 112,

114, 123, 127, 138, 145, 193,
  199
decapitation, 1, 16, 47, 74, 75,
  92, 96, 100, 129; interrupted,
  1, 30, 193
demon. *See* Satan and lesser
  demons
denial of god, 3, 109, 166
discovery of lost relative. *See*
  relative, lost, discovery of
disease, epidemic or loathsome,
  107, 162, 165, 207
disinterment, 33, 66, 72, 135,
  159, 206, 207
dismemberment: arm, 74; ear,
  192; finger, 70, 100, 192;
  hand, 2, 4, 65, 99, 103, 139,
  150, 206; leg, 89, 199. *See
  also* decapitation
door, secret (including panels,
  passages, and trapdoors), 1,
  5, 7, 10, 18, 20, 24, 28, 29,
  30, 31, 33, 47, 60, 62, 70,
  74, 75, 76, 77, 78, 86, 97,
  99, 100, 107, 108, 118, 119,
  121, 122, 123, 124, 128, 133,
  135, 136, 137, 138, 139, 145,
  151, 154, 155, 168, 170, 172,
  174, 186, 190, 191, 193, 199,
  200
doppelganger, 59, 66, 77, 187
dream: erotic, 99, 117; prophetic, 5, 9, 14, 28, 29, 30, 31,
  33, 38, 41, 45, 47, 51, 59,
  64, 65, 66, 69, 74, 75, 76,
  83, 84, 85, 97, 99, 102, 107,
  108, 117, 119, 121, 130, 132,
  137, 140, 161, 164, 165, 180,
  183, 190, 193, 194, 203
dressing, cross-gender. *See*
  cross-gender dressing, non-
  erotic
drugging, 3, 28, 30, 31, 33, 38,
  44, 47, 59, 61, 64, 68, 69,
  70, 71, 74, 83, 85, 86, 87,
  90, 99, 106, 111, 119, 125,
  134, 148, 155, 162, 170, 174,
  186, 190, 192, 202, 207. *See
  also* opium
drunkenness, 1, 9, 10, 24, 29,
  36, 42, 47, 48, 49, 51, 54,
  57, 60, 64, 66, 67, 70, 73,
  79, 82, 85, 86, 92, 95, 97,
  99, 109, 111, 112, 114, 115,
  119, 129, 130, 138, 139, 149,
  168, 170, 175, 177, 180, 189,

191, 194, 201, 202, 204, 207
dueling and other single combat,
8, 11, 13, 24, 35, 39, 41, 46,
54, 57, 59, 62, 64, 66, 71,
73, 77, 81, 83, 84, 86, 87,
92, 109, 111, 114, 120, 123,
126, 127, 130, 132, 136, 137,
138, 140, 144, 145, 149, 152,
154, 168, 176, 177, 182, 187,
190, 191, 193, 196, 205, 207;
averted, 50, 62, 68, 79, 104
dungeon, 1, 4, 5, 6, 18, 19, 20,
21, 22, 24, 25, 28, 29, 30,
31, 32, 33, 34, 46, 50, 51,
53, 54, 56, 59, 62, 63, 74,
75, 76, 77, 78, 86, 90, 91,
95, 97, 99, 107, 109, 112,
116, 119, 122, 123, 127, 129,
130, 133, 135, 138, 139, 155,
160, 162, 165, 167, 177, 178,
180, 191, 200, 201
dwarf, 3, 46, 56, 69, 98, 111,
165

earthquake, 19, 82, 108, 119,
129, 135, 162, 169, 207
eclipse, 19
elopement, 1, 12, 40, 41, 49,
56, 57, 65, 71, 90, 100, 104,
112, 122, 130, 144, 150, 152,
154, 163, 171, 182, 185, 199,
204; bungled, 99, 128, 174,
183, 185; prevented, 59, 99,
138, 177
execution, 1, 3, 14, 28, 47, 49,
76, 83, 87, 92, 96, 110, 119,
161, 167, 174, 179, 192
exhumation. See disinterment
exorcism. See curse, release
from
explosion, 31, 67, 69, 90, 162,
175
eye: corpse's swollen, 168;
evil, 3; fiery, 80, 82, 152;
Satan's, 129; seen through
crack, 9, 16
fainting: female, 1, 3, 4, 6, 7,
8, 9, 10, 11, 12, 13, 16, 18,
24, 28, 29, 32, 33, 34, 36,
41, 44, 45, 46, 47, 48, 54,
55, 56, 57, 58, 59, 60, 62,
64, 66, 69, 70, 71, 74, 75,
76, 78, 80, 83, 84, 86, 90,
92, 95, 100, 106, 108, 109,
111, 112, 116, 118, 119, 120,
122, 127, 128, 129, 130, 132,

133, 134, 135, 136, 137, 138,
140, 142, 145, 149, 150, 151,
152, 154, 155, 162, 165, 166,
168, 170, 172, 173, 174, 175,
177, 178, 182, 183, 187, 188,
189, 190, 191, 193, 195, 199,
204, 207; male, 1, 3, 4, 9,
11, 29, 33, 37, 42, 43, 53,
54, 56, 58, 59, 62, 64, 65,
71, 76, 80, 83, 86, 90, 97,
99, 100, 107, 109, 112, 114,
119, 127, 128, 129, 130, 132,
134, 135, 137, 139, 149, 152,
155, 166, 168, 169, 174, 177,
180, 182, 187, 201, 203, 204,
207
falling: almost, 29, 43, 100,
134, 138, 151; delusory, 35;
dream about, 55, 137, 199;
from heights, 3, 11, 12, 38,
53, 54, 66, 67, 78, 83, 99,
100, 104, 107, 129, 139, 149,
178, 184, 190; in holes, 1,
19, 29, 43, 54, 59, 82, 83,
85, 97, 108, 121, 123, 144,
178, 206, 207; off horse, 62,
74, 88, 94, 132, 148, 185,
199; into river, 100, 161,
165; worry about, 9, 43, 97,
136
false appearance. See masking;
shapechanging
false philosophy, 35, 37, 38,
68, 83, 96, 104, 111, 128,
135, 167, 183
feeblemindedness, 5, 12, 69, 86,
132
feud, interfamily, 47, 133, 138
filicide, 9, 45, 49, 76, 100,
116, 119, 120, 123, 177, 193
fire: auto da fé, 74, 75, 109,
173; accidental death by, 70,
107, 144, 160, 169; apparently
supernatural, 2, 3, 5, 10, 88,
102, 119, 121, 136, 190, 206;
house, 1, 19, 29, 31, 33, 34,
48, 50, 51, 53, 64, 65, 70,
79, 81, 82, 86, 91, 94, 95,
97, 99, 107, 109, 114, 118,
121, 125, 127, 139, 144, 152,
161, 162, 168, 169, 174, 207;
ship, 34, 151
flagellation, 48, 54, 64, 65,
66, 71, 74, 75, 87, 90, 103,
109, 120, 127, 129, 149, 150,
162, 176, 187

flood, 108, 165
fratricide, 29, 32, 44, 66, 74, 80, 99, 101, 107, 123, 125, 127, 129, 135, 137, 145, 150, 155, 174, 180, 186, 191, 200, 207
funeral: attended accidentally, 57, 100, 119, 130; clandestine, 186; gorgeous, 114; sham, 3, 6, 65, 70, 75, 92, 99, 138, 191

gaming, 7, 10, 15, 20, 31, 35, 36, 37, 38, 40, 41, 45, 50, 52, 59, 60, 61, 64, 68, 70, 86, 87, 104, 108, 111, 114, 118, 119, 120, 126, 128, 130, 131, 136, 137, 145, 147, 149, 157, 162, 166, 168, 169, 171, 172, 173, 174, 176, 177, 182, 187, 188, 190, 199, 206
garden as scene of temptation, 35, 36, 99, 109
ghost: with baby, 29; bleeding, 16, 99, 134; dancing or singing, 107, 206; fiery, 33, 76, 79, 80; in flaming boat, 34; hairy, 9, 187; helpful, 24, 26, 29, 30, 31, 56, 67, 75, 82, 90, 102, 130, 158, 187, 188, 194, 200; juvenile, 29, 187; lower-class, 101; murderous, 207; mutilated, 2, 75, 206; nonhuman, 43, 75, 79, 83, 128; skeletal, 75, 76, 193, 206; tangible, 177; of victim, appearing to murderer, 1, 7, 9, 10, 29, 33, 55, 56, 70, 76, 82, 99, 108, 135, 139, 178, 188, 194, 199, 201, 202; wearing chains, 191
ghoul, 3, 56
gluttony, 3, 67, 101, 107, 111, 129
god, denial of. See denial of god
grave: double occupancy of, 33, 116; dug with bare hands, 130, 139; hidden by boards, 28; leaping into, 6, 100; lying on, 109, 130; open, 6, 29, 33, 93, 136; parental, fondled, 11, 149; as playground, 159; poison plants on, 82; robbed of ornaments, 70; shallow, 48; of suicide, 53, 66; talking

to, 153. See also body snatching
guest: perfidious, 35, 38, 86, 127; uninvited and sinister, 10, 42, 75, 187
gypsy, 14, 52, 83, 99, 115, 160

hag. See witch or hag
hair: bandage, 95; given to dead, 100, 132; jewelry, 9, 20, 63, 69, 77, 80, 81, 83, 132, 148, 152, 172, 186, 189, 203; shaving off, 148; shirt, 69; tearing, 9, 47, 48, 58, 76, 92, 100, 105
hand, cold, seizing heroine, 154
hand, severed. See dismemberment
hangman, 48
harem, 1, 24, 54, 82, 127, 179
harem girl, 1, 107, 178
harlot. See loose woman
heart: as horrid memento, 33, 69, 123; parental, broken by child, 20, 36, 45, 74, 90, 118, 120, 146, 187, 204
hell, 3, 9, 82, 109, 165, 206
hell-mouth, 43, 99, 129, 165
heresy, 74, 75, 107, 109, 165, 177, 189
hermit's narrative, 1, 24, 47, 60, 62, 87, 118, 122, 123, 191; prevented by muteness of hermit, 86
highwayman, 37, 63, 68, 73. See also banditti
hole. See falling in holes
homecoming, tragic, 1, 8, 19, 43, 44, 49, 70, 87, 95, 97, 100, 112, 117, 118, 122, 130, 136, 142, 164, 171, 179, 185, 191, 193, 206
homosexuality. See cross-gender dressing, confusion of affections resulting from
hook or nail, heroine caught on, 136, 150
human: as commodity, 1, 7, 10, 12, 48, 54, 63, 64, 82, 85, 87, 118, 120, 129, 136, 139, 140, 142, 146, 165, 166, 206; as food, 3, 48, 101 (See also cannibalism); as prey, 79 (See also vampire); as sacrifice, 3, 82, 102, 107, 109, 129, 174
hunchback, 3, 119, 129

idolatry, 19, 82, 109
illegitimacy, 5, 9, 16, 20, 31,
  36, 44, 45, 49, 52, 57, 61,
  64, 65, 66, 71, 72, 74, 80,
  81, 85, 89, 90, 92, 95, 99,
  109, 111, 113, 114, 115, 116,
  117, 120, 127, 128, 129, 130,
  132, 137, 142, 145, 146, 166,
  167, 171, 177, 205
illness, emotionally induced, 1,
  3, 7, 13, 20, 28, 30, 31, 41,
  43, 47, 48, 49, 50, 51. 57,
  62, 64, 69, 75, 80, 83, 84,
  86, 92, 94, 95, 96, 97, 99,
  100, 109, 111, 112, 114, 118,
  119, 122, 123, 127, 128, 130,
  133, 135, 136, 137, 140, 145,
  149, 160, 162, 164, 165, 168,
  171, 174, 175, 177, 180, 182,
  183, 187, 188, 191, 199, 204,
  206, 207. *See also* death,
  emotionally induced
impalement, 28
imprisonment. *See* confinement
incest: actual, 20, 29, 47, 99,
  129, 130; literary flirtation
  with (including false alarms,
  foiled attempts, threats, and
  unconsummated incestuous passion), 5, 16, 21, 22, 23, 28,
  32, 33, 40, 48, 56, 64, 75,
  78, 79, 85, 87, 88, 89, 90,
  92, 103, 106, 109, 113, 116,
  120, 125, 128, 129, 135, 137,
  143, 145, 148, 154, 165, 171,
  186, 189, 190, 191, 192, 193,
  200, 207
infant, nonflammable, 101
infanticide, 44, 65, 83, 98,
  109, 120, 129
Inquisition, 5, 27, 28, 31,
  38, 47, 50, 53, 61, 69, 74,
  75, 76, 78, 85, 91, 99, 106,
  108, 109, 117, 129, 135, 155,
  165, 167, 171, 173, 174, 180,
  207
insanity. *See* lunacy
insurrection. *See* sedition, insurrection, and treason
invisibility, 38, 59, 77, 91,
  108, 158

jilting, 46, 56, 83, 84, 109,
  110, 120, 149, 207

kidnapping. *See* abduction

laudanum. *See* opium
letter: burned, 8, 42, 174;
  in casket, 119; concealed in
  lemon, 88; dropped from window, 26; forged, 25, 33, 38,
  49, 71, 119, 154, 174, 177,
  204; intercepted, 36, 49, 54,
  99, 137; from murderer, 72;
  poisoned, 206; stolen, 42;
  swallowed, 32. *See also*
  message; warning
levitation of armor, 9
libertine, 11, 16, 30, 35, 36,
  41, 47, 49, 57, 61, 62, 64,
  68, 69, 70, 71, 80, 81, 83,
  92, 97, 99, 101, 104, 108,
  119, 126, 129, 130, 131, 137,
  138, 140, 143, 145, 149, 150,
  151, 154, 160, 162, 165, 174,
  175, 180, 185, 188, 207
light, mysterious, 2, 3, 10, 29,
  43, 59, 86, 108, 118, 125,
  133, 138, 154, 172, 177, 187,
  191
loose woman, 7, 20, 24, 31, 35,
  49, 54, 57, 60, 61, 63, 64,
  66, 69, 85, 86, 108, 111, 113,
  114, 119, 125, 129, 130, 154,
  172, 177, 192, 204, 206. *See
  also* brothel; villainess
lost: in castle, 9, 33, 136,
  139; in woods, 29, 33, 48, 76,
  132, 136, 177, 201
lunacy, 1, 6, 12, 13, 14, 19,
  28, 29, 30, 33, 36, 37, 39,
  43, 44, 45, 48, 49, 50, 52,
  57, 64, 65, 70, 71, 77, 79,
  83, 89, 90, 92, 97, 98, 100,
  105, 106, 109, 110, 119, 120,
  123, 127, 128, 142, 144, 146,
  147, 149, 153, 154, 155, 158,
  162, 165, 169, 172, 174, 175,
  177, 180, 181, 187, 189, 191,
  199, 204, 205, 207

madhouse, 36, 68, 73, 109, 119,
  128, 129, 144, 177, 192, 204
magical object, 3, 66, 82, 99,
  145, 201
magical process, 3, 38, 43, 50,
  65, 67, 69, 85, 99, 107, 108,
  134. *See also* miracle; occult
  arts; warlock or wizard;
  witch or hag
mariticide, 1, 87, 188
masking, 7, 9, 10, 29, 31, 32,

masking (*continued*):
41, 42, 46, 52, 57, 59, 69,
71, 74, 76, 77, 83, 86, 96,
99, 108, 113, 119, 126, 132,
134, 135, 143, 154, 155, 158,
174, 175, 177, 182, 186, 187,
205, 206, 207. *See also* shape-
changing
matricide, 57, 66, 74, 90, 99
memento mori, 31, 47, 77, 121,
136
mendication, 57, 76, 96, 109,
119, 199
message: in blood, 59, 128, 158,
174; in fire, 5, 43, 85, 91,
109, 121, 134, 180, 190. *See
also* letter; warning
miniature, 1, 5, 9, 11, 16, 24,
28, 29, 30, 36, 41, 47, 48,
49, 60, 62, 63, 69, 73, 76,
77, 83, 84, 86, 88, 90, 92,
94, 99, 106, 108, 109, 113,
118, 119, 123, 124, 128, 129,
130, 133, 134, 135, 136, 137,
138, 144, 147, 149, 150, 151,
152, 154, 155, 161, 168, 171,
172, 173, 178, 180, 183, 189,
191, 192, 196, 199, 201, 204,
206, 207, 208
miracle, 19, 31, 43, 69, 87, 92,
99, 109, 194
miser, 32, 56, 84, 92, 109, 119,
140
mob, 48, 50, 66, 67, 99, 106,
109, 114, 129
monastery: child raised in, 1,
60, 75, 86, 99, 117, 178, 190;
escape from, 60, 109, 180;
forced or tricked into, 29,
31, 109, 180; penitent man going into, 9, 62, 93, 111, 150,
191, 193; as prison, 194; as
refuge, 95; as scene of revelry, 95, 97, 138; as solution
to delicate situation, 86,
191. *See also* convent
monk, unusually mysterious, 5,
70, 74, 75, 76, 85, 101, 119,
135, 139, 171, 181
mummy, 3
murder. *See* ax murder; filicide;
fratricide; infanticide; mariticide; matricide; parricide;
poison; regicide; sororicide;
suicide; uxoricide
music, mysterious, 6, 9, 10, 24,
28, 29, 33, 38, 41, 43, 47,
59, 74, 77, 82, 99, 102, 105,
109, 133, 134, 136, 149, 170,
177, 185, 206
muteness, 1, 86

noble savage, 48, 109
novel reading, dangers of, 35,
37, 64, 111, 204
novice or nun: debauched, 31,
69, 75, 99, 100, 101, 117,
137; destined from infancy,
54, 99, 170; determined to
take veil, 6, 65, 87, 108,
127, 207; eloped, 1, 184;
ruined, 29, 60, 69, 70, 99;
wicked, 9, 29, 99, 117, 154.
See also abbess; convent;
veil-taking
nudity, 3, 85, 109, 177
nun. *See* novice or nun

occult arts, pseudo-sciences,
and parlor tricks: alchemy,
67, 140; astrology, 69, 71,
108, 187, 193; cabalism, 10;
necromancy, 79, 129, 161;
phrenology, 115, 148; sorcery, 99, 130, 174; ventriloquism, 6, 187. *See also*
magical process
occult knowledge, 109, 190
opium, 39, 52, 69, 70, 89, 111,
125, 164, 207; fatal overdose,
148; suicide by, 40, 204
orphan, 12, 15, 24, 30, 32, 33,
41, 45, 49, 50, 51, 56, 63,
65, 76, 77, 97, 105, 111, 112,
127, 130, 135, 136, 140, 144,
145, 149, 151, 153, 159, 161,
162, 165, 168, 169, 172, 177,
181, 183, 189, 191, 201, 207

paralysis, 48, 125, 186
parricide, 21, 70, 75, 77, 88,
93, 95, 108, 109, 119, 129,
167, 187, 206
passage, subterranean, 5, 6, 9,
10, 18, 24, 28, 29, 32, 33,
44, 59, 70, 74, 75, 76, 77,
90, 92, 97, 99, 108, 109, 119,
121, 129, 133, 134, 135, 136,
137, 138, 155, 170, 172, 189,
191, 193, 201, 207
peasant or apparent peasant of
noble demeanor, 25, 31, 56,

59, 63, 65, 76, 85, 88, 89,
91, 102, 117, 123, 133, 141,
146, 154, 162, 165, 170, 174,
193, 201, 206
philosopher's stone, 50
piracy, 1, 19, 24, 29, 33, 47,
54, 55, 95, 105, 119, 122,
125, 129, 136, 174, 176, 179,
193, 206
plague. *See* disease
poison, 4, 5, 24, 28, 33, 36,
38, 45, 58, 70, 75, 78, 99,
100, 101, 118, 119, 135, 136,
150, 155, 166, 167, 172, 180,
190, 193, 200; blade, 135,
145, 194; chaplet, 121; kiss,
187; letter, 206; orange, 206;
plant on grave, 82; sacramental wine, 70, 107
portrait: animated, 134, 193;
changing, 9, 128, 187, 191;
falling, 129, 187; fascinating, 9, 16, 28, 71, 99, 109,
193; frightening, 108, 109,
187; of hero as child, 149;
hidden, 136, 151; hiding behind, 1; with keyhole, 1;
with matching ghost, 102,
134, 142, 187; mistaken for
ghost, 208; morally support-
ive, 120; revelatory of incest, 130; sad, 187; saved
from financial ruin, 81; in
unlikely place, 47. *See also*
miniature
precipice. *See* falling
presentiment, 9, 19, 29, 31, 33,
37, 41, 47, 51, 54, 64, 71,
75, 76, 92, 127, 132, 135,
136, 154, 162, 188
prophet, seer, or sibyl, 3, 5,
9, 19, 28, 55, 56, 72, 75, 83,
99, 109, 160, 165, 170, 206,
207. *See also* dream, prophetic; gypsy; occult arts;
warning
prostitution. *See* brothel;
loose woman
pulp, bloody: formerly abbess,
99; formerly baby, 129; formerly devotees of Juggernaut,
109
putrefaction, 9, 16, 23, 28, 30,
46, 72, 74, 76, 93, 99, 116,
119, 123, 129, 139, 161, 166,
168, 207; accelerated, 38, 93,

100, 107, 116, 129, 168;
waxen, 136

rape, 7, 24, 27, 47, 64, 70, 74,
88, 98, 99, 129, 191, 192,
202, 207; attempted, 5, 9, 18,
23, 24, 25, 28, 29, 30, 31,
33, 38, 51, 55, 64, 68, 75,
76, 91, 93, 95, 107, 119, 135,
138, 139, 140, 154, 168, 177,
200
rebellion. *See* sedition, insurrection, and treason
regicide, 97
relative, lost, discovery of, 1,
4, 5, 6, 9, 15, 16, 19, 20,
21, 22, 24, 25, 30, 31, 33,
36, 38, 40, 43, 44, 46, 47,
50, 53, 59, 61, 62, 63, 65,
73, 74, 77, 80, 83, 85, 86,
87, 90, 91, 97, 99, 100, 106,
107, 108, 114, 115, 122, 123,
124, 125, 129, 130, 136, 139,
143, 144, 150, 152, 154, 155,
160, 168, 171, 173, 174, 178,
179, 183, 186, 191, 193, 199,
200, 204, 207, 208; on verge
of murder, 24, 70, 88, 135; on
verge of rape, 16, 23, 36,
136, 168
relics, holy, 74
reputation, loss of, 7, 9, 15,
29, 47, 49, 56, 57, 62, 74,
80, 83, 84, 92, 96, 97, 112,
127, 128, 129, 130, 133, 135,
149, 151, 154, 162, 168, 172,
175, 177
resurrection, apparent, 2, 10,
16, 29, 33, 43, 47, 59, 83,
96, 132, 134, 170, 177
revenge. *See* vengeance, vow of
riot. *See* mob

sacrilege, 3, 4, 19, 53, 70, 83,
93, 97, 107, 109, 129, 135,
178, 180, 193
sadism, 69, 120, 129, 170
Satan and lesser demons, 3, 9,
10, 38, 43, 53, 54, 61, 66,
67, 70, 82, 85, 98, 99, 101,
117, 129, 130, 158, 166, 206
scar, identifying, 40, 65, 86,
90, 100. *See also* birthmark
secrecy, oath of, 6, 25, 29, 31,
33, 38, 41, 47, 49, 51, 54,
56, 59, 74, 75, 76, 77, 85,

secrecy, oath of (*continued*):
89, 90, 100, 116, 119, 125,
127, 129, 135, 138, 139, 154,
170, 180, 206, 207

sedition, insurrection, and
treason, 3, 9, 16, 29, 33, 42,
75, 96, 110, 123, 129, 162,
206, 207

seduction: of female by male, 9,
20, 24, 35, 36, 38, 41, 43,
45, 48, 49, 57, 59, 61, 64,
65, 66, 71, 73, 82, 83, 85,
86, 95, 99, 100, 101, 104,
114, 115, 119, 120, 124, 127,
129, 131, 143, 152, 153, 154,
166, 167, 168, 174, 177, 181,
182, 185, 189, 204, 207; of
male by female, 38, 64, 74,
89, 119, 128, 129, 207

selling. *See* human as commodity;
soul, selling of

sensibility: counterfeit, 167;
dangers of, 83, 111, 136, 142,
167, 178

setting, supernatural shift of,
2, 9, 38, 43, 75, 79, 82

shapechanging, 1, 38, 43, 66,
67, 82, 99, 101, 107, 108,
158, 187

shipwreck, 1, 9, 12, 14, 19, 32,
34, 41, 48, 49, 54, 55, 56,
75, 82, 87, 92, 95, 98, 101,
106, 108, 109, 119, 133, 135,
136, 138, 150, 152, 162, 165,
168, 170, 175, 176, 179, 207

skeleton: animated, 80, 82, 88;
at banquet, 121; in bed with,
1; of child, 34; in closet,
191, 205; costumed, 28, 208;
in dungeon, 122; hand of,
clutching murder weapon, 139;
hanging, 158; in quantity, 3;
spectral, 75, 76, 193, 206; in
trunk, 16, 31, 108, 137; wearing familiar ring, 28

skull, 16, 29, 47, 85, 99, 109,
168, 170; as base for cauldron, 75; at feet of demon,
10; food in, 21; kicked, 70;
object made from, 53, 82, 109;
rat in, 80; talking, 187;
transformation of, 187

slavery. *See* human as commodity

sleepwalking, 74, 107, 172, 178

smuggling, 177, 189

snake or snakes: bite of, 99;

dancing with, 82; large and
menacing, 48, 100; mangled and
rotting, 75; as mat for idol,
109; pit of, 155; around
witch's cabin, 10. *See also*
bosom, viper in (figurative)

society, secret, 59, 116, 206

sororicide, 62, 99, 185, 206

soul, selling of, 38, 53, 66,
67, 99, 102, 129, 166

spider, supernatural, 82, 158

spirit, benevolent, 43, 59, 66,
77, 82. *See also* ghost, helpful

starvation, 31, 33, 35, 36, 44,
47, 50, 67, 75, 76, 83, 84,
97, 99, 109, 119, 130, 162,
186, 194

statue, peculiar: animated, 2,
75; with bleeding nose, 193;
with disappearing helmet, 193;
with secret button, 1, 99;
silver, with holy relics, 74;
unexpected, 47, 62

storm, 9, 12, 13, 18, 24, 28,
29, 30, 32, 33, 34, 37, 38,
43, 45, 47, 48, 49, 50, 53,
54, 55, 56, 57, 59, 60, 62,
65, 68, 69, 75, 76, 77, 81,
82, 83, 86, 88, 90, 94, 95,
97, 98, 99, 105, 108, 109,
116, 119, 122, 125, 129, 130,
132, 133, 134, 136, 137, 138,
146, 149, 150, 151, 152, 154,
158, 159, 160, 161, 162, 165,
166, 167, 172, 173, 174, 175,
177, 180, 182, 187, 188, 189,
190, 191, 192, 193, 200, 201,
205, 206, 207

subterranean passage. *See*
passage, subterranean

suicide, 1, 17, 20, 21, 24, 26,
28, 30, 31, 35, 36, 37, 38,
40, 46, 47, 49, 55, 56, 59,
64, 66, 69, 70, 71, 76, 78,
81, 82, 83, 85, 88, 89, 92,
95, 98, 100, 101, 104, 107,
110, 116, 117, 119, 127, 129,
135, 137, 138, 146, 147, 150,
162, 164, 166, 167, 168, 174,
177, 178, 180, 186, 190, 192,
195, 199, 204, 205, 206, 207;
attempted or contemplated, 9,
21, 35, 39, 43, 49, 52, 58,
62, 68, 71, 80, 89, 91, 144,
148, 159, 166, 167, 199;

threatened or faked; 33, 87,
99, 111, 129, 149, 164, 204
sword, unusual: outsize, 95,
193; Melchior's, 82; with
message on blade, 134, 193;
self-propelled, 3

talking in sleep, 88, 135, 166
teeth: fanglike, 48; shot out by
former abductee, 63. *See also*
snake, bite of; vampire
torture, 31, 33, 47, 48, 49, 53,
74, 75, 87, 97, 100, 106, 109,
116, 129, 130, 135, 158, 165,
167, 173, 174, 180, 186, 206,
207; instrument of, 42, 75,
96, 106, 109, 116, 129, 135,
136, 155
twins, 54, 71, 74, 86, 88, 89,
92, 109, 118, 119, 130, 169,
174, 185, 187

underground passage. *See*
passage, subterranean
usurpation, 3, 5, 12, 18, 20,
22, 23, 25, 29, 30, 31, 33,
42, 52, 56, 62, 77, 78, 80,
85, 86, 91, 95, 102, 104, 107,
110, 123, 137, 139, 141, 142,
150, 160, 174, 178, 180, 186,
193, 194, 200, 201
usury, 56, 111, 120, 165
uxorcide, 9, 10, 24, 49, 62, 76,
85, 88, 119, 125, 136, 148,
177

vampire, 109, 131
veil-taking, disrupted, 29, 54,
135, 190
venereal disease, 64, 192
vengeance, vow of, 29, 30, 31,
33, 37, 41, 44, 46, 70, 71,
74, 75, 86, 87, 88, 89, 100,
108, 122, 133, 166, 167, 177,
180
villain. *See* clergyman, evil;
libertine; villain, gauche
villain, gauche: dagger caught
in cloak, 33; discovered with
monastic equivalent of pants
down, 99
villainess, 1, 10, 28, 29, 35,
36, 37, 38, 40, 41, 46, 61,
71, 83, 93, 97, 120, 123, 127,

129, 135, 138, 144, 149, 166,
170, 184, 188, 196, 206. *See
also* abbess, bad
vision. *See* dream, prophetic
voice, mysterious, 6, 9, 19, 26,
29, 31, 33, 42, 43, 45, 47,
54, 64, 70, 72, 75, 76, 77,
82, 83, 90, 107, 108, 109,
119, 122, 127, 128, 129, 134,
136, 137, 147, 150, 151, 154,
158, 170, 172, 174, 178, 181,
184, 185, 187, 207
volcano, 47, 54, 108, 120, 138,
206
vortex. *See* whirlpool
vow. *See* secrecy, oath of; veil-
taking; vengeance, vow of;
wedding

wanderer, preternatural, 19, 50,
55, 99, 109, 166, 207
warlock or wizard, 5, 43, 67,
119, 170, 190
warning, anonymous or pseudony-
mous, 13, 28, 31, 35, 37, 41,
42, 49, 59, 70, 71, 76, 86,
97, 118, 128, 130, 152, 184,
187, 207
wedding: aborted prior to ceremony, 6, 19, 24, 56, 138, 149,
199; clandestine, 1, 8, 28,
29, 40, 56, 60, 64, 86, 88,
92, 99, 108, 109, 112, 114,
116, 119, 120, 126, 127, 128,
139, 140, 149, 168, 169, 174,
180, 183, 186, 193, 199; counterfeit, 11, 29, 31, 35, 115,
142, 149, 171, 183, 198;
forced, 1, 5, 6, 33, 45, 46,
61, 62, 76, 82, 83, 85, 87,
92, 95, 97, 101, 107, 112,
116, 122, 125, 139, 144, 147,
148, 151, 179, 181, 185; interrupted, 6, 9, 26, 29, 31,
33, 61, 62, 69, 80, 86, 88,
92, 95, 97, 116, 117, 122,
129, 134, 135, 139, 152, 178,
187; by specter clergyman,
109, 139
werewolf, 107, 158
whirlpool, 19, 29, 43, 48
witch or hag, 3, 9, 10, 43, 50,
67, 69, 71, 75, 82, 100, 107,
128, 129, 165, 174, 201

Index of Characters

My restriction of characters into categories serves two purposes: first, it avoids the crowds of hermits, aunts, faithful servants, and passing cavaliers, whose names the reader is unlikely to want; second, it makes more accessible the sometimes entertaining habits of Gothic christening and alias-taking. Simplification, however, has its price, since all the headings, and especially "hero," are subject to ambivalence. Do I, the reader may well ask, mean by "hero" 1) the protagonist, 2) the right-thinking chap who helps justice prevail, or 3) the male romantic lead? I ordinarily mean 3), which nearly always involves 2) and sometimes 1), but I have included even 1)'s whose principles have so faltered that they require double listings as villains. Similarly, heroines are usually female romantic leads, frequently protagonists as well, but protagonists can double as villainesses. By an arbitrary decision villains and villainesses are deliberate rotters: I do not include characters acting on misguided principles, or demonic visitants.

A number of characters appear in the index under a single name. Although this phenomenon may occasionally represent a lapse in note-taking, it can usually be accounted for by the quantities of orphans, foundlings, mysterious pedigrees, and one-word aliases essential to Gothic plots.

Numbers refer not to pages but to summaries.

Heroes

Abellino (alias for Count Rosalvo), 96
Adolphus, 25
Adrian, 162
Alciphron, 121
Alford, Edwin, 7
Alhamet, 55. *See also* Cassimir; Gialdini; Lorenzo; Lovinski; Ozembo; Penrose, Edward
Alleyn, 133
Almanza, Prince, 145
Alphonso, 198
Alphonsus, 87, 207
Altamont, Lord, 94
Amamore, Sir Lucius, 73
Ambrosio, 99. *See also* under Villains

Archdale, Sigismund, 205
Arlingford, Henry, 41
Armirald, 107
Atheling, Lord, 103
Aubrey, 131
Augustine, 30
Augustus, 24
Avignon, Louis d', 185
Avinzo, Huberto, 75
Avondale, Henry Mowbray, Earl of, 83
Avondel, 196

Barozzi, Rosalva, 174
Beaufort, Eugenius de, 183
Beraldi, Ormando, 20
Berchtold, Ernestus, 130

206

Berenza, 38
Bertram (alias for Isabel),
  194
Bertrand, Sir, 2
Bethel, Ormsby, 111
Beverly, Edward, 182
Bleville, the Earl of, 126
Blondeville, Gaston de, 134.
  See also under Villains
Bouville, de, 125
Brooks, Everard, 100
Browning, Octavius (later Duke
  de Valentois), 113

Caesario, 54
Calini, 24
Calzolaro, 187
Carlos, 59
Carlostein, 120
Cassimir (alias for Alhamet), 55
Castruccio, 165
Cisternas, Raymond de las, 99
Claridge, Alfred de, 146
Claudio, 85, (really Louis) 129
Clermont, 150
Colwan, George, Jr., 66
Connal, 110
Corbet, Sir Henry, 144
Cornwall, Mr., 8
Courci, Edgar de, 123
Courtenay, Edward de, 43
Cronstadt, the Count de, 140
Cyphon, Theodore, 192

Darlowitz, Count, 37
Darnley, Sir Clement, 208
Darrell, Sir Francis, 39
Delacour, Captain, 152
Delamore, William, 148
Delancey, Ethelred Winbyrne,
  Lord, 186
Desmond, 110
Donald, 201
Douglas, James, 67
Douglas, Lionel, 80
Dubois (really Count St. Blan-
  chard), 112
Dunamore, Lord, 147
Duncan, 63
Duntrone, Alan, 122

Edgar, 170
Edward, 40, 88, (The Black
  Prince) 9
Egbert, Sir, 43
Eldred, 122
Endymion (alias for Ines), 110
Essex, 92

Falkner, John, 159
Fauconbridge, Philip (later Earl
  of Monmouth), 5
Ferdinand, 127
Fernandez, 53
Ferrara, Don Lorenzo de, 190
Fitzalan, Oscar, 149
Fitzallan, Edward, 206
Fitzallan, Hector, 71
Fitz-Auburne, Arthur, 30
Fitzeustace, 166
Fitzmaurice, Edward, 204
Fitzowen, Henry, 43
Fitzrivers, Algernon, 34
Fitzwalter, 65
Fleetwood, Casimir, 49
Flodoardo (alias for Count
  Rosalvo), 96
Florilmo, 26
Fortescue, Edward, Lord, 41
Francis, 187
Frankenheim, Osbright of, 100
Frankenstein, Victor, 161
Frederick, 197, 206

Gialdini (alias for Alhamet), 55
Glenmorris, Captain, 181
Glenwark, Lorrimond, Laird of, 56
Godwin, William, 64
Gonzari, Martini, 75
Grant, Alan, 63
Gray, Thomas, 128

Hamilton, Graham, 84
Hanslape, Baron, 184
Hanson, Jason, 192
Harley, Charles, 48
Haro, Alphonso de, 28
Hellfried, 79
Henley, Frank, 68
Henri, 24, 154
Henry, 22
Herman, 79, 158
Hoffmann, de (earlier Leopold
  Sternheim), 65
Honorio, 188
Horatio, 21, 116
Howard, Charles, 153
Hubert, 184, 199
Huberto, 180

Isidore (alias for Hemel-
  fride), 180

Jefferson, Mr., 52
Julio, 86

Kais, 116

L, Edmund, Lord, 124
Le Forester, Godfrey, 12
Leicester, 92
Leonard, 123
Leontini, 46
Leopold, 91
Lima, Frederico de, 106
Lindamore, Frederick, 70
Lioni, 54
Lodore, Henry, 163
Logano, Napolo di, 17
Lorenzo, 117, (alias for Al-
   hamet) 55
Louis (also called Claudio), 129
Lovel, Edmund Twyford, Lord, 141
Lovinski (alias for Alhamet), 55

Marcellus, 93
Marchmont, Mr., 175
Maserini, Alfred, 118
Maserini, Percival, 118
Maximilian, 42
Medina, Lorenzo de, 99
Melford, Charles, 89
Mellas, Osmund de, 119
Melmoth, John, 109
Melvil, Renaldo, 177
Millward, Edward, 60
Millward, Henry, 60
Monmouth, Philip Fauconbridge,
   Earl of, 5
Montague, Clement, 80
Montalto, 139
Montbrasil, the Marquis of, 182
Montferrat, Enrico, 171
Montfort, Henry, 97
Montmorenci, Henry, 43
Montorio, Annibal, 108
Montorio, Ippolito, 108
Montville, Horatio de, 151
Morney, Edwin de, 6
Mortimer, Lord, 149
Mountflorence, 151
Mowbray, Henry (Earl of Avon-
   dale), 83
Munro, Osmond, 152

Neville, Gerard, 159

O'Carroll, John Oceanus,
   Lord, 169
O'Mara, Reginald, 4
O'Neill, Eugene, 148
Ormond, the Earl of, 170
Osbert, 133
Oswald, Egbert, 154
Ozembo (alias for Alhamet), 55

Paladour, Sir, 107
Pemberton, Henry (called Pem-
   broke), 115
Penrose, Edward (alias for
   Alhamet), 55
Pin, Ignatius du, 191
Pole, Arthur de la, 179
Porta, Marcello, 74

Raby, Lord, 62
Radmill, Henry, 168
Ravenspur, the Earl of, 78
Raymond, Lord, 162
Rayneer, Eugene, 16
Rhinaldo, 18
Ricardo, 117
Richmond, 182
Rimauldo, the Conde Don, 76
Rimini, Clementine, 11
Rinaldo, Prince, 47
Rosalvo, Count, 96
Rosenheim, Adolphus, 70
Rosorio, Ferdinando d', 61
Rotaldo, 25
Rozendorf, Baron, 37
Rudolpho, 200

S--, Count, 59
St. Alvars, Bertrand, 77
St. Blanchard, Count (earlier
   called Dubois), 112
St. Elmer, 35
St. Evremond, Richard de, 44
St. Julien, Ulric, 1
St. Julien, Valentine, 1
St. Leon, 50
Salathiel, 19
Salisbury, Longsword, Earl of, 95
Saltoun, Edward, Lord, 78
Savani, Alberto, 45
Savani, Alphonso, 45
Saville, Edward, 143
Sevigne, de, 150
Seymour, Frederick, 203
Sigismorn, 33
Sigismund, Valentine, 90
Smith, Dick, 197
Somerset, 15
Southampton, Lionel, 157
St**, Baron, 58
Stanton, 109
Sternheim, Leopold (afterward
   De Hoffmann), 65
Sunderland, Arthur, 57

Theodore, 137, 158, 178, 193
Timoska, Count, 202

Twyford, Edmund (later Lord
  Lovel), 141

Urbandine, Constantine, 29
Urbino, Lorenzo, Duke d',
  155

Val-Ambrosio, Lorenzo, 31
Valancourt, 136
Valentois, Octavius Browning,
  Duke of, 113
Vallenstein, Casimir, 69
Valmont, the Marquis of, 32
Varano, 173
Vathek, the Caliph, 3. *See also*
  under Villains
Vereza, Count, 138
Verezzi, 167
Verney, Lionel, 162
Villars, Edward de, 194
Villers, Mr., 147
Villiers, Edward, 163
Vivaldi, Vincentio di, 135

Walter, 6
Warbeck, Perkin, 160
Warren, Raymond, 194
Warwick, Captain, 176
Weimar, Count, 37
Werdenberg, Herman of, 97
Williams, Caleb, 51
Willmot, Leonard, 73
Willoughby, Clarence, 132
Willoughby, Sir Ralph, 14
Wilson, Wilson, 104
Wolfstein, 166
Woodvile, 13
Woodville, 164
Woodville, Charles, 169
Wringham, Robert, 66. *See also*
  under Villains

Xavier, 207
Yates, Frank (later Lord
  Caerleon), 114
Zeluco, 120. *See also* under
  Villains

Heroines

Adelaide, 97, 151, 172
Adelaine, 43
Adelais, 191
Adeline, 137
Aigline, 132
Alethe, 121
Alexa, 24
Aliagra, Isidora di (usually
  called Immalee), 109
Alizra, 207
Allenberg, Theresa d', 127
Almeria, 106
Almira, 25
Alphonsine, 54
Alto, Morella de, 27
Amanda, 21
Angelina, 93
Angellina, 117
Aprieu, Jennet, 80
Arieni, Cazire, 35
Armida, 110
Arnhalt, Adela, 188
Arnhalt, Isabella, 188
Aspasia, 26
Athelia, 105
Azelia, 73

Barozzi, Rosalina, 174
Barville, Mary Jane (earlier
  called Radmill), 168

Belford, Aurelia, 94
Bennet, Charlotte, 199
Bensadi, Eve, 192
Berchtold, Julia, 130
Blanchard, Adelaide, 11
Brindoli, Hersilia di, 24
Brisac, Mrs., 206

Calantha, 83
Carmilla, 129
Catherine, Lady, 201
Cecilia, 173
Charmont, Lucy, 103
Christiana, 190
Circesia, 24
Cisternas, Antonia de las, 99
Claudina, 127
Clermont, Madeline, 150
Cleveland, Maisuna, 52
Clifford, Charlotte (later
  Seymour), 203
Clifford, Elinor, 208
Clifford, Julia, 203
Clifford, Mary de, 13
Constanza, 76
Cornelia, 190
Courtenaye, Isabelle de, 107

Dacres, Althea, 175
Darlowitz, Amelia, 37
Darnford, Mrs., 142

Delaval, Rose, 41
Delmington, Clarentine, 15
Dinwoodie, Rosilda, 56
Doni, Louisa, 130
Douglas, Elinor, 80
Draulincourt, Margaret, 56

Elcour, Adelaide d', 112
Eleanora, 25
Elfrida, Princess, 105
Elinor, 92
Ellen, 197
Elmira, 59
Eloise, 166
Elrington, Emily, 57
Elvington, Agnes, 182
Elvington, Constance, 182
Elvington, Elenor, 182
Elvira (called "the Rose of
    Vancenza"), 145
Emily, 104
Emma, 30, 123
Emmeline, 97
Endermay, Jacintha, 154
Ethelind, 170
Euthanasia, 165

F**, Albertina of, 58
Falieri, Rosa (alias for Rosalina
    Barozzi), 174
Falkner, Elizabeth, 159
Fanny, 104
Farnham, Anna, 115
Felicia, 198
Fiormonda, 82
Fitzalan, Amanda, 149
Fitz-Auburne, Ethelwina, 30
Fitz-Owen, Emma, 141
Fitzwalter, the Baroness, 170
Fitzwalter, Margaret, 65
Florentina, 187
Fortescue, Amelia, 71
Frene, Laura de, 16

Genevieve, 107
Gertrude, 78
Glenmorlie, Rosalind, 147
Gorden, Marian, 41
Gosmund, Leonora de, 119
Grenville, Issena de, 1

Hanslape, Isabel, 184
Hanson, Eliza, 192
Helena, 151, 183
Hemelfride (earlier called
    Isidore), 180
Henderson, Amelia, 48
Herbert, Emma, 197

Hersilia, 31
Honeywood, Adela, 149
Howard, Maria, 43

Ianthe, 131
Ida, 187
Immalee (properly called Isidora
    di Aliagra), 109
Imogen, 33
Ines (earlier called Endymion),
    110
Ingonda, 202
Irza, 98
Isabel, 53, (earlier called Ber-
    tram) 194
Isabel, Princess, 18
Isabella, 193

Julia, 123, 167
Julie, 171
Juliette, 178

Latimer, Eleonora, 90
Laura, 120, 133
Lauretta, 87
Laurette, 171
Lavenza, Elizabeth, 161
Leila, 116
Lindamore, Adeline, 70
Lodore, Ethel, 163
Loredani, Victoria, 38. See also
    under Villainesses
Louisa, 117, 127, 146

Macneil, Mary, 49
Madelina, 181
Madeline, 6
Malvina, 200
Mandaville, Emily, 196
Marchfeldt, Louisa, 69
Margaret, Lady, 67
Margaretta, 89
Mary, 133
Maserini, Clementina, 118
Maserini, Matilda, 118
Masham, Elinor, 124
Mason, Emily, 12
Mathilda, 164
Matilda, 22, 43, 92, 153, 193
Mazzini, Julia, 138
Medina, Agnes de, 99
Melville, Henrietta, 8
Meredith, Harriet, 126
Miranda, 17, 116
Monimia, 177
Montague, Emma, 126
Montgomery, Ellen, 81
Montgomery, Madeline, 81

Montgomery, Matilda de (later St. Evremond), 44
Monti, Rosalita della, 179
Montmorency, Gabrielle, 36
Montolieu, Athanasia, 111
Mora, 56
Mordaunt, Rose, 148
Mordent, Mrs., 205
Morney, Mary, 128
Morney, Roseline de, 6
Mortimar, Ella di, 5
Mowbray, Rosaline de, 88
Munro, Elizabeth, 152

Neville, Alithea, 159
Nouronihar, 3
Nunez, Isabella de, 187

O'Neill, Grace, 148
Orrenberg, Blanche of, 100

Paulina, 42
Peggy, 63

Radmill, Mary Jane (later discovered to be Barville), 168
Ravenspur, Geraldine, née Fitzhugh, 78
Raymond, Cordelia, 152
Rhodiska, 91
Rhone, Mary de, Lady, 34
Roberts, Emma, 60
Ronilda, 75
Rosa, Maddalena, 74
Rosabella, 96
Rosalba, Ellena, 135
Rosalina, 139
Rosaline, 77
Rosalviva, 46. See also under Villainesses
Rosamond, 181
Roussillon, Corisande de, 185

St. Aubert, Emily, 136
St. Aubuspine, Roselma, 32

St. Evremond, Matilda, née de Montgomery, 44
St. Ives, Anna, 68
St. Julien, Julia, 1
St. Orme, Emily, 147
St. Oswythe, Rosaline, 29
Salmoni, Etherlinda de, 20
Santa-Maria, 47
Santarre, Cornelia, 163
Saville, Augusta, 39
Selina, 9, 204
Seymour, Charlotte, née Clifford, 203
Stanley, Blanch, 65
Strictland, Mrs., 142

Tempest, Laura, 169
Torrenburg, Elizabeth, Countess of, 97
Tracy, Rosalind de, 189
Tylney, Caroline, 8

Una, 102
Urbino, Valeria, 86

Vaena, Juliana, 60
Valenza, 75
Vancenza, Carline, 145
Venosta, Urania, 97
Verney, Idris, 162
Verney, Perdita, 162
Vernon, Althena, 156
Victoria, 54
Villars, Eleanor de, 194
Viola, 155
Volker, Jacqueline, 140

Wallace, Jane, 122
Warwick, Isabella, 176
Weimar, Julia, 37
Weimar, Matilda, 125
Widdrington, Margiana, 186
Williams, Maria, 195
Woodley, Ellen, 7

Villains/Villainesses

A--, the Marchioness of, 40
Adolpho, 32
Agatha, 117
Agnes, 29
Aignon, Theodore d', 87
Albani, Count Angelo d', 36
Alderton, 199
Allanrod, 88
Alverani, the Conte, 180
Alwena, 10
Ambrosio, 99

Angerville, 183
Antonia, 89
Ardolph, Count, 38
Arnaud (also called Julian), 129
Arnhalt, Octavia, 188
Astolpho, 18
Augusta, 149
Austin, 44

Badajos, Diego de, Marques, 76
Barbarossa, Hayradin, 179

Barnard, William, 72
Barozzi, Augustino, 174
Barville, 168
Belgrave, 41
Belgrave, Colonel, 149
Bernardo, 117
Berresford, Mr., 52
Blondeville, Gaston de, 134. *See also* under Heroes
Bolton, Betsey, 128
Bracciano, Vittoria, 74
Brazilio, Father, 180
Brindoli, Vincentio di, 24
Bromley, 153
Bruce, Mrs., 52

Carathis, 3
Carlsheim, Ethelbert, 97
Cleveland, Sir Joseph, 81
Clifton, Coke, 68
Conrad, Father, 47
Contarini, 47
Corbet, Holly, née Howard, 141
Cyphon, Squire, 192

D'Alembert, 150
Danby, Mr., 8
De Courcy, 62
DeLauné, 172
Delavel, Margaret, Lady, 83
Deloraine, 111
Delphina, Lady, 111
Delvalley, Aubrey, 204
Desmond, Lord, 9
De Weldon, 43
Donald of the Isles, 122
Doni, Olivieri, 130
Dunbeth, Etheldart, Lord, 33

Eastwood, Mr., 114
Emeric, Sir, 9
Etheldart (Lord Dunbeth), 33
Euphrasia, 149

Fathom, Ferdinand, Count, 177
Felgrove, Lord, 208
Fitzallan, Baron, 93
Fitzallan, Edmund, Lord, 123
Fitzowen, Robert, 141
Fitzparnel, Ingelrica, 184
Francisco, 200

Gifford, 49
Glenarvon, 83
Godolphin, Percival, 90
Golfieri, Conte, 46
Gondez (originally Giovanni Maldachini), 75

Gonzari, Nicolo, Cardinal, 75
Gordon, Adeline, 71
Greville, Mrs., 154
Gusman, 60

Harcland, Sir Reginald, 170
Hardyknute, Count, 102
Henri, 129
Hildebrand, Sir, 194
Hippolita, 41
Holbruzi, 24
Hortensia, 31

Ilford, Earl of, 9

Jocelyn, 52
Joseph, Don, 207
Julian, 21, (really Arnaud) 129

Koenigsmark the Robber, 158

La Braunch, Baron, 10
Lafranco, 91
Lafroy, 150
Larina, 129
Laura (alias for Antonia), 89
Le Forester, Hugh, 12
Leonora, 113
Lindamore, Leopold, 70
Lindorf, Count, 35
Loredani, Victoria, 38. *See also* under Heroines
Lumm, Peter, 13

M--, Rosalie de (alias for Hippolita), 41
Maldachini, Giovanni (later called Gondez), 75
Mal-Leon, Count, 95
Manfred, 193
Manfroné, 139
Marauder, 104
Marchioness, the, 157
Markham, John, 141
Matilda, 167
Maurice, 25
Mazzini, Ferdinand, the Marquis of, 138
Mellas, Orlando de, 119
Millborough, 36
Monckton, William, 71
Mondovini, Signor, 189
Montalt, the Marquis de, 137
Montalva, Stephano, 61
Montalvo, 11
Montaubon, 178
Montferrat, the Marchese de, 171
Montoni, 136

Montorio, Orazio, Count of (later called Schemoli), 108
Morcar, Chief of Stroma, 33
Mordaunt, Mr., 148
Mortemar, Marie du, 107
Murchardus, 201

Nerina, 120

Oakendale, Lord, 16
Obando, 53
O'Connor, William, 146
Oldham, George, 126
Ollifont, Count d', 118
Oriano, 36
Orlando, 188
Ortano, 70
O'Sinister, Lord, 152
Oswald, 1
Otto, 119
Owen, Mr., 206

Parma, the Prince of, 31
Paulina, 29, 196
Perouse, 172
Peter the Cruel, 28
Petrozi, the Marquis, 145
Polygon, 106
Punlada, 28

Ramsey, Ann, 10
Ravenspur, Henry, Lord, 78
Raymond, 95
Reis, Ada, 82
Rhodolpho, 18
Rhodophil, 127
Ricardo, 20
Richmore, Lord, 126
Rinaldo, 45
Roberto, 155
Rochemonde, de (alias for Adolpho), 32
Roderigo, 45
Rodolpha, 1
Rosalviva, 46 (female), 93 (male)
Rosendorf, Countess, 35
Rosorio, Ferdinando d', 61
Roussillon, the Marquis de, 185
Rupert, Father, 78
Ruthven, Mr., 152

St. Angouleme, Count, 172
St. Evremond, Matilda, née de Montgomery, 44. See also under Heroines

St. Ivor, Leopold, Lord, 30
St. Julien, Reginald, 1
St. Oswythe, Rudolph, 29
St. Pierre, 4
Sanguedoni, 31
Savani, Montavole, 45
Sceloni, 24
Schedoni, 135
Schemoli (really Orazio, Count of Montorio), 108
Schneider, Peter-Paul, 140
Scorpino, 27
Sebastiano, 76
Sigismund, Hildebrand, Sir, 90
Skeffington, 73
Streou, Edrie, 105
Stroma, Morcar, Chief of, 33
Strozzi, Megalena, 38

Theodore, 198
Theodosius, Father, 119
Toulouse, the Bishop of, 107
Triphosa, 60
Tylney, Lucy, 8
Tyrell, 50

Ubaldo, Padre, 74
Uglio, 33
Urbandine, Gondemar, 29

Valdetti, Alberto de, 86
Vampyre, 175
Vathek, the Caliph, 3. See also under Heroes
Venome, Madame, 24
Vivaldi, the Marchesa di, 135
Volkert, 79

Wallace, James, Sir, 122
Walleran, 43
Wandesford, 110
Weimar, 125
Wenlock, Richard, 141
Winifred, 170
Wolfenbach, 125
Wolfram, Count, 127
Wolfsteïn, Warbeck of, 69
Wringham, Robert, 66. See also under Heroes

Zastrozzi, 167
Zeluco, 120. See also under Heroes
Zittaw the Cruel, Prince, 202
Zulmer, Appollonia, 37

Index of Titles

Numbers refer to pages.

The Abbess 80
The Abbey of Saint Asaph 86
Abbot of Montserrat, or, The Pool of Blood 59
Ada Reis 88
The Advantages of Education, or, The History of Maria Williams 185
The Adventures of Ferdinand Count Fathom 169
The Albigenses 109
The Algerines, or, The Twins of Naples 59
Alibeg the Tempter 61
Ancient Records, or, The Abbey of Saint Oswythe 35
Anecdotes of Two Well-Known Families 125
An Angel's Form and A Devil's Heart 46
Anna St. Ives 74
Ariel, or, The Invisible Monitor 84
Astonishment!!! 91
The Balance of Comfort, or, The Old Maid and Married Woman 154
Barozzi, or, The Venetian Sorceress 167
The Black Robber 16
The Bloody Hand, or, The Fatal Cup 19
The Bravo of Venice 100
Bridal of Dunamore, and Lost and Won 145
The Brothers, or, The Castle of Niolo 76
Bungay Castle 20
The Castle Chapel 146
The Castle of Otranto 183
Castle of Wolfenbach 125
The Castles of Athlin and Dunbayne 133
The Cavern of Horrors, or, Miseries of Miranda 29
The Children of the Abbey 147
Clarentine 27

Clermont 148
The Confessional of Valombre 170
Confessions of the Nun of St. Omer 42
Contrast 149
The Corsair's Bride 171
Count Roderic's Castle, or, Gothic Times 29
Count St. Blanchard, or, The Prejudiced Judge 113
The Dagger 64
The Danish Massacre 108
Deception 58
The Demon of Sicily 118
Di Montranzo, or, The Novice of Corpus Domini 171
The Discarded Son, or, Hau..t of the Banditti 150
Don Raphael 181
Duncan and Peggy 69
The East Indian, or, Clifford Priory 194
Ellen Woodley 21
The Epicurean 123
Ernestus Berchtold, or, The Modern Oedipus 131
Ethelwina, or, The House of Fitz-Auburne 36
The Exiles, or, Memoirs of the Count de Cronstadt 139
Falkner 155
The Farmer of Inglewood Forest 69
The Fashionable Friend 22
Fatal Revenge, or, The Family of Montorio 110
Fatal Secrets, or, Etherlinda de Salmoni 30
Fatal Vows, or, The False Monk 50
Feudal Tyrants, or, The Counts of Carlsheim and Sargans 101
Fitzallan 77
Fitzmaurice 190
Fleetwood, or, The New Man of Feeling 54

The Forest of St. Bernardo   66
The Fortunes of Perkin Warbeck   156
Frankenstein, or, The Modern
    Prometheus   156
Gaston de Blondeville, or, The
    Court of Henry III   133
Glenarvon   89
Gondez, the Monk   81
Graham Hamilton   90
Grasville Abbey   119
Gwelygordd, or, The Child of Sin
    106
The Haunted Castle   182
The Haunted Cavern   123
The Haunted Palace, or, The Horrors
    of Ventoliene   192
The Haunted Priory, or, The For-
    tunes of the House of Rayo   34
The Highest Castle and the Lowest
    Cave, or, Events of the Days
    Which Are Gone   50
The History of Miss Meredith   126
Horrible Revenge, or, The Monster
    of Italy!!   31
Horrid Mysteries   65
The Horrors of Oakendale Abbey   28
The House of Ravenspur   85
The Idiot Heiress   79
The Infernal Quixote   107
The Invisible Enemy, or, The Mines
    of Wielitska   97
The Irish Guardian, or, Errors of
    Eccentricity   108
The Isle of Devils   102
The Italian, or, The Confessional
    of The Black Penitents   135
The Italian Banditti, or, The
    Secret History of Henry and
    Matilda   31
Italian Mysteries, or, More Secrets
    Than One   92
Italian Vengeance and English Fore-
    bearance   47
Julia   190
Klosterheim, or, The Masque   48
The Knights of Calatrava, or, Days
    of Chivalry   187
The Last Man   158
Le Forester   26
The Libertine   43
Literary Hours, or Sketches Criti-
    cal, Narrative, and Poetical   48
Lodore   159
Longsword, Earl of Salisbury   99
Madelina   172
Madeline, or, The Castle of
    Montgomery   87
The Maid of the Hamlet   151
Manfroné, or, The One-Handed Monk
    138

The Marchioness!!! or, "The Matured
    Enchantress"   154
Marchmont   168
Margiana, or, Widdrington Tower
    177
Mary De Clifford   26
Mary Jane   163
Mathilda   160
Melmoth the Wanderer   111
The Midnight Bell   94
The Midnight Groan, or, The Spectre
    of the Chapel   117
Midnight Weddings   115
The Milesian Chief   112
The Monk   103
The Monk of Udolpho   37
Montalva, or, Annals of Guilt   67
Montbrasil Abbey, or, Maternal
    Trials   173
More Ghosts!   128
Munster Abbey   99
The Mysteries of Udolpho   135
The Mysterious Freebooter, or, The
    Days of Queen Bess   94
The Mysterious Monk, or, The Wiz-
    ard's Tower   19
The Mysterious Murder, or, The
    Usurper of Naples   31
The Mysterious Wanderer   142
The Mysterious Warning   127
Mystery   95
The Mystery, or, Forty Years Ago
    53
The Mystery of the Black Tower
    124
The Necromancer, or, The Tale of
    the Black Forest   86
Netley Abbey   184
The Nocturnal Minstrel, or, The
    Spirit of the Wood   164
Nocturnal Visit   151
The Nun of Santa Maria di Tindaro
    174
The Old English Baron   140
The Orphan of the Rhine   165
The Passions   44
Priory of St. Bernard   68
The Private Memoirs and Confessions
    of a Justified Sinner   72
The Prophecy of Duncannon, or, The
    Dwarf and the Seer   62
Pyrenean Banditti   166
The Recess, or, A Tale of Other
    Times   97
The Red Barn   78
The Refusal   186
Rimauldo, or, The Castle of Badajos
    83
Ringrove, or, Old Fashioned Notions
    186

Roche-Blanche, or, The Hunters of the Pyrenees 132
The Romance of Smyrna, or, The Prediction Fulfilled!!! 193
The Romance of the Appenines 153
The Romance of the Forest 136
Romantic Tales 32, 104
Rosalind De Tracy 180
Rosalviva, or, The Demon Dwarf 51
St. Botolph's Priory, or, The Sable Mask 38
St. Irvyne, or, The Rosicrucian 161
St. Leon 56
St. Margaret's Cave, or, The Nun's Story 71
Salathiel 29
Santa-Maria, or, The Mysterious Pregnancy 52
The School for Widows 141
A Sicilian Romance 137
The Siege of Kenilworth 175
"Sir Bertrand. A Fragment" from Miscellaneous Pieces in Prose 17
Sir Ethelbert, or, The Dissolution of Monasteries 41
Sir Francis Darrell, or, The Vortex 45
Sir Ralph Willoughby 27
The Sisters of St. Gothard 25
The Skeleton, or, Mysterious Discovery 33
The Son of the Storm 163
The Spectre Chief, or, The Blood-Stained Banner 98
The Spectre of Lanmere Abbey, or, The Mystery of the Blue and Silver Bag 187
Spectre of the Turret, or, Guolto Castle 33
The Spectres, or, Lord Oswald and Lady Rosa, Including an Account of the Marchioness of Cevetti Who Was Basely Consigned to a Dungeon beneath Her Castle by Her Eldest Son, Whose Cruel Avarice Plunged Him into the Commission of the Worst of Crimes, That Stain the Annals of the Human Race 188
Story of Morella de Alto, or, The Crimes of Scorpino Developed 33

A Suffolk Tale, or, The Perfidious Guardian 144
Tales of Terror 106
Tales of the Dead 177
Theodore Cyphon, or, The Benevolent Jew 182
Theodosius De Zulvin, the Monk of Madrid 120
"There Is a Secret, Find It Out!" 116
Things As They Are, or, The Adventures of Caleb Williams 57
The Three Brothers 128
The Three Ghosts of the Forest 179
The Three Perils of Man, or, War, Women, and Witchcraft 73
Treachery, or, The Grave of Antoinette 176
The Two Mentors 141
The Unknown, or, The Northern Gallery 96
Valperga, or, The Life and Adventures of Castruccio, Prince of Lucca 160
The Vampyre 132
Vancenza, or, The Dangers of Credulity 143
Vathek 18
The Veiled Protectress, or, The Mysterious Mother 117
The Wanderings of Warwick 169
Warbeck of Wolfstein 75
The Watch Tower, or, The Sons of Ulthona 39
The Water Spectre, or, An Bratach 189
Who's the Murderer? or, The Mystery of the Forest 167
The Wild Irish Boy 112
A Winter's Tale 22
The Witch of Ravensworth 23
The Wood Daemon, or, "The Clock Has Struck" 106
The Woodland Family, or, The Sons of Error and Daughters of Simplicity 63
The World We Live In 191
Zastrozzi 162
Zeluco 122
Zittaw the Cruel, or, The Woodman's Daughter 189
Zofloya, or, The Moor 45